William Turner Coggeshall

Stories of Frontier Adventure in the South and West

William Turner Coggeshall

Stories of Frontier Adventure in the South and West

ISBN/EAN: 9783337146818

Printed in Europe, USA, Canada, Australia, Japan

Cover: Foto ©ninafisch / pixelio.de

More available books at **www.hansebooks.com**

OF

FRONTIER ADVENTURE

IN THE

SOUTH AND WEST.

BY

WILLIAM T. COGGESHALL,

AUTHOR OF "HOME HITS AND HINTS," "POETS AND POETRY OF THE WEST," ETC. ETC.

NEW YORK:
FOLLETT, FOSTER AND COMPANY.
J. BRADBURN (SUCCESSOR TO M. DOOLADY),
49 WALKER STREET.
1863.

Entered, according to Act of Congress, in the year 1868, by
WILLIAM T. COGGESHALL,
In the Clerk's Office of the District Court of the United States for the Southern District of Ohio.

DEDICATORY LETTER.

To William D. Gallagher:

When I went to Cincinnati, in the Spring of 1847, seeking the humblest place in the editorial corps of a daily newspaper, indulging, at the same time, slight hope that, one day, I might see my name over articles in literary periodicals, I was anxious to see and know you, because I had been informed that, holding an humble post in an influential journal, you had risen to the chief post, and had, meantime, added wealth to the literary store of the West.

Because, when, afterward, I was a worker with you, in the same office,* I found, contrary to what had been told me, that you were a friend to striving young men; and because you were the first literary man who encouraged me, by just criticism and good advice, to write something more pretending than "items," I dedicate to you this volume of Tales and Sketches, designed to illustrate frontier life and char-

* Daily Cincinnati Gazette.

acter—to you, who, in my judgment, have written about, and for the West, from just impulse, with just purpose—to you, who have made no small sacrifice for—Ah, me! Western Literature.

However justly those terrible fellows, the critics, may find fault with my unpretending romances, you will have charity for them, because you know they were written when "local" matters of fact commanded a large share of my days and nights; and you know, too, that they are now republished from the columns of the newspapers and magazines in which they first appeared, with only such revision as could be made on proof-sheets.

Accept, then, this frank epistle, and its intention, as an honest acknowledgment that, if there be any merit in this volume, it was developed under your encouragement.

With highest regards,
Your indebted friend,
WILLIAM T. COGGESHALL.

COLUMBUS, OHIO,
May, 1860.

CONTENTS.

	PAGE
THE EVERGLADE HEROES—*A Tale of Florida*	1
FLEET FOOT—*A Legend of Kentucky*	89
HUNTER BIRTY; OR, THE HALF-BREED COLONY OF ILLINOIS	113
GOLDEN BIRD OF MENOMINEE	211
THE COUNTERFEITERS OF THE CUYAHOGA—*A Buckeye Romance*	217
THE BRIGHT EYE OF THE SETTLEMENT	307

LIST OF ILLUSTRATIONS.

DESIGNED BY BILLINGS, AND ENGRAVED BY ANDREW.

	Page
FRONTISPIECE: Death of Major Bertram.	
ARREST OF BRINTON BY THE OUTLAWS,	70
FLEET FOOT,	104
HUNTER BIRTY,	160
THE GOLDEN BIRD OF THE MENOMINEE,	216
DISCOVERY OF THE COUNTERFEITERS,	236
TICKEL SHOT AT BY THE COUNTERFEITERS,	296

The Everglade Heroes.

A TALE OF FLORIDA.

CHAPTER I.

INTRODUCTORY.

At the time General Jackson was Governor of Florida, soon after the treaty of "amity, settlement and limits" had been ratified between the United States and the Spanish governments, an officer of the American army was on his way from St. Augustine to Pensacola, with a large sum of money in his charge, which was to be placed in the government coffers, over which Jackson had superintendence.

This officer had arrived within one day's journey of his destination. It was an autumn afternoon. The atmosphere of that southern clime was laden with those odors which the famed trees and shrubs of West Florida exhale. The young man, who had never enjoyed so agreeable a treat of that character, was enchanted with the beautiful scenes on which his eye rested, and the delicious sweets on which other senses regaled.

He had traveled the King's road—at that time the only highway in Florida which deserved the title of road—from St. Augustine to St. Mary's river, and there, with an accession to his escort, had taken the most direct trail for Pensacola. The country having for some time been quiet, the company traveled with little fear of molestation from marauding Indians or other depredators.

To enjoy fully the delights which air and scenery afforded, the officer had fallen behind his escort, and in the distance gaining a view of a wide-spread lagoon, he diverged from the trail to contemplate more immediately the wild fowl that rested on its waters, the grasses that waved within it, and the bright-colored flowers with varied hues that hung in festoons on its borders. Endeavoring to find his path back to the trail, after riding a few miles, he entered a pine barren, through which he had wound but a short time when it became evident to him that he had missed his reckoning, and would be unable to direct his course towards his company.

Night was fast coming on. Already the last rays of the sun, setting far away in the lagoon that the officer had been viewing, were gilding the tops of the tall pines beneath which he wandered; yet he had no fears for his safety, knowing that his men would encamp and wait for him. He had often *bivouaced* in the forest, and, determining to await the coming of morn to find the trail, he prepared to spend the night among the pines. Fastening his horse to a limb where he could conveniently browse—for there was nothing to graze—he took from his back the portmanteau containing the government funds, placed it upon the moss growing around the trunk of a massive pine, then gathering an armful of brush, struck a fire and prepared for repose.

When darkness enveloped the forest, he lay down to rest as calmly as if he had been in his own tent, surrounded by a numerous encampment. As he slept, the silver rays of a waning moon fell tremblingly through the pine foliage and revealed his form, wrapped in a hunter's blanket, stretched on the green moss.

Had he known that his wanderings were that day followed, he had not slept so sweetly; he had been standing guard over his treasure, or he had hid himself in some bushy glen or dale.

A few days previous, the "Everglade Heroes" had heard of his passage through the country, had ascertained the amount of treasure with which he had been entrusted, and they had determined that Jackson should never possess it, if a score of lives was the forfeit. The captain of these "Heroes," as they styled themselves, was now on the track of the officer. He was acquainted with Florida from the keys of the south-east to the bogs and rivers of the northwest. His band had been following the government soldiers for several days, and had a number of times meditated an attack, but prudence bid them be cautious, for they wished to commit the robbery without letting the robbed see by whom it was done. They had been watching for a favorable opportunity, until they knew that another day would cut off their chances entirely, and the captain had decided that the night following the day on which our story opens, should be the time of attack, at all hazard. What was his gratification when he saw the officer fall behind his company —then diverge from the trail! Leaving his "Heroes" to watch the escort, the captain followed the officer.

The hour had come when the captain's schemes were to be put into execution, but he disdained to rob and murder a sleeping man. Slipping to the place where the officer's steed was fastened, he cut the cord that made him a prisoner, and with a yell that rung among the pines, started the affrighted animal at a swift gallop through the forest. The officer was awakened and he sprang to his feet, expecting that

Indians were upon him. He reached for his trusty rifle, but it had been removed; his sword was at his side, however, and he quickly drew it. Before him appeared a man of swarthy hue, dressed in the Indian fashion; but he was neither Seminole nor Creek, as the officer expected.

"Lieutenant Bertram," cried the outlaw, "I discovered who you are this afternoon. We have met, as I have long wished. I am the captain of the "Everglade Heroes"—the man you struck twelve years ago, for calling you a villain, when he was orderly sergeant under you. His Spanish passion then vowed revenge. He has since gratified it by plundering the government that would not give him justice; and he'll now satisfy that revenge *fully* with your life and the funds you have with you."

To this defiant speech the lieutenant made no reply. He was a brave man and a skillful swordsman, and, determined to die valiantly, he rushed upon his antagonist. The outlaw was prepared to meet him, and for more than ten minutes the clashing of their swords rang upon the night air. By his desperation and skillful swordsmanship the lieutenant was making the result of the contest doubtful, when by a skillful movement, the outlaw threw him off his guard and ran his sword through his body. He bent over him as he fell to see that it was a fatal wound; then tearing open his garments, traced two letters in blood on his breast, and muttering between his teeth, "*You'll insult no more women,*" grasped the portmanteau that contained the treasure and speedily fled.

Major Bertram (for, though the outlaw called him lieutenant, and we adopted the title, he *was* major, having risen in rank during the twelve years to which his murderer referred,) survived but a few moments. He had not weltered in his blood half an hour, before a scout from his company found him. He had bivouaced within a mile of their encampment, and though every means had been taken to find him, his men had no suspicion that he was near them, until his horse galloped through their camp a few minutes after he had been liberated by the outlaw, chance or the instinct of the animal having led him to this rendezvous. The guards had raised the cry of Indians; but when the company was aroused, and it was found to be their major's steed that had caused the alarm, the officer in command dispatched scouts in every direction, fearing there had been robbery and murder. This officer found the major's body, and was startled by its appearance. He was a wicked man, and he exclaimed furiously:

"The torments of hell take them! The Everglade Heroes have done this! There are the characters traced in blood on the poor major's breast. The devil will be to pay when we get to Pensacola."

For two years previous to the date of this chapter, maledictions of this kind had been frequent in Florida. The ominous letters, "*E. H.*," with the sign of a cross, had been regarded with terror by many who had been robbed in their camps and cabins, and upon more than a hundred corpses had they been traced, along the trails which traversed the wilds of the peninsula. They were a watch-word of terror more dreadful than the title of the bloodiest Seminole. It was not known whether the "*Heroes*" were Americans, Spaniards or Indians, but they were supposed to belong to a secret band of Spanish banditti.

When the scout who had discovered the major had called

a couple of companions to his aid, a litter was prepared, and the body was carried to the trail and buried in a spot which, for many years, was marked by a rude stone. Wild flowers grew on his grave, and birds built their nests in the branches that hung over it; but Major Bertram, though a wicked man, had been a valuable officer, and he was not forgotten.

On the evening of the day following the occurrence of these events, the company arrived at Pensacola and reported the ill success of their expedition.

A liberal reward was immediately offered for the arrest of any *one* of the "Everglade Heroes;" and the high offense of murdering a major in the United States Army, and robbing the government of a large sum of money, was soon told along all the trails between Pensacola bay and St. John's river. But no officer, Indian or hunter, was able to claim the handsome reward. The murderer was secure at the retreat of his "Heroes," amid an extensive everglade on the south-western slope, drained by the Coloosatchee river.

Upon an island, approached by a strip of hard earth on which the grass grew scantily, three men had for several years hidden ill-gotten treasure, and retreated when danger threatened them. They were all of Spanish descent. Their leader, as we have intimated, had been a soldier in the United States Army, and had deserted. He was a bold and desperate man, and he had led his men on desperate expeditions and bold exploits, which had yielded them an immense amount of booty. They carried to their island retreat nothing but gold and silver or valuable jewels, and they had amassed enough to make three large fortunes. Every possible means had been taken to ferret out their hiding place; but they understood the art of disguise—the condition of the country had been favorable to their exploits, and though many times hotly pursued, they had eluded all search; and there was no suspicion of the true situation of their headquarters among any of the people of the peninsula.

This band had been organized for two years. The period of the wicked copartnership had expired, and, having become richer than they anticipated, they were about to separate. The captain had already calculated the division of spoils, and they assembled to apportion the shares, before their rude cypress hut on the everglade island, with the tall grass waving about them, the fragrant wind rippling the waters of a pond on which swam myriads of wild fowl amid blossoms of the lily and lotus, bathing their varied plumage in the bright sunshine that came down from an almost Italian-clear sky. The chief counted out to each man the share of blood-stained booty which had been accorded him, and then the "Heroes" threw off their Indian dresses, changed in many respects the savage appearance they bore, packed their horses, and, in European costume, emerged from their everglade haunt. They traveled for a couple of days through secret paths, then boldly struck into a trail leading towards the St. John's river, and pursued their way to St. Augustine, determined, as their conversation seemed to disclose, to separate as soon as they arrived at the city, give up their wicked course of life, invest their money in the purchase of lands, and become agriculturists—*in name, at least.*

CHAPTER II.

THE PATGOE PARTY.

Twelve years have elapsed since the cession of Florida to the United States.

The scene of our history now lies near the noble river St. Johns, within a few miles of St. Augustine—the oldest city of the United States.

Embowered in a grove of orange, lime, guava, citron, fig and palm trees, to which extended a wide avenue, lined on either side with ancient live oaks, and ornamented with bowers of roses, were, five years previous to the opening of the Seminole war, the ruins of an English mansion that had been the residence of a gentleman of the nobility, during the time the British nation considered the peninsula among its possessions.

It had been purchased by a wealthy Floridian, who, without heed of war, rumors of war, or Indian depredations, repaired all the devastations time and negligence had made, and added to its groves, gardens and walks, under the direction of a skillful gardener, such improvements as had rendered it the most enchanting residence of the St. John's district. When the odorous trees were in blossom, the luxuriant flowers in bloom, or the tropical fruits had ripened, it was a palace which vied in delightful associations with the famed oriental villas that have been the "burden of song and verse" ever since Persian descriptions first glowed on the pages of traveled authors.

The owner of this place was Cabot Conere, a gentlemen whose Spanish ancestors had been among the first emigrants to Florida. He had arrived at the meridian of an eventful life, and, while the country about him was in commotion, was settled peacefully with his family, consisting of his wife, and a daughter verging into womanhood, at a home surrounded with all the sources of ease and enjoyment that wealth, in that favorable clime, could command.

From a tributary to the St. John's that flowed across one portion of his plantation, a number of small streams had been led meandering among shade and ornamental trees, and through flowery paths and fruit walks—and from this circumstance, with the approval of its master, the mistress of the mansion had named it Rillwood.

Conere of Rillwood was a remarkable personage. He had all the fire and impetuosity of a Spaniard, tempered with the cool, calculating judgment of the plodding Englishman. He was tall of stature, commanding in bearing, and prepossessing in manner; but there was always about him an air of reserve, which chilled confidence, and his most intimate associates knew nothing of 'his history previous to the period when he made Rillwood his home.

His mansion, or villa, was celebrated the country round as the residence of the most daring and skillful sportsman of St. Augustine vicinage, the most accomplished woman of north-east Florida, and the loveliest girl that had visited the gay assemblages of the ancient city for many years.

Isabelle Conere was a Spanish beauty, with the vivacity and energy of an American girl. She had the translucent olive complexion, the full dark eye, fringed with languishing lashes, belonging to the Castilian blood, with the lithe limbs and roundly developed muscles that are the heritage of the maiden of North America, who loves the rough gallop before sunrise, and the hill-chase after sunset, better than needle-work or sentimental reading.

Senora Conere—as her husband persisted in calling her, although she was a Virginia lady, of English descent—was one of those mild, excellent women, who are ministers of goodness and charity, beloved by all the poverty-stricken and sorrow-laden. She had never been what the world would call beautiful; indeed, at the period when we commence her history, although there was a matronly grace of manner about her, a majority of persons, whose tastes are formed on conventional principles, would have considered her homely—and *homely* she was, in the true sense of the term.

Homely—what an abused term, taken in connection with the associations clustering around the first syllable! Richardson defines it, "Pertaining to home; having the plainness and simplicity of home;" and Milton says in Comus:

> "It is for homely features to keep at home;
> They had their name hence."

The most cherished pleasures of the mistress of Rillwood sprang from the enjoyments of her own home, and the gratification of laboring to make other homes happy. Her pleasing, affectionate manner fitted her for charitable duties; and wherever there was poverty or suffering, she was the angel of mercy and hope that brought relief and consolation. She was the very antipode of Conere. What a contrast between this calm-natured, fragile woman and the muscular, strong-minded Spaniard—a summer zephyr contrasted with the northern blast of midwinter; it was the mating of the dove with the eagle. Yet she loved him truly, and he appeared to return her affection; but his was that love which power may be expected to bestow upon a dependent idol.

The daughter had her father's wild and fitful spirit, with her mother's good-heartedness. The two natures were singularly blended in Isabelle. She appeared frank and ingenuous; she *was* independent; but when she had a purpose to gain, she was crafty and secretive; and she had often wayward moods, over which her mother had long ceased to attempt a control.

It is an evening in early autumn. Breathing a "hushed and charmed air," an atmosphere redolent with the fragrance of tropical fruits and the perfume of rare flowers, upon the seat of an arbor, shaded by a pomegranate tree, and overhung with clustering vines, Isabelle Conere reclined. She awaits a trysting hour, when she expects to meet one who will assist her to persuade her father to come home on the morrow—her eighteenth birth day—which is to be commemorated by a Patgoe Party.

She is becoming impatient, when upon her attentive ear falls the melody of a familiar tune, sung sweetly in low tones. She falls in with the singer and softly follows the tune with a delicious voice, until the vocalist has approached within a few steps, then springing from her reclining position, she accosted him:

" 'Tis past the hour, and if something had not detained father at the city, I should not have to thank you for aiding me in getting his consent to be with us to-morrow."

" I was here an hour since, but knew your father had not come, and failing to find you, I wandered to the orange grove, and there I met Conere. I told him that you waited for him. His brow was dark, and he bid me tell you that he could not see you, and you must not expect him at the festivities to-morrow. Before this time he has returned to St. Augustine."

" He gave you no explanation—no other message ?"

" None."

" There has been something preying on his mind of late. Does mother know that he will be absent to-morrow ?"

" I believe she does not."

" Let me seek her."

The young man who held this conversation with Isabelle Conere was a native of trade-driving Connecticut—a scion of Puritan stock—attracted to this southern land by a handsome property bequeathed him by an uncle, who had been one of the early English settlers on the St. John's river.

This property was situated within half a mile of Rillwood. Ledyard Brinton had lived at Windsor (thus named by his loyal uncle) nearly four years. His household was governed by a widowed aunt, and his plantation was controlled by a creole, who managed it in a manner that yielded profitable returns to its owner. Brinton had "southern policy" enough not to meddle with other people's business, and he made no enemies among his neighbors, by interfering with their "peculiar institutions." He had, probably, not made Florida his permanent home, if an accidental acquaintance with Isabelle Conere, had not rendered the country one of peculiar interest. He was a frequent visitor at Rillwood, and, seemingly, a favored companion of the proprietor, as well as of his daughter.

Conere was adverse to forming intimate associations, and he did not cultivate Brinton's acquaintance without an object. On the night in which they met in the orange grove, Conere had applied to him for the loan of a large sum of money. Brinton was unable to accommodate him at the hour, but Conere attributing his refusal to unwillingness, abruptly bid him a good night, telling him to inform Isabelle that he should be absent on the morrow.

The mother and daughter were not surprised at the decision brought them, for latterly Conere had made them accustomed to sudden departures, and many times, when he returned his moods were in no wise agreeable. For six months he had been sadly in trouble about his pecuniary affairs. He had engaged in numerous speculations — the country was in an unsettled state, and he found it difficult to "keep up appearances" that would deceive his friends and the acquaintances of his family. It was to keep from foreclosure, mortgages which would have exposed his circumstances, that he was obliged to absent himself from his daughter's birth-day festival. She was grieved at his absence, because she loved her father with a wild love, which she had reason to think was sincerely returned — and she had given herself much pleasure in calculating upon his enjoyment in the festivities that would commemorate her majority.

The pleasures of the day were to spring from a Patgoe party — and what is a Patgoe party?

It was a festival common in Florida at the time of which we write, as the introduction to a dance, the popular amusement of the Floridians. A wooden bird, fixed upon a pole, was carried through the neighborhood. Each lady, to whom it was presented, made an offering of a piece of ribbon, choosing the color and style. The bird is soon decked in gaudy style, and at an hour appointed, gallanted by their beaux, bearing their rifles, the fair patrons of the Patgoe assemble at a spot selected. The bird is put up as a mark, and the sportsman who buries the first ball in its novel plumage is proclaimed king of the entertainment. He presents the Patgoe to the lady of his choice, and she is crowned queen. On Isabelle Conere's birth day, Ledyard Brinton was the fortunate marksman, and she was chosen his royal consort.

A large company had assembled at Rillwood. Upon the lawn, in front of the mansion, the festivities were proceeding—here a dancing party—there a bevy of waltzers—away, beneath the shade of an orange or pomegranate tree, were lovers engaged in "converse sweet;" and all was joy and hilarity, befitting the occasion, conducted, as it was, with regal splendor by the king and queen.

As the shades of evening began to gather, a horseman was seen urging his steed at a swift gallop up the main avenue towards the mansion. Isabelle, who had painful forebodings, fled precipitately to the house. When she arrived the messenger was already in her mother's room, and she was obliged to await his reäppearance in the hall, which she no sooner perceived than she flew to him.

"Is father harmed? Where is he, Benjamin? You

must tell me!" exclaimed the girl, with fearful energy and startling wildness of manner.

"He is at St. Augustine, and unharmed," answered the man.

"Why came you here then in such haste?"

"To get papers which it is necessary for your father to have immediately, for the settlement of some important business."

"Will he be home to-day—answer me fairly?"

"I will, Isabelle," said the messenger, trembling as she laid her hand upon his shoulder, "Your father cannot come home to-day, nor perhaps to-morrow; but by that time I hope all his difficulties will be settled. You must question me no farther, for I am forbidden to tell you."

"Then mother *shall*," cried the excited girl, hastening in quest of her parent. But she could obtain no satisfactory information. Her mother did not know what detained Conere; but from the character of the documents the messenger had demanded, she feared that he had fallen into serious trouble.

The festivities were now without the spirit of their queen— an army foraging for pleasure bereft of their commander—and the party broke up and the guests departed much earlier than had been anticipated.

Isabelle sought Brinton, to ascertain if he could enlighten her on the suspicious conduct of the messenger. He could give her no assistance, but strange surmises were aroused, and he determined to know whether these surmises were well founded.

In an hour he was galloping towards St. Augustine.

CHAPTER III.

THE FATAL MEETING.

When Conere parted from Brinton, at the orange grove, he walked rapidly to a bye-path where his horse was fastened, mounted and spurred him eagerly along the road towards St. Augustine. Within a mile of the city, when it was near dark, he turned off the main road into an obscure trail. Along this he galloped speedily for several hours, and then reined up at a low uninviting palmetto hut, and forthwith entered without ceremony. He remained for more than an hour, and when he came out, appeared anxious to get beyond hearing before any one should follow him; but as he was about to mount his jaded steed, a torch-light flashed from the hut and a voice hailed him.

"Remember, at two o'clock to-morrow afternoon."

"I'll be there," replied Conere with evident impatience, and the sound of his horse's hoofs soon died away at the hut.

We will not follow the Spaniard in his wanderings that night. About noon of the following day, he slowly approached St. Augustine. He paid no heed to the burning sun, and though he was much oppressed, it was not on account of the sultry air, that had covered his tired horse with white foam. He stopped at a mean looking house, in the suburbs of the city, flung his bridle to a negro in attendance, hastily turned a corner, and rapidly pursued his way towards the heart of the city. He proceeded to the public square, which opens on Mantanzas Sound, and striding before the monument dedicated to the constitution of the Spanish Cortez, which rears its front in the center, struck directly to what the French call a *cafe*, situated near one of the corners. Addressing a few words to the swarthy-looking attendant at the bar, Conere walked up a flight of narrow stairs. The *cafe* was a two story building, erected of coquina, (a peculiar sea-shell, employed extensively for building purposes some years ago along the Florida coast,) and in the rear of the second story was a low, dark room, to which Conere directed his steps. He entered without knocking, and throwing his sombrero on the table, surveyed the apartment. Upon a bench near the window, he espied a rough-looking man, perhaps thirty-five years of age, who gazed upon his dark brow a moment, and then very indifferently remarked:

"You're punctual, Cabot—no doubt you're prepared."

"Have you the papers?" returned Conere, with ill-feigned annoyance, disdaining the seat to which his companion pointed him.

With the most unconcerned manner, the rough man answered, "If I haven't, my pocket's been picked since I lay down here. Ah! here they are, all right!"—producing a roll of documents from a large pocket in his coarse coat, and throwing them on the table.

"What are the sums?" said Conere, still standing, with a struggle to appear calm.

"Enough to play the devil with you, if you are not prepared to cancel them. Conere, these are very different circumstances from what you and I calculated on when we did business together, some years ago. You were master then — the tide's changed."

"*You* will not taunt *me*, Espard. You have reason to fear me, if I *am* in your power just now. You know what I *have* been — I feel one of my old moods to-day."

"It will become you, Conere, to keep cool. I am not here unprepared, and *you* know what *I* have been," answered Espard, with the most imperturbable coolness, still reclining on the bench.

Conere, every moment falling into a deeper passion, looked wickedly at his tormentor, and replied, "*You must* not taunt me, or you shall know what I can be *now* — but are you ready to settle this business?"

"Are you?"

"Yes."

"All right, then," said Espard, slowly raising himself up and drawing the bench towards the table, when Conere arrested his movements.

"But I am here without a dollar. You must give me more time, or do your best, and abide by the consequences."

"Threats, eh? if I make you pay your honest debts, that have been due these six months. I'll have the last picayune. I'll not wait another day. Your property shall pay me, if it takes the night-cap off your beauty, and your Virginia lady has to accommodate herself to a cabin. We'll see who'll be gentleman then."

Espard had thrown off his indifference, and these words were uttered as if he gloated at the prospect of making Conere a beggar. The Spaniard saw this, and felt that all his calmness was requisite. In the mildest tone he had used during their interview, almost in a whisper, he replied:

"No word of my family, Espard, or by heavens you die!" In a menacing attitude he approached his creditor, who sprang to his feet and drew a pistol, crying, "Beware, Conere; I know what I say, and I mean it. If your pet has to take the street, her beauty will be a good market, and you will have no more need of money-lenders who *take care of their funds.*"

These words were uttered with a peculiar bitterness, which Conere fully understood; he was livid with rage, and exclaiming, "The torments of hell take the wretch!" he dashed aside the table which stood between them, and sprang upon his insulter.

Espard instantly fired his pistol, slightly wounding Conere in his right side. The door of the room was broken open by persons from below, who had been alarmed at the noise made in the scuffle; but before they reached the combatants, Espard fell heavily upon the floor, with Conere's dagger in his breast. A portion of the party appeared to be friends of the fallen man, for immediately they took him up and conveyed him from the *cafe*, as Conere and all the inmates supposed, dead.

Without the movement of a muscle, or an effort at concealment, Conere saw his victim borne away. He was about to follow the company, when his eye fell upon the roll of papers about which the difficulty had commenced, lying near the upturned table. He hastily grasped them, and hiding them beneath his coat, muttered, "The man who would have conspired has gone to the devil, and Isabelle and her mother are safe."

By this time officers had arrived, and Conere was taken into custody. His Secretary happened to be in the city, and soon heard of the affray and hastened to the magistrate who had Conere in durance. He would make no effort at a release — attempt no palliation — he had calmly determined to let matters take their course and meet his fate. But he was glad to see his Secretary, because there were certain papers at Rillwood of which the peace of his family might require *him* to be possessed.

Of the Secretary's reception at Rillwood, during the Patgoe party, our history has made mention. When he returned to St. Augustine he found Conere in a strange mood. He would answer no questions satisfactorily, and had none to ask about his family. The Secretary importuned him for permission to tell his wife that night what was the cause of his absence. At length, knowing the knowledge must soon come to her, and wishing that she should communicate the sad news to Isabelle, he consented.

The wound he received had been dressed and gave him little annoyance. It was in no degree dangerous. He was not confined in the common jail, but had been provided with a room in an old fort fronting on the Mantanzas, and was provided with all the conveniences he desired. Soon after his Secretary departed for Rillwood, he called for a cigar, had it lighted, and throwing himself upon a couch, composedly drew a cloud of thin smoke around him. When the guard had retired to his place outside the door, taking from his pocket two rolls of papers, he opened them, and after looking at them a few minutes ignited them, piece by piece, and watched them slowly burn, till every particle had been reduced to ashes; then, in the most determined manner, he paced his room, muttering:

"Let them do their worst now — let them hang me *if they can*. I ought to die; I've lived long enough in *this* world. They cannot expose me. Espard is dead, thank God, and the only man whom I need fear is far away. Isabelle and her mother are secure; they have the richest plantation about St. Augustine, and they can do without *me*. It is best I should die now, for there's no telling what *may* happen when the news that I killed Espard gets abroad. I'll wait patiently for what does come, but I have lived too long in this world not to know what will save me from an ignominous *public* death."

CHAPTER IV.

THE DAUGHTER'S RESOLVE.

ISABELLE CONERE passed a restless night, and when the soft air of early morn breathed into her apartment, she arose from her couch and sat down by a window overlooking the orange grove. The fragrance of those trees, exhaling deliciously from the dew drops which trembled on their leaves and blossoms, hung in the pure air about her. Sometimes she leaned her head on the window sill, as if in deep revery; then she watched the faint streaks of dawn appear in the eastern sky, as the sun neared the verge of the horizon, and again she cast her eyes confidently up to

"The blue eye of God, which is above us."

Near one of the rills that murmured around the mansion,

"A mocking bird, wildest of singers,
Swinging aloft on a willow spray that hung over the water,
Shook from his little throat such floods of delicious music,
That the whole air, and the woods, and the waves, seemed silent to listen.
Plaintive at first were the tones, and sad; then soaring to madness,
Seemed they to follow or guide the revel of frenzied Bacchantes.
Single notes were then heard, in sorrowful, low lamentation;
Till, having gathered them all, he flung them abroad in derision."

The restless girl listened, enraptured, feeling that, in the natural eloquence of sympathy, the wild singer expressed her emotions.

She had determined that the day should not pass without bringing full knowledge to her of what had befallen her father, and of the troubles she foreboded that were to fall upon their house.

As soon as the servants were stirring, leaving untouched the morning meal that her maid had brought her, she sent a request that her mother would meet her in the parlor, and walked out on the lawn. She had heard the Secretary return to the mansion in the night, and knew that he had called for her mother, and she hoped to meet him in some of the walks; but in this she was disappointed, and she returned to the house with the fears of the night in no degree allayed. When she entered the parlor, her mother awaited her. Her first salutation was:

"Mother, *will* father be home to-day?"—taking her parent by the hands, and looking, through fast flowing tears, into her face. Her mother was moved, and answered, with much feeling:

"I fear, daughter, you will not see your father *at home* for many days—perhaps for years."

"What has happened to him?" said Isabelle, wildly.

"I cannot tell you now, child. I will see you when you are more calm."

And the mother's overflowing heart revealed its deep emotion in scalding tears and suppressed sobs, for Conere did not tell the Secretary that he had not committed premeditated murder. Under this impression his wife suffered, and she ended this painful conference by abruptly withdrawing from the parlor, leaving Isabelle in an anxiety of mind which impelled her to fathom the mystery at any hazard.

This mother, with all her good-heartedness, was one of those women who never can freely communicate with their children upon afflictions that may befall the family — counsel them on the stern duties of life, or instruct them fully upon its cares and griefs — and Isabelle had grown to womanhood as unsophisticated in all these matters as the child of the forest.

No sooner had the door closed behind her mother, than Isabelle was out on the lawn again. The fresh air was pleasant upon her fevered brow, and she became somewhat calmed in her ramble, before she found the Secretary; but yet, with a profusion of dark ringlets hanging disheveled about her fair neck — her face pale with watching, and her eyes sparkling with the lustre of anxiety, her appearance startled him, when he met her in a garden path, back of the mansion. With an arch grace of manner, she accosted him:

"You had a pleasant ride this morning?"

"Rather," was the laconic reply.

"Is not the air sweet and pure?"

The Secretary was embarrassed. He had expected a a storm when he saw Isabelle approach him. She was now so strangely calm, he feared she might have heard of her father's arrest, and become partially deranged, and he was considering how to answer her, when her expression changed, and she drove his speculations all out of his head, by inquiring:

"Did father send me anything?"

"Nothing," replied the wondering servant.

"Where did you leave him, Benjamin?"

"At the city."

"I know *that*, Benjamin, and you cannot evade me. I *will* know where he is, and you *shall* tell me!"

"I dare not, Miss Isabelle."

"But I have said you *shall*," replied the girl, with a wild energy which made the Secretary quake.

"It's dreadful, and you would curse me."

"I'll thank you—I'll like you, Benjamin. If it's dreadful, so much the more should I know all about it—*will you tell me*, Benjamin?"

As if forced from him with a great effort, the Secretary uttered the words:

"He's in prison."

"In prison!" echoed Isabelle. As upon the wings of the wind, she flew along the garden paths, and in a few minutes burst into her mother's room.

"Why is my father imprisoned?" were her first words.

"Imprisoned, daughter, who told you?"

"Benjamin; I forced it from him. But, mother, quick—I must know—my brain's on fire!"

In broken sentences, and with frequent interruptions, by the repressing of deep emotion, the mother revealed to her daughter what the Secretary had related at their interview during the night. When Isabelle had learned the dangerous circumstances under which her father was placed, she walked backwards and forwards for some minutes, with her hands pressed on her brow, then stopping before her mother, she cried:

"It is false—it is a conspiracy. I don't believe a word of it. The man who is dead was a bad man, and if father killed him, he had cause for it. He shall not die. He *shall* be liberated!"

"My daughter, be calm," interposed the weeping mother. "You do not know what you are doing."

"But I *do*, mother—I am in earnest—it shall *not* be so!" And with impotent passion the afflicted daughter clasped her hands and wept scalding tears upon her mother's neck; then in a moment sank by her side, and rested her head upon the ottoman on which the mother sat.

Suddenly a violent storm had come up, and the rain began to fall heavily upon the roof. Its dull, regular music seemed to soothe the stricken mother and daughter. Isabelle raised her head—

"Mother, I read in that French history Benjamin lent me, of a young girl, who left her home, in devotion to her country, and went to Paris, determined to deliver the land of her birth from the mad passions of a man who, she believed, was the great cause of the social evils that oppressed the people. She killed him, mother—*killed* the bad man. It is nobler to *save* a father. I shall never rest till my father is saved. I know he is not a murderer—I will never believe it."

The mother had no power to restrain her daughter; she had been unaccustomed to maternal restraint in her childish sports;—what influence could the parent now have over the wild frenzy which distracted the young girl's mind? She could only say, mildly:

"You must go to rest, Isabelle. You do not know what you talk about. Sleep would compose you."

"Sleep, mother!—I'll go to my room, but not to rest."

Isabelle retired. She loved her mother, and would always obey her implicitly, when her wild passions were not stirred. She threw herself upon a couch, and lay with her eyes fixed on the ceiling, as if she would count the rain-drops as they pattered upon the roof.

Isabelle Conere had taste, if she had not meekness. She loved flowers—she loved the birds—she loved nature in its calmest as well as wildest aspects; and, hanging about her room, were representatives of all these tastes, that would not have discredited a much more pretending boudoir.

In an hour, the mother called to see if her daughter rested. She found her, as it were, in a trance; but the parent's footfall aroused her, and springing to her feet, she exclaimed:

"The storm is past, mother. I shall see father this afternoon."

"Not calm yet, my child?"

"Not calm? No! Mother, I wonder how you can be so calm; but you are older—you have had more experience—you can control your feelings."

"And you must learn to do so, Isabelle, or you will find this a sad world."

"It is a lesson I cannot learn now, mother. I know this *is* a sad world. What a proof I now have—my father in prison! Mother, I will go with you to see him to-day."

The mother knew that it would be useless to deny Isabelle this privilege, and perforce she answered:

"If you wish it."

"You know I *do*, mother. I made Benjamin promise, this morning, if you would go, to take us to the city this afternoon; and if he had not consented, I should have sent for Brinton."

Before five o'clock that afternoon, under the escort of Benjamin, Isabelle and her mother applied for permission to see Conere. Their request was cheerfully granted. Isabelle was pressed to her father's heart. She looked up fondly into his face; it was careworn.

"You grieve, father, that wicked men persecute you, but you shall be liberated," she remarked, affectionately, half soliloquizing.

"I fear not, my daughter," was his reply, in a tone which chilled her.

Isabelle glanced around the dreary room, so different from that to which she had been accustomed, and through dripping eyelashes gazed at her father.

"But you are innocent, father. You *must* be rescued."

The father had practiced deception all his life, but he dare not deceive Isabelle. He was thinking, and did not answer her promptly.

"Tell me you are innocent, father. Say they have persecuted you. What made them do it?"

"I would not deceive *you*, Isabelle. I do not feel myself guilty, but I did kill Espard."

"Was it premeditated? Did you do it without cause?" eagerly asked the daughter, tightening her grasp on her father's hand.

"Neither," he replied coolly. "He insulted me basely. I threatened him—he fired his pistol at me, and I stabbed him."

"I knew it—I knew it. Thank God, you *shall* be rescued."

"But this I cannot prove, my daughter. My dagger was found in his breast."

"I care not," she answered thoughtfully. "A way will come; a way *must* come."

At this moment Benjamin entered, and told them that

the hour of their privilege had expired, and the guard demanded his prisoner. Conere took a tender leave of his wife and daughter, and Benjamin escorted them back to Rillwood.

This Benjamin was a New England boy who had followed Brinton to Florida. He had been a school-mate, and his father having been an old friend of the Brinton family, Ledyard took the boy south with him, to enable him to get a "start in the world." At first he had a great "notion" of fighting the Indians, but Brinton convinced him that this business would be poor "pay," and he gave up the idea, to become the secretary of Conere, and a sort of "general help" about his family. He had determined on "making his fortune" before he returned to New England.

He had not yet proceeded very far towards the "goal of his ambition," but perhaps brighter days are in store for him. He was working like a man who means to "rise in the world." He had a respectable quantum of Yankee economy, and every odd picayune he could spare, went towards the purchase of some rare book. Conere and Brinton both had large libraries, but Benjamin had, long since, made himself acquainted with all the congenial lore they contained; and with a *carte blanche* to all the lawyers' and doctors' offices of St. Augustine, as well as to a number of private libraries, he was reaping all the advantages of book learning, which the times and his circumstances allowed. He was a fellow of rough manners, from early association, but naturally quite a gentleman in his address. He took great pains to give himself the air of a well bred citizen, and it had begun to be apparent that communion with men and books was giving his manners a polish and his conversation a point; and about the time of which we write, it was whispered that Benjamin had enough of the genuine Yankee in his composition to make a stir in the world some day. He was now about twenty years of age, was tall and sinewy, had dark hair that hung in graceful wavelets, and a bold black eye that possessed a general-observation expression, which gave his countenance quite the look of a man of the world. He had labored diligently and watchfully to conquer New England mannerisms, but he could never so remodel the outward character, stamped upon him by nature and education, that he would not at first " guess " have been " reckoned " a Yankee, by all who had the slightest familiarity with the habits, manners and peculiarities of that class of the *genus homo*.

CHAPTER V.

THE POSEY DANCE.

Had Isabelle Conere been called to follow to the grave the remains of a father who had died in honor, though the affliction had set heavily upon her, she could have borne up against it without palor of cheek, dimming of eye, or decline in the elasticity of her step; but to see him whom she had loved, with that trusting affection that believes its object can do no wrong, buried within the thick walls of a dismal cell,—if she did feel that he deserved not the punishment which the laws put upon him,—was the germ of a grief that immediately began to sap the buoyant spirits that had blessed her girlhood. She had not given up the strong determination, taken hastily in an hour of violent passion, that her father should be liberated. She had formed no idea how this deliverance was to be effected—she reflected not *of* the means—she determined, with all the power of an uncurbed will, *upon the end.*

Conere had been a prisoner in the castle of St. Mark, now called Fort Marion, nearly six months. This castle, commanding the approach to St. Augustine, between Anastasia Island and the main shore, was, at the time of which we write, used as a civil and military prison.

It is the oldest fort in the United States, having been built in 1756. With its grass-grown walls, lofty turrets and massive battlements, which give it an air of antique romance,—with the stories told of some of its dungeons, that they were at one time used for the purposes of the Spanish Inquisition, it forms a great attraction to the "sight seekers" who visit the Peninsula. The casemate in which Conere was confined was that from which, some years subsequently, the Indian Coacoochee, youngest son of the renowned and subtile chief Philip, escaped through an embrasure; and many curiosity-lovers have walked over its damp floors, who had no thought of the bitter tears shed profusely upon them, by a devoted daughter.

The Spaniard had been arraigned before an inferior court, and remanded to prison to await his trial, before the proper tribunal, for the amazing crime of murder in the first degree. He had employed no counsel; he made no explanation, attempted no palliation. Brinton had used every effort possible, in his behalf, but Conere would second no scheme for his release.

It is strange that he made no full confession of all his circumstances to his family; but when the thought was suggested, or it came up in his mind, his universal soliloquy was, "Ashes are not mortgages." And when Brinton urged him to make preparation for his approaching trial, he answered:

"I cannot, *would* not tell *you* why; but it is best they should do their worst. I shall be prepared."

The people believed that Conere was a base murderer. They knew him to be a man of dark passions, with a Spaniard's disregard of the life of an enemy; and there were those who, notwithstanding all that Madam Conere had done, as an angel of mercy and charity, circulated base rumors, and alienated many friends.

Though the blight of crime had fallen on the master of Rillwood, in what were his wife and daughter changed? Nothing but devotion. But the purblind world cannot recognize nice distinctions unless they happen to be in a desired favor; and there were few of Isabelle Conere's friends who regarded her the more tenderly because she appeared prepared to sacrifice her life at her father's order, to save him from his impending fate.

Madam Conere, tender-hearted, mild-natured, grieved sorely at the coldness of former intimate acquaintances; and she was dying, as the tropical plant dies in a chill clime, for the want of that life-giving nourishment necessary to bind her closely to earth—sympathy in the rendering of good deeds—that had made her life blessed. Isabelle said of all who grew distant:

"Let them go, mother, they are not worth having."

But the mother could not find in her heart a shade of feeling akin to her daughter's cynicism; and every day her cheek grew paler, her form became more attenuated, and at the return from each sad visit to her imprisoned husband, it was evident another of the ties that bound her to earth had been broken. There were true friends among the poor and lowly minded, who were welcomed to her household, and their anxious concern did much to soothe her sorrows; but they could not bring back her waning strength, nor restore the lustre to her listless eye.

But it must not be said that all the influential, who, in prosperity, had been friends of the Rillwood family, now deserted them. There were those who did not vanish when adversity fell upon Rillwood, as the early blossom vanishes when the cold mountain air comes upon it, as,

> "Winter still lingering on the verge of Spring,
> Retires reluctant, and from time to time
> Looks back."

Foremost among the true ones, should be mentioned Brinton and Benjamin.

Isabelle had counseled with Brinton. She had declared her determination that at all hazard her father should be released from prison, before the threatening vengeance of the law fell upon him, hoping to gain the aid of his strong mind and worldly experience, in devising the means by which her object was to be accomplished; but when she had revealed all to him, with amazement he exclaimed:

"It cannot be, Isabelle, honorably, except by means of a pardon, and of that you know there can be no hope."

"It shall be, Ledyard Brinton," returned Isabelle, in a tone which made him shudder, "with or without a pardon; and if *you* now desert me, I must seek aid where I can place my confidence."

"I *will* aid you, Isabelle—will do all an honorable man can do; but my self-respect requires me to tell you that your project is a mad one."

"I am resolved, Ledyard. I know you too well to believe you could now give me your confidence; and the counsel I expected from you, I must seek from a stranger. But do not plead with me; it will avail nothing."

These words were uttered by Isabelle with deep emotion,

as she walked with Brinton along the avenue leading from the Augustine road to Rillwood mansion. They were unanswered for some moments. Brinton had absented himself from festivities proceeding at his house, under the direction of his aunt and her daughter, to spend half an hour with Isabelle, and they had been walking some time when the conversation we have detailed, occurred. We will not describe their parting that night, but let the conduct of Brinton reveal his feelings, when, an hour afterwards, he returned to Windsor.

The Posey Dance had opened with spirit, and a "merrie companie" were whirling its giddy mazes with general delight. Benjamin appeared to be master of ceremonies. We shall see how it happened.

The Posey Dance, not like the Patgoe, is a favorite, particularly of west Florida. The ladies of a household, wishing to gather their friends, erect an altar, decorated with bouquets and festoons of flowers, which is understood by the gentlemen as an invitation to call and admire the taste and skill of the fair architects. The lady of the house, culling a rare bouquet, presents it to the gentleman of her choice, and if he accept the honor, he becomes master of the festivities, chooses the lady as queen of the ball, and then follow Spanish dances and whirling waltzes.

Brinton's English cousin had chosen Benjamin as the gentleman with whom she was best acquainted, and the aspiring New Englander felt his consequence as much as if he had been king of all the Spaniards, instead of superintendent of Spanish dances for a few hours.

Brinton had no heart to join the gay assemblage of dancers, and he wandered towards a bower in the garden, from which, on the calm night air, floated sounds of delicious music.

His aunt was a passionate lover of music, and she had inspired him with much of her enthusiasm. She had an exquisite ear and a finely cultivated voice, and, from the families in the neighborhood, she had collected half a dozen young girls and several gentlemen, who often, under her direction, made vocal with enrapturing strains the orange groves about Windsor. Brinton delighted in these parties, but he could have no pleasure in this one. Isabelle should have been there to sing with him wild and melancholy songs. He stood beside his friends in the arbor, and followed the tunes they sang, but he could not sing *with* them. His aunt observed his change of manner, and when the singers were prepared to join the dancers in the mansion, she took his arm, and they wandered along a garden walk.

The aunt wept over the nephew's growing attachment for Isabelle Conere, because her notions of happiness, in married life, were formed upon a much different standard from that generally regarded in Florida, and feeling that Brinton's impulses were with hers, she warned him, that if Isabelle Conere became his wife, he would never have a home, and counseled him tenderly, not to allow himself to be *entrapped*, as she considered it.

Brinton felt that his aunt did not understand Isabelle, and he did not heed her warnings, though he received her counsels kindly. On the night of which we now speak, she knew from Brinton's manner, that something of no trivial character had disturbed him, and she suspected that it concerned Isabelle. When they had walked where their conversation would not be overheard, after referring to Isabelle's absence, and the sad cause, she inquired:

"But, Ledyard, is the girl as wild as ever?"

"Wild!" he returned, speaking as if his thoughts had been echoed. "If you had seen her to-night, you had not asked me; but it is over now — all over."

"What is over, Ledyard?"

"Our intimacy — we have separated."

"Then you have taken my counsel — you believe that she should never be your wife?" said the aunt, eagerly.

"No, aunt. No. You do not understand Isabelle. I am rejected."

"Rejected!" repeated the lady.

"Yes, rejected," said Brinton, bitterly.

"Has she been a coquette — has she deceived you?"

"Not deceived *me*, aunt, but she deceives herself. She confessed that she loved me — that were it not for her father's ill fate, I would be her choice. But she is mad, aunt. She says her father shall be liberated — that his prison doors shall be opened. I told her it was impossible, except by force; but she would not hear me, and when I said she should have some one to counsel with her — to be her true friend, in the troubles that had fallen upon her house, and begged her to let me be her protector, she answered wildly, 'You are not the man, Ledyard.' I told her, all that an honorable man could do I was ready to perform. But it would not answer. She declared that marriage must be subservient to the object, for the attainment of which she had devoted her life, and she would have no man for a husband who would not consecrate himself to that work, at all risk. Oh, she is mad! I pleaded with her a few minutes, then the expression of her dark eye grew terrible—I shall never forget it—and she fiercely bid me never dare to mention marriage to her again. I cannot see her destroy herself. What shall I do? What a woman she would be, if her powers were directed in the proper channel."

And the young man looked up confidently to his aunt, as if expecting that she would propose a scheme that would banish all his painful thoughts; but if he had a thought of this character, it vanished when the stern woman replied:

"I am sorry for her, Ledyard, but I rejoice for you. It is strange you are not convinced that my counsel is for your good."

"You do not know how I love her, aunt. I would do anything but sacrifice my honor to her, and this she would not have me do. She is mad. Hers is the purpose of a crazy woman, and I must save her from it." Saying these words, Brinton turned, as if to go back towards the mansion.

"You would not go to her again, Ledyard?" said the aunt.

"I must walk alone," he returned, sadly. "I am half distracted—perhaps I have madly loved this girl, but I cannot see her madly destroy herself." With these words, as they approached company, Brinton disappeared from his aunt's side. She whispered as he left:

"Go not now, Brinton, or I shall think you as mad as Isabelle."

But her words were unheeded. High in the heavens rode the full moon, but Brinton knew not whether he walked in sunlight or moonlight. He emerged from an orange grove near Rillwood, just as a party of revelers, returning home from Windsor, passed along a neighboring path, and not wishing to be observed, and knowing that he would not now be missed at home, he sat down beneath one of the trees and endeavored to reflect; but his thoughts were not at his command, and he sat gazing towards the spot where he supposed the object of his anxiety to be, when a dark form appeared on the front steps, and was admitted by Isabelle. Feelings which he could not explain, gave him an impulse to speak one word to her, at least, before she reflected for the night, on the strange conversation they had held together in the early part of the evening.

He appeared at the entrance to the main hall. Isabelle was in the parlor, and answered his summons alone. Her manner startled him.

"To what," she said formally, "am I indebted, Mr. Brinton, for this visit? I thought we had parted."

"I come to talk to you, Isabelle."

"I'll listen to you here, then; but our conference must be brief."

"I have a great deal to say, Isabelle. You know not what I have suffered in the last hour. Let me counsel you."

"You mistake me, Mr. Brinton. Did I not tell you that I was resolved. The command of one from the grave could not change me. Above us swings the cage of a parrot, which you taught to speak four words—it repeats them unceasingly, as long as the light of each day lasts. Go near it when you will, it is crying '*Polly wants to fly;*' and it has never uttered any other words. There is one confined, for whose release I shall labor as unceasingly as that parrot begs, and unless he fly from his prison, never, until the light of life goes out, will I relinquish my task. When you would talk to me, think of that parrot. You made your choice.

Until you can tell me you would alter it, I command you, speak to me no more of love. Good night."

Isabelle disappeared, leaving Brinton in a state of mind which he alone could describe, who experienced its peculiar perplexity and embarrassment. He walked slowly from the mansion, and sat down in an arbor on the main avenue. He continued with his thoughts for an hour or more, when voices disturbed him. He looked towards the hall door, and by the broad moonlight which streamed into it, he recognized two persons whom he had little expected to see thus together. He cursed himself for having stopped in that place; then he reflected:

"All is over—it's no matter now."

In a moment, the gentleman had passed him; he could not be deceived. It was Benjamin, and he had kissed Isabelle's hand at parting. Conjecture and speculation were at fault entirely, in divining the object of this meeting; and Brinton was more in wonder than ever at the strangeness of Isabelle's conduct.

A great change had come over this man Benjamin in the period intervening between this time and his first introduction in our history. He was no longer secretary to Conere. He was regarded, at St. Augustine, as a shrewd Northerner, who had recently taken the license to peddle pills and feel pulses. Benjamin possessed that sly way of getting along through this world which gives men the reputation of being "smart fellows." It is not exactly on the principle by which a miller or a chimney-sweep gets through a crowd, but it is by making shrewd use of the faculty of reading other men's characters and dispositions. It is a faculty of incalculable advantage to the demagogue—he knows all men truly, while they think him anything but the man he really is. This power enables the "wire-puller" to prosecute his "cunningly devised schemes;" it is, too, of great benefit, many times, to the orator; and by it the lawyer is enabled to make out a "hard case" and let his client go "scot free." In all business relations it is available, and, to a great extent, is the secret of most men's success; and although it may not be always employed with a view to the maxim that "honesty is the best policy," we have no doubt it is frequently the "policy" of dignitaries whose position should be above trickery. The Scottish bard thought it of no inconsiderable importance, when he gave the following advice:

> "Conceal yoursel as weel's ye can
> Frae critical dissection,
> But keek through ivery ither man
> Wi' sharpened slie inspection."

CHAPTER VI.

RESULTS.

Spring had departed — that season when Florida puts forth the vernal display, from which Ponce de Leon, the Spanish adventurer, in 1512, gave it its name, when, pursuing the fiction of a Carib girl, he sought a fountain whose waters would rejuvenate the man of hoary brow, and restore the beauty of maidenhood to the careworn matron.

Ledyard Brinton was extensively popular among the young and active men of the district. He was well versed in matters of state polity, and though he did not often appear in courts, was deeply learned in the law. He had entered the arena of politics, to some extent, at the earnest solicitation of influential friends, who admired his liberality and independence, and, consistent with his views, among the people by whom he was surrounded, his course had been such as to secure him the confidence of the mass. He was a reformer, but he was not one of those Hotspurs, who cannot live but in the heat of angry agitation; and though he would have had changed, in one day, many social evils which oppressed a people in the State of his adoption, he knew that to hope for such a revolution was vain, and he chose not to make enemies by bitter upbraidings and ascetic censures upon his neighbors. His object was to conciliate friends, and when he had gained their confidence, cautiously put before them such facts as would demonstrate what was practical and profitable.

He had been selected as a candidate for a seat in the Legislature, and the election was to be held in a few months.

Brinton was what may be properly termed an independent man — not one whose independence consists in a mulish obstinacy, but one who thinks and acts for himself, as an honest man should—one who is not trammeled by prejudice —who does not travel in the *beaten track* because he was so educated, but who has no fear of breaking from conventional customs, when he would follow the right because of the right. He is the independent man, who comports himself as circumstances justify, according to the highest standard of right and justice, whether before the world, or in his closet—

> "Whose armor is his honest thought,
> And simple truth his utmost skill."

Conere had been tried. The testimony was positive, and there was no escape, in the common course of events, from the fate of a murderer. To his friends, Conere's conduct was inexplicable. He met the verdict, condemning him to death, with stolid indifference; and, except that his manner was reserved, nothing about him betokened the least concern at the anxiety of his friends, the grief of his family, or the dreadful end which awaited him.

Brinton had been a regular visitor at Rillwood since the evening of the Posey dance, but, though Isabelle received him kindly, her manner gave him to understand, unmistakably, that her determination was unchanged.

Her conduct was an enigma to him, as much as that of her father. He could not but feel that, to all outward semblance, for one who loved a parent wildly as she loved her father, she bore bravely the troubles he had brought upon his household, yet he could not consider hers that noble struggle against adversity, which meets trials sternly, but meekly, and prepares to profit by their lessons. She did not give him her confidence, and he misunderstood her, while her heart's emotions breathed, towards her father, Moore's impassioned words—

"Oh what was love made for if 'tis not the same
Thro' joy and thro' sorrow, thro' glory and shame?"

It was the Sabbath following the conviction of Conere. Gloom, like a pall, settled over Rillwood. Like the fading away of a sweet odor, had gone out the life of its mistress, sadly, but almost imperceptibly. She was buried with simple ceremony, at the foot of a cypress tree in the garden, beneath which she had loved to sit. The spot was marked only by flowers that "poured out their souls in odors," but it was dear, as no sculptured urn could have made it, to the sad hearts of those whose afflictions Madame Conere had softened by her charities, and whose griefs she had assuaged by well-timed kindness. *Her* virtues had not been written in water, and *her* good deeds did not die with her.

CHAPTER VII.

THE DOCTOR.

Since the death of Madame Conere, Benjamin, by his cunning and intrigue, upon the profession of sincerest friendship, had become a confidential visitor at Rillwood.

After her mother's death, in looking over some papers in a secret drawer of her father's *escritoire*, Isabelle found a letter, the persual of which caused her to exclaim:

"My God! Why had I not found this sooner? Now my father *shall* be liberated. I feel that there can be no doubt. It is strange father had not told me something of this."

Rising, she rang for a servant. The summons was promptly answered by a trusty negro, and she said to him:

"Go to St. Augustine immediately, and tell Doctor Benjamin that I wish to see him at Rillwood as soon as he can conveniently come."

The servant hastened away, and in an hour had properly delivered his message. Benjamin gladly received it. He had that day been informed that the time of Conere's execution had been fixed for the 20th of the following month; and suspecting that Isabelle had received the terrible news and wished to counsel with him, hoping that something would occur to further the designs he entertained, before the hour had come, when

>—" Twilight lets her curtain down
And pins it with a star,"

he was on his way swiftly to Rillwood. He found Isabelle beneath an airy veranda extending east from the mansion, rose-wreathed and vine-encircled. She received him rather affectionately, remarking:

"We have good news, Doctor. The scheme which I partly revealed to you, must succeed."

"Then you have not heard"——

. "What, Doctor?"

"I had best be plain — you must expect it. It has been fixed that the execution shall take place on the 20th of next month."

"Before that time, my father shall have a pardon. His release will be honorable, and then we can show that he stabbed Espard in self-defense. To consult you in the selection of a legal adviser, I sent for you to-day."

"But how is this to be done?" inquired Benjamin, with a perplexed manner.

"We will walk into the house, and I'll show you," answered Isabelle.

When they were seated by a lamp, which threw a soft light over the richly furnished apartment, Isabelle handed the doctor a letter, remarking:

"You know that, for important reasons, the Government is anxious to discover the man who murdered Major Bertram, some years ago, near Pensacola, and carried off certain state papers, which, in the prosecution of the Seminole war, have become of much moment."

"Yes," answered Benjamin, "I read it all in the Augustine paper yesterday."

"That letter will tell you that Cabot Conere, in some way, knows who this murderer was. It must be the man whose name is signed there," returned Isabelle.

Benjamin read the document, examined the name, and exclaimed.

"Eureka! This *must* be the fellow. He is fighting with the Indians, against our forces. If Conere can give testimony that will convict him, I know the Governor will grant him a pardon. Brinton has influence with the Governor — shall I not see him to-morrow?"

"Speak not to me of him, Benjamin — him on whom I depended — he deceived me — I would not now be beholden to him."

A gleam of light burst upon the doctor, as Isabelle spoke these words, which almost made him utter an exclamation of delight; but suddenly his natural cunning came to his aid, and he said, mildly:

"It can be done without him. I have influential friends."

Emotions had been awakened, which almost rendered Isabelle forgetful of the immediate business with the doctor, and she walked several times rapidly across the room, and then, stopping at the window, pressed her hot brow on the cold glass.

The doctor gazed at her strangely for a few moments, and then approaching her, rested his arm on the window sill. She did not know that he was so near her until he whispered,

"Isabelle."

She turned her weeping eyes upon him, wondering what brought him so near, and perplexed at the peculiarity of his look.

"Isabelle, you have not been scornful lately; you sent for me to-day; you have confided in me. I know your secret. You would get your father from prison; let me help you."

"I expect you to do so, Benjamin—what mean you?"

"Isabelle, I have dared to love you. I loved you when you were a little girl. I knew it was madness then. I have worked, Isabelle, to be worthy of you. I am not what I once was. I'll devote my life to you."

The doctor's tones were eloquent—his looks were impassioned. He endeavored to take Isabelle's hand, but she lifted both to her forehead, and, as was her wont when wild thoughts surged in her brain, pressed them over her eyes, and sinking upon a low seat, she said:

"Benjamin," in a tone that made him tremble, "are you sincere, or would you only be lord of this mansion? I know you are ambitious. Have you considered that I am a convict's daughter—that I have been exiled from society?"

"All—all," he answered, impetuously, "but you are not the less beloved. I love you the more for your devotion to your father, the man who first helped me. Were it not for what you described, I should never have dared to address you. As I expect to be judged, believe me honest."

Isabelle was silent for a few moments, while the tears flowed fast from her downcast eyes, then she rose to her feet, and presenting her hand to the doctor, said firmly:

"Give me a trial—rescue my father, and this hand is yours."

The doctor pressed her hand passionately between both of his, and answered:

"Your father was a friend to me, for his sake I would do much; but for your sake, I swear that I am at your command—that I will be your slave."

Without attempting to release her hand, Isabelle looked into Benjamin's eyes and answered:

"I have only to ask that you will shrink from nothing to liberate my father from prison — *mind* nothing. Can you swear it?"

"As I hope for Heaven, I can," said Benjamin.

"Then understand me. Remember, I have not loved you —I know not that I ever can love you; but if you rescue my father, I *will try* to love you. I sacrifice my love and fortune for that purpose. If you deceive me, it will be terrible for you."

The doctor quailed beneath the look Isabelle gave him, as she spoke these words, but he answered instantly:

"May it be terrible for me if I deceive you."

"The work should commence to-night. I would be alone. Go now, Benjamin, and to-morrow bring me word of whom you have chosen for a legal adviser."

The doctor kissed her hand, and was in a few minutes on the road to Augustine. He traveled it in such exultation as he had never before experienced.

Isabelle Concre's emotions were the very antipode of her lover's, in all except hope that her father's prison doors would soon be opened, and the dread execution, thought of which chilled her heart's blood, averted.

When the doctor reached the city, he proceeded to a hotel, where a political club met, and was soon breathing an atmosphere redolent of liquors and tobacco fumes.

CHAPTER VIII.

THE LEGAL ADVISER.

It was the eve of an election, which, at this time, though the country was filled with soldiers, and the Indians were every day committing depredations, was an era in the history of St. Augustine; one, too, that contrasted strangely with many customs that had been observed when the Spaniards ruled over the ancient city. The happy constitution of our government puts all men on a level at these periods, and often those who have the least real consequence, feel the most importance.

In a drinking saloon closely filled with such characters, Benjamin appeared, when we parted from him in the last chapter. It was not exactly a caucus, or a club, or a cabal, but an irregular gathering, at which politics was the theme. The discussion was on the candidates, and one of the "crowd," whose face like that of Shakspeare's Bardolph, it had cost many a copper to keep in color, was answering one of his party, in this wise:

"You're right; this feller as is up for the Legislater, aint the chap what we wotes for. He'd make us give up licker. He can't stand among folks as likes liberty."

"That he can't, stand 'mong us," returned another of the

party, who was only able to keep his feet by leaning against his friends, or holding by the tables. "We're goin to exercise the right of suffrage for independence; if we can't, what's the use in the Declaration?"

"It's the doctor's treat," exclaimed a toper who then had been treated till he scarcely knew anything but the way to the bar.

"So it is," chimed in half a dozen voices, and the doctor could do nothing else than make a sudden retreat, or attend to the call on his "patriotism." A dozen or more arranged themselves where they could be served with their drinks, and the doctor addressed them:

"It's a fact, boys, Brinton aint just the chap we want for a legislator. He's a clever fellow in some things, but I don't think all his notions just agree with this country. You're right on liberty, boys. Such notions whipped the old British—got this land from the Spanish—and they will put the Seminoles where they can't molest us any more. Here's a health to Squire Lifty—he'll beat Brinton, slick."

The party tossed off their glasses, when a man, sitting at one end of the tables, who had yet taken no part in the conversation or drinking, quietly observed:

"A d——n pretty fellow you are, Doctor, to desert a man who brought you here, and made you all you can boast of. It's not a week since you were electioneering for him."

"Turn him out!" exclaimed several of the "voters" who had drank the doctor's liquor; but his shrewdness was not at fault, and he very deliberately replied, although he was much nettled:

"No, no, boys. Let him go it. Because I'm independent, I expect to be abused. If I saw I was on the wrong side, I had a right to wheel about. In politics, a man can't always be with his personal friends."

"Right, Doctor—right again. We honor you for your independence. We'll stand by you, too, till you're a candidate some day," said the spokesman of the drinking party. In the meantime, the individual who had thrown "the firebrand" disappeared, and Benjamin, finding it not necessary to keep up further intercourse with the "sovereigns," said to the man who sold them drink:

"Give the boys another round, at my expense. I have an appointment in the next room, and you will excuse me till I have seen Squire Lifty."

He stepped out as the party drank his health, and in a moment was among a company that was concocting plans for the defeat of Brinton's party on the morrow.

"Good evening, Doctor," said one of the schemers, "we were just counting upon you."

At this, the nominee of the company, Brinton's opponent, came forward, and shaking the doctor's hand vigorously, said:

"Your conversion to our cause, has given us great pleasure. If it had been sooner, we had been surer of success. But you know our plans; are they right?"

"I think they're the best you could invent," returned Benjamin, stepping aside. "But, mind you, Brinton has conducted himself so carefully that people wont believe much against him. They know, at least, he will do only what he thinks best for them, all things considered; and he is popular among the liberalists, and you know there are plenty of them. But, Squire, d——n politics, to night—I am here on other business. I want to defeat Brinton in another way.

I have a chance for you to make a handsome fee. Excuse yourself to the club, and meet me, in half an hour, at the *cafe*, near the Barracks. I'll have things right there."

Benjamin hastened to prepare for the squire, and the would-be legislator immediately excused himself to his followers present, on the plea that there were other friends to counsel with, and he must be stirring about. He had drunk deeply, but he could bear up against a big load, and he was not yet too dull for a scheme, out of which there might come a prospect of money.

Over a bottle of wine and a cigar, Benjamin revealed to Squire Lifty, Isabelle's plan for the rescue of her father, and telling him all about the important letter, and offering a liberal fee if he would manage it successfully, inquired what he thought the hope of success.

"It can be done as easily as I shall beat Brinton to-morrow, and when I am elected, I'll have influence with the Governor. I'll undertake it, any how," returned the lawyer.

"Then," said Benjamin, "you must see Isabelle as soon as the election's over. I'll tell her, to-morrow morning, that you are engaged. She'll give you all the documents."

The new friends separated, the squire pleased with the prospect of a good office and a fat fee, Benjamin with the prospect of an accomplished and beautiful wife, a large fortune, and the getting of Brinton out of his way, in his design of making a stir in the world some time.

The election took place, with many a dispute, many a squabble, much drunkenness, intrigue and misrepresentation; but the candidate popular among the dram-drinkers, one of that class of politicians who can "wire in and wire out," as expressed by a well known, homely couplet, was signally defeated, and Brinton received official notice that he had been honored with a seat in the Legislative Council of his adopted State.

The doctor, at the time appointed, duly advised Isabelle of the selection of the squire, as legal adviser; and knowing nothing of the man, and having confidence that Benjamin would exercise his best judgment, she had no reason to be dissatisfied.

On the day after the result of the election had been announced, the doctor conducted the squire to Rillwood, and introduced him to Isabelle.

He was not in quite as good spirits as he would have been, had he been able to consider himself a law maker, as well as a law mystifier; but he had a little revenge to gratify, and having been informed of Brinton's former relation to Isabelle, and the doctor's hopes, his crafty nature was well pleased with the scheme of which he had been advised, and the handsome reward its execution promised.

He had a long conference with Isabelle — examined the important letter, and, assuring her that there could be no doubt of a pardon, on the ground she proposed asking it, prepared the form of the necessary papers, and left her, with the advice that she forthwith see her father, acquaint him with her intentions, get what information he could give, visit the Governor, and in person sue for the pardon.

CHAPTER IX.

THE INTERVIEW AND THE PARDON.

It was a refreshing morning in early winter, when Isabelle Conere left Rillwood, attended by Doctor Benjamin, for the castle of St. Mark's.

The foliage of the orange groves, the majestic palms, the lime, the pomegranate and the fig, deepened, not embrowned, as the frosts of a Northern clime change the summer green, gently stirred by breezes balmy as those that "blow soft o'er Ceylon's isle," almost burthened the atmosphere with delicious fragrance. Flowers by the wayside, of varied hue and conformation, with their leaves and petals drooping, gave out, ere their decay, sweetest perfume; and bright plumaged birds twittered and sung in the branches of all the trees; but Isabelle was not awakened from the thoughtful revery by the invigorating air, the prospect of the groves, nor the charms of the fields. Winter was in her mind, and its desolateness resembled more the condition of Northern landscapes, bleak and drear, beneath chilling winds, than the luxuriance of that Southern clime. But she did not despair, for hope presented a spring time, near at hand, in which her joys would bloom afresh in the delights of home associations. In all, there was but one object, around which did not gather affections in keeping with the scene, and that object presented itself whenever Doctor Benjamin, or his service, was suggested.

Conere was always glad to receive visits from Isabelle, but he had seemed peculiarly so since the death of Madame Conere. He welcomed her with more than wonted affection on this morning. She had fear to open the object of her visit, which she could not account for; but the devotion of a life was cast on this hour, and she must proceed. When they were alone, without explanation, she presented Conere the papers Squire Lifty had prepared. He read them with evident emotion — his breathing grew quick, his eyes flashed strangely, and he exclaimed wildly, grasping her hand:

"My daughter, where, in the name of God, did you get this information?"

"From this letter, father; but why are you so agitated?"

He snatched the letter she handed him (that found in his *escritoire*), and after looking at it a moment, he became more calm, and asked her:

"Do you know who this man is, and where he is?"

"Benjamin says he is the Indian called Hulkwa-nuntokay, who leads a party of Mickasukies in the cypress swamp."

"How does Benjamin know this?"

"He says an officer of the army told him that this chief was a white man who was suspected of having been engaged in depredations before the Americans possessed Florida. He lived a short time in Augustine, and he was then known as Herpez. Mr. Lifty says he has seen him, and knows that he was a bad man," answered Isabelle, wondering why her father put such questions; but she had been accustomed to moods that no present circumstances could explain, and she dare not interrogate him in regard to them.

"He *is* a bad man, daughter—that's what the Indian name he has chosen means—but I believed the man Herpez was in another country. He told me he would go; yet if he *is* here, and finds that Espard is killed"——

As Conere spoke these words, he stood before his daughter, and taking both her hands, gazed intently upon her a few moments, then thoughtfully continued:

"You can save me from an awful death, child. You can make my life, which has been a burden for many years, from constant fears, peaceful and happy, if, by love or money, you can have this Indian leader arrested."

Isabelle did not understand her father fully, but she answered with determination—

"I *will* save you, father, and I know the Indian can be arrested. Benjamin will seek him, and he has the promised aid of the Indian Agent."

"You have planned well. I'll sign these papers, and you will hasten, to-morrow, in person, to present them to the Governor. Let them be seen by no one else." With these words, Conere was about to part from his daughter, when she affectionately said:

"What had you to do with this Indian white man, father? How came he to send you the letter? He confesses a knowledge of the crime of murdering Major Bertram, but he does not confess himself the murderer."

"But he *was* the murderer," interrupted Conere. "You must not now ask me what I had to do with him. You shall know all, another time."

"There are many things I wish to know, father, and I

have heard things which, when I think of them, frighten me; but this land is full of wicked men, and, when I have saved you, we will leave it."

"Yes, daughter, we *will* leave it. But go now—my guard is coming."

"In a few days, Benjamin shall bring you word that I have your pardon." Isabelle took tender leave of her father, and, conducted by the guard, joined Benjamin in the outer court.

When Conere was alone, he soliloquized—

"Yes, we *will* leave this land. Oh, what a land it has been to me. Why did I have a family? I might defy them, but all must be deceived now. The Americans would like to get this Indian. What do I care whether he is Herpez or not? Prejudice is against him. I can invent a story that will fix him—but I believe it *is* him—if it is, how I shall triumph! Espard dead—Herpez hung. It was lucky Isabelle found that letter—but when she showed me the papers, I thought she might know too much. She's a brave girl, and she'll get the pardon. I shall be free—no fear of man's tongue shall haunt me hereafter. Would that Brinton had stood by us. I rather suspect secrets have been told to him; but Benjamin will work hard, and if he arrests that infernal Indian, Isabelle and her fortune—that fortune Espard would have had—shall be his. I'll wait—patiently, *if I can*—to hear from him."

Isabelle Conere, escorted by the aspiring doctor, lost no time in visiting Tallahassee. The Governor happened to be at home. She waited upon him, and plead, as only a daughter can, for the life of a father. Her papers had been judiciously prepared, and when she laid them before his Excellency, after he had heard her story, he assured her that he would take the matter into immediate consideration, and send word of his determination, at her hotel, on the following evening.

Tediously dragged the hours, until the period appointed for the Governor's report. Isabelle was alone in her room—she paced it slowly, and as the dim shadows, thrown in gigantic shapes from her person by a flickering lamp that sat on a low stool, flitted to and fro, she fixed her eyes upon them, and exclaimed:

"Can it be that now my hopes are fleeting, unsubstantial as these shadows—that in a dim light I have been groping, and all my visions, for the future, are but dreams, shadowy dreams? If it prove so, I shall go mad. But I did not plead well with the Governor, perhaps. I told him my father confessed that he had killed the man Espard, but I knew he did it in self-defense. I did not ask a pardon out of pity—my father wants no man's pity—but I asked it because he could render the government valuable aid. I demanded it as the price of service rendered. I have heard that to great criminals pardons have been rendered, for testimony that would convict greater criminals. The Governor said he would grant the pardon, if my father could do what he promises—I know he can—the Governor was gracious to me—the pardon will come—hark! I hear a summons below —some one comes up the stairs. I know the step—it is Benjamin."

The almost frantic girl hastened to the door of her room, hastily opened it, and met the doctor. He handed her a package of papers. She said to him:

"Leave me alone for an hour, Benjamin, and I will summon you."

As he retired, she threw herself upon a lounge, and nervously broke the seal of the papers. A letter bearing the Governor's signet, met her view; she opened it, and read:

"My Dear Madame:—I return you the papers which you entrusted to me, with the assurance that it is consistent with my duty to the nation, and a proper regard to the laws, to say to you, under my official seal, that your friends shall have every aid I can render; and if the Indian Hulkwa-nuntokay can be arrested, and your father, Cabot Conere, shall present before the proper tribunal, such evidence as will convict him of the murder of Major Bertram, an unconditional pardon shall be granted him.

"I shall countermand the order fixing the execution for the 20th inst.

"I remain, with sentiments of high respect, your obedient servant,

——— ———,

"*Governor of the Territory of Florida.*"

When Isabelle had read this letter, without stopping a moment for reflection, she summoned Benjamin, acquainted him with the purport of the Governor's communication, and said to him:

"All rests with you now, Benjamin—you have a dangerous task, but you chose it without solicitation. The Governor will order men to escort you. I will leave you here to-morrow. Proceed immediately to arrest this Indian—you must accomplish it by stratagem. Take trusty guides and brave men. Bring him to Tallahassee, and when the trial is had, this hand is yours. I will carry the news of pardon to father, myself."

Benjamin kissed the hand she offered him, and vowed that he would never return to St. Augustine alive without Hulkwa-nuntokay.

On the morrow, the doctor prepared to visit the cypress swamps, and Isabelle returned to Rillwood in company with a party of Augustine acquaintances. They little suspected the object of her visit to Tallahassee.

At the earliest possible hour, Conere had the privilege of reading the letter, securing him pardon, on the conditions we have described. Loading his daughter with thanks and caresses, he assured her, that on the day of trial he should vindicate himself.

He was a dark minded and dangerously deceitful man. His daughter loved him too blindly to understand his true character.

CHAPTER X.

THE ARREST AND THE DISCOVERY.

Doctor Benjamin, with a faithful escort and experienced guides, had journeyed three days from Tallahassee. He began seriously to reflect, that following Indian trails, through swamps and thick woods, was not as pleasant as rolling pills in St. Augustine. It was not the *way* he proposed walking to distinction in this world. In his solitary hours he grew desponding many times, but love and fortune cheered him on, and before his men he maintained a brave exterior.

From a friendly Indian, the commander of the escort had learned that Hulkwa-nuntokay, as the leader of a small party of Mickasukie Indians, had a camp near the southern boundary of the Big Cypress swamp, which was subsequently the rendezvous of many parties of hostile savages, who retreated thither during the Seminole war, and defied the American soldiers.

Hulkwa-nuntokay's band had been in the practice of marauding on the weaker planters along the rivers, and in the smaller towns; and the chief, as he was considered, was much feared as a daring and blood-thirsty savage. He had no regular connection with any band of Indians, and it was well understood that the only way to entrap him would be by stratagem. The doctor was directed by a party of six men, besides the guides and three friendly Indians, who knew the country, and the dangers they might expect to encounter.

Herpez was one of those singular, misanthropic men, who appear to despise comfort, and delight in crime—who exile themselves from society, and seek the deep forest. He had been in Florida, under different names, many years; and, from threats which he had thrown out, it was suspected that he had been always a foe to the Americans; and, from expressions that had escaped him while at one time in St. Augustine, it was surmised that he had in his possession important secrets. These things were known to the Governor, and for this reason he readily believed Cabot Conere's story, and promised him pardon, on the conviction of the Indian Spaniard. There was no Indian blood in his veins, but he had so long followed the habits of the red man, and worn his costume, that, except by the few who knew his history, he was supposed to be a Seminole, as his name indicated, giving, at the same time, his character, Hulkwa-nuntokay, as intimated by Conere, in his conversation with Isabelle, signifying *bad man*. Herpez was a man of great muscular power and agility, and a renowned marksman. His men were desperate Indians, who had scattered from different parties of that tribe, who, according to Indian tradition, murdered the first white man that was ever seen in Florida, believing him to have sprung from the foam of the ocean, thrown upon the beach. They discovered his trail on the shore of Lake Okeechobee, and, struck by the peculiar print of his shoe, followed it until they overtook him, and were led, by their natural thirst for blood, to take his life, though he besought peace.

When the party approached the swamp, they were very nearly surprised by a band of Creek Indians, and this admonished them to proceed watchfully, taking every precaution not to alarm the enemy.

One night, when the escort was encamped on the border of a pond covered with water-lilies, and from which proceeded the bellowing of alligators, so loudly as to interfere, very uncomfortably, with Doctor Benjamin's design of having a good night's rest, after a hard day's march, one of the Indian scouts, who had been sent out in the afternoon, returned with a pony, which, he declared, belonged to the Indians they were seeking. He had taken the animal near a settlement, at which, he believed, the band was now gathered.

On the following morning, various plans were proposed for the capture, and much speculation was had on the most feasible methods; but at length it was decided that they should first ascertain if Hulkwa-nuntokay was at the settlement— if so, they would that night attack it from various quarters, awe the Indians by surprise, disperse them, and so guard Herpez's hut that escape would be impossible. Dr. Benjamin had command of the squad that was to be relied upon to make the capture. There was but one man in the party who could identify Herpez, or Hulkwa-nuntokay. In the afternoon, he reported that he had seen the victim, and knew which was his hut.

The settlement was hid by tenebrous boughs and trailing mosses, in a dense cypress hammock. The attack was so well planned, and so cautiously managed, that the Indians were completely surprised, but they fought with desperation. Three men belonging to the escort were killed, and several received severe wounds. How many of the Mickasukies were slain, could not be ascertained. One of the men belonging to the escort was killed by a blow from the knife of Hulkwa-nuntokay. When the war-cry was given, the chief sprang to the door of his hut, and was met by the Indian guide, who gave a concerted signal, and attacked him. The chief was too skillful and muscular a warrior for his foe, who fell at his feet before assistance reached him, but Benjamin and his men were near at hand, and closing around the chief, they soon overmastered him, although he fought desperately with his knife, wounding a number, and among them the doctor.

As soon as the party could be rallied, after the defeat of the Indians, it was decided that rapid flight from the scene of the battle, was the policy they should adopt. They proceeded through the swamp in hasty marches, without molestation, except from a small band of Spanish Indians, who were soon routed. The second day they struck the trail for Tallahassee. About the time they began to fear pursuit, fortunately they fell in with a party of friendly Indians, who had been at war with the Mickasukies, and rejoiced to see their terror, Hulkawa-nuntokay, a prisoner. They now advanced in more easy marches, and allowed the men to recruit.

Herpez had maintained a dogged silence, and did not yet know that he had been taken prisoner on a particular charge. He supposed his numerous depredations on the whites, to have instigated the attack on his men. He knew his fate under such circumstances, and was prepared to meet it with Indian fortitude. Benjamin endeavored, several times, to engage him in conversation, without success, until one evening, when he stood by him in the camp, he said:

"Herpez!"

And at this sound, one which he had not heard for years, and which sent a torrent of wild thoughts through his brain, the disguised Indian started to his feet, and gave the doctor a look that caused him to step back a pace, but he continued,

"Did you ever know or hear of a Major Bertram, murdered some years ago, near Pensacola?"

"Who are you, that calls me this name, and asks me these questions?" demanded Herpez authoritatively.

"I am known as Doctor Benjamin, of St. Augustine—but you have not answered me."

"You have no business to question me. It's none of your business what I know, but I'll answer you. I did know Major or Lieutenant Bertram, and I know who murdered him, but the United States shall never know. The inquisitors could not make *me* tell."

"It is not expected that you will tell—but I am surprised to hear an Indian speak so good English," returned the doctor, provokingly. He could not move the Spaniard, who said, coolly:

"I followed another life than this, once—but what has my arrest to do with Major Bertram?"

"You shall know when we reach Tallahassee," answered the doctor, and the conversation was closed by the appearance of the commander of the escort, who had a duty for the doctor to perform, in the care of one of the wounded men, who had not yet recovered. Herpez held no more conversation with any of the party during the journey. When he was lodged safely at the capital, he was fully acquainted with the charge against him, and was ordered to prepare for his trial, which had been set for the following week. When inquired of if he desired counsel, he asked:

"What for?"

"To defend you," was the reply.

"Defend me? The devil could only do that. I'll have no defense. The Americans are determined to kill me—let them do it by hanging. A hundred lives shall pay the forfeit of mine. My Indians will avenge their chief—they will burn dwellings and pillage towns. But who is my accuser?"

"Cabot Conere, of Rillwood, who is in the fort at St. Augustine, for the murder of one Espard," answered the civil officer, who had visited him to learn his wishes in regard to counsel, for it had become known that he was far from being an Indian in early, if he had been in late education.

"Cabot Conere, of Rillwood," said Herpez—"I knew him once by a name not quite as high sounding. He killed Espard; to get his neck out of a halter, he would kill me. Well, if he chooses, he can do so—I shall be legally murdered, for if he could not make me guilty of this murder, he could tell enough against me besides to hang a small army— but my men shall have word, and they shall avenge my blood terribly."

The day appointed for the trial of Herpez would dawn on the morrow. Cabot Conere, released from his casemate at Castle Marco, but under a watchful guard, was at Tallahassee, with his daughter, in quarters where he was less constrained than he had been for a few months past. Squire Lifty was his adviser, and was to aid the Government in the prosecution of Herpez. Conere had so prepared himself, that he had no fear of the result of the trial.

* * * * * *

In company with a number of friends, Ledyard Brinton journeyed from Augustine to Tallahassee. They expected to reach the capital on the evening before the trial. It was late in the afternoon. Brinton, reflecting on the causes which had led him to Tallahassee—on the probable result of Conere's release—on Doctor Benjamin's hopes—was in no mood for gay company, and had fallen some rods behind his party. He knew that Isabelle did not love the doctor—knew that she was sacrificing herself for his aid in the rescue of her father, because her old lover had disappointed her in his honest expression that there was no hope of honorable release for Conere. Had Brinton entertained a suspicion of the course events had taken, no man could or would eagerly have done more than he to bring to justice the murderer of Bertram, and rescue Conere; but the accident, that gave Isabelle the knowledge upon which she had acted, came when he was estranged, and no opportunity had been given him to lend his aid or influence. Such reflections engaging him, he rode without perceiving how far his companions were in advance, when, as he passed a grove of undergrowth orange trees, a man in Indian garb, "armed to the teeth," sprang from a clump of bushes at the road-side, and, before Brinton saw his intention, grasped his horse by the bridle-bits, and exclaimed in good English:

"Ledyard Brinton, I have business with you."

Brinton was unarmed, excepting a brace of pocket pistols, and he knew resistance at this time would be vain. Though staggered at the man's strange and violent salutation, he did not lose his presence of mind, but answered promptly:

"You have chosen a novel manner of introducing yourself. Perhaps your business is with my purse."

"D——n your money," answered the outlaw. "I have a bigger scheme than taking money, on hand, and you must help me work it."

"*Must,*" said Brinton, "then you possess more power than I think you do; but I have no time to bandy words. What is your business?"

"You are going to Tallahassee to see one Herpez tried for a murder that took place some years ago."

"How do you know this?"

"No matter. This Herpez was taken on the information of Cabot Conere, who would get his neck out of a halter for the murder of one Espard. Conere has a daughter—you love her."

"Are you a wizard?" thought Brinton, aloud.

"Not quite—nor an Indian, as you may be convinced, but a Spaniard, who knows all about both these murders—who knows that Herpez did not kill Major Bertram, and that Conere stabbed Espard in self-defense."

"And what do you propose doing with this information?" said Brinton.

"If you will help me, I mean to show who the murderer of Major Bertram was, and clear Conere and Herpez from the charges against them."

"Can I trust you?"

"It can do no harm to try me."

"And what do you expect me to do?"

"Take this piece of coin," answered the Spaniard, giving Brinton an old Spanish dollar, on which were stamped the letters "E. H." "Go to the place where Herpez is confined, give it to him, tell him you got it from Don B., who will be in court to-morrow, and you must be his counsel—you are a lawyer."

"I cannot appear against Conere."

"Not to save him, and rescue his name from infamy?"

"But I have my suspicions that all is not right. Why do you tell these things to me? Why do you not let the Government know them?"

"Because I do not choose to. I alone have the information that will make all right. I chose to make it known in court to-morrow, through you. If you will not aid me, Herpez will suffer for a crime he is not guilty of, and Conere will be forever cursed as a murderer."

"Does not Conere think Herpez the murderer?"

"How can I tell what Conere thinks? But will you aid me?"

"What do you wish me to do in court?"

"The trial must not be had," answered the Spaniard. "When all is ready for the witnesses, I want you to say to the court that there is a man present who can clear up all the mystery about these murders, and give positive testimony as to who the murderer of Bertram was, as well as show that Conere is not a murderer. Will you do it?"

"I fear it is a mad proceeding, but I will take the risk."

"You are a man of honor, Ledyard Brinton. You will see me beside the prisoner to-morrow."

The Spaniard darted into the bushes, and was out of sight in a moment.

Brinton, called to himself by the deepening twilight that had began to gather while he parleyed with the Spaniard, spurred his horse, and, with indescribable emotions, galloped swiftly towards the capital. When he had proceeded a few miles, he met two of his traveling companions returning to seek him, having become alarmed at his absence. They inquired anxiously as to the cause of his detention, but he gave them no satisfactory answers.

When he reached Tallahassee, after calling on Isabelle to congratulate her on the expected happy events of the morrow, he lost no time in seeking Herpez's place of confinement. When he announced himself as counsel for the prisoner, he was admitted without delay, and the guard informed Herpez that his lawyer wished to see him.

"I want no lawyer," was his dogged answer; but Brinton, not to be daunted, walked into the cell, when the wicked man looked up and exclaimed:

"Damnation take the man who would force himself on me, to learn my secrets!"

"You mistake me, sir," said Brinton, mildly; "I had that from a man who wished me to see you to-night," handing him the stamped dollar.

"Great God! Where is he?" cried the prisoner, wildly, "and who are *you?*"

"My name is Ledyard Brinton. I promised Don B., as he called himself, that I would appear in your behalf to-morrow."

"I don't want you without him. Will *he* be there?"

"He declared that he would."

"He'll do it—he'll do it. We may die, but not unavenged," said Herpez, clenching his fists and grinding his teeth.

"Why this rage?" said Brinton.

"You look like an honest man, but my experience has taught me to trust no man. I could tell you secrets—you would then understand my rage; but I won't tell you.

You'll hear them at the trial. You will give Don B. a chance, at court, in my behalf."

"I have so promised, but I fear it was done rashly."

"Not so—you will expose great villains. But I would think alone. My thoughts must be spoken, and no man shall hear them."

Brinton retired, and walked to his hotel in great perplexity, but determined, at all hazard, to fulfill the promises he had made, and wait patiently for the morrow to solve the singular mystery which seemed to hang around the prisoner, and the man who had stopped him on the Augustine road.

CHAPTER XI.

THE TRIAL.

At the opening of the Seminole war, Tallahassee had become a town of considerable importance, although the first house was erected as late as the spring of 1824. A handsome building for the capitol was nearly completed—various religious societies had been established, and other associations, calculated to give the city importance, were rapidly progressing. During the winter of which we write, a respectable body of troops was quartered near it, and as the Legislative Council was to sit in a few days, the regular population had been much increased about the time fixed for the trial of Hulkwa-nuntokay.

Major Bertram had been generally respected in the army, and a number of officers at Tallahassee remembered him as a brave soldier and a true friend, although, in youth, he had sustained an unenviable character for *intrigue*, as the French use this word. His death and the Government robbery had been talked about a great deal, and much speculation had been indulged in regard to the Everglade Heroes. To ferret them out, had long been a strife among the civil as well as military officers of the Territory; but prior to Isabelle Conere's appeal before the Governor, no reliable information had ever been received in regard to any one of them. It was generally supposed that Herpez must have been an important man among the Heroes, and a general exposure of the band, and their operations, being expected through the investigations at his trial, it had awakened intense excitement throughout the city and adjacent settlements.

On the morning appointed for the commencement of the investigation, the building, in which the court, was held was completely crowded with a body of men of varied grades and stamp, all eager to hear the details of the secret and terrible crimes.

Conere, with Isabelle by his side, sat within the bar, near Squire Lifty. Brinton occupied an obscure seat at the foot of a long table, on which lawyers' books were so piled as to exclude him entirely from Isabelle's view. He was not yet prepared to be known in the case, and he did not wish to be observed by Conere or his daughter until he knew surely whether Don B. would make his appearance.

The prisoner bore himself like a man who had no concern in what agitated the mass about him. Excepting a peculiar compression of the lip, there was nothing to be remarked upon in the expression of his countenance. He endeavored many times to catch Conere's eye, but the witness had no intention that he should do so, and his gaze was directed everywhere but toward the prisoner.

Conere was not the same hale man who had left Rillwood on the day of the fatal meeting. Reminiscence and reflection, in confinement, had changed him much, but had served only to increase that peculiarity of look, which seemed ever to regard all on whom it rested, with suspicion. His bearing was that of a man who fears that every gesture, each change of position, every direction of his eye, or quiver of his lip, may militate against him in a cause wherein he has deep interest.

When the formalities of the court had been observed, Squire Lifty stated briefly what the prosecution expected to accomplish through the witness Conere, with corroborating testimony that he had directed, and proposed that the oath be administered to him.

Ledyard Brinton now arose, and appearing from behind the legal shield that had protected him as he desired, while Isabelle was amazed and alarmed, and Conere fixed on him a most crushing look, remarked:

"May it please the court, I appear as counsel for the prisoner. I am prepared to show that he is not guilty of the crime charged. It is a proceeding without precedent, but as the circumstances are peculiar, and as there is now within this court room a man who can not only clear the prisoner at the bar, but show that Cabot Conere is not guilty of the crime for which he has been condemned, and point out also, clearly, the true murderer of Major Bertram, I move you that he be now heard."

There was a sensation produced by this speech, throughout the court room, that cannot be described. A strange fire glowed in the prisoner's eye. Cabot Conere's countenance was "ashen and sober" as the sky of a damp morning ere sunrise, and Isabelle, from some unaccountable dread, was as pallid as if her life had suddenly gone out.

The judge said:

"This is a remarkable announcement, Mr. Brinton. Let the witness be called; we shall then determine whether to hear him at this stage of the trial."

A tall man, painted and dressed as a Seminole Indian, appeared on the witness stand.

"Is it an Indian you would thus informally introduce?" demanded Squire Lifty, prompted by Doctor Benjamin, who sat trembling at his side.

"Ask him," replied Brinton, quietly.

"Your name, sir?" demanded the clerk of the court, while the spectators were crowding, deeply excited, around the bar and the prisoner's box.

"The Indians call me Chitta, or Snake—but I was not known by this title, when, many months ago, I was carried out of St. Augustine to be buried."

"Explain, sir!" cried the presiding judge. Conere started to his feet, and would have advanced toward the Indian, had not Isabelle clung to him.

"More than a year ago," said the Indian, speaking as good English as most men do, "I was engaged in a fight in a *cafe* in St. Augustine. I was stabbed, and left for dead. Some friends conveyed me to a dwelling, and when all had abandoned me, a trusty servant prepared to give me a burial. He discovered signs of life, and using what restoratives he could command, I became enabled to speak. I told him I wished terrible revenge on my opponent—begged him to remove me secretly where he could take care of me, but let no one know that I had not been buried. The plot succeeded. I recovered. *The servant died a few days after I was able to dispense with his care*, and my secret was safe. My murderer was tried and condemned. I have been an Indian since. Before, I was known as Manuel Espard, and Cabot Conere was my murderer."

At these words, Isabelle uttered a piercing shriek, and

Conere sank powerless on the seat from which he had risen when the witness began to speak.

"This has nothing to do with the cause in question," said the prosecutor.

"I come to it," returned Espard. "The captain of the Everglade Heroes murdered Major Bertram; the band shared the Government money. *They are all now in this court room.* The hour has come—justice shall be done. That band, terrible in all this country, consisted of but *three men.* Here are the men—the *prisoner* and the *witness.* There is the CAPTAIN!" He made a significant gesture. All eyes were fixed in the direction Espard pointed. The report of a pistol rang through the court room. Cabot Conere fell dead upon the floor—a groan of agony was heard, and Doctor Benjamin weltered in his blood. All was consternation for a moment, and then the cry went up:

"*The Indians have escaped?*"

Espard had shot Conere—Herpez had stabbed Benjamin; and then they sped like lightning, while attention was directed to their victims.

Isabelle Conere had swooned—attention was given her by her immediate friends, while numbers went in pursuit of the murderers. They had some distance the start, and were fleet runners. As they approached the stream that winds along the eastern border of the city, many musket balls whistled after them, but none reached the mark. The "Heroes" soon disappeared where the stream leaps into a gulf, whence, taking the woods, their pursuers were baffled. But "the race is not always to the swift." A few hours after these wicked men leaped from the court room at Tallahassee, as they skulked through the forest, a company of soldiers, returning from a hunting party, taking them to be marauding Indians, fired upon them, and both fell mortally wounded. Herpez never spoke, but Espard, as he writhed on the ground, cried out:

"Tell the people of Tallahassee you have finished the Everglade Heroes."

Thus perished three men, whose lives had been eventful of terror and bloodshed—who had been hardened in crime—who had amassed fortunes in the shedding of innocent blood—who had followed chosen pursuits many years unsuspected, but upon whom, at length, as upon all the unrepentant wicked, sooner or later, it must come, fell retributive justice; and society was avenged, as far as their *death* could atone for their infamous *lives*.

CHAPTER XII.

DESOLATION AT RILLWOOD.

The season when "bursting buds look up" had returned again, but it was that spring time succeeding the coldest winter ever known in East Florida, and the vernal ray had no power to call the groves or the gardens from gloom. In the last winter month, a "withering frost" threw over the rivers and lakes a thin curtain of ice—affording a most novel spectacle for that tropical clime—and beneath the cutting influence of a driving northwest wind, the fruit trees were stripped of their foliage, and their life-currents so congealed that a midsummer sun shone powerless on leafless branches. The groves and gardens of Rillwood were as desolate as the heart of its mistress—drear as a Siberian forest. Where beautiful flowers had attracted the humming-bird and the bee, rising from terrace and lawn, were strewn withered stalks and sere leaves; and where had hung clustering boughs of dark and golden fruit, beneath whose shade and from whose fragrance lovers imbibed pleasure, and invalids drank in strength, unsightly poles, with rugged bark, were seen. Where the red-bird built his nest—the mocking-bird sung his ever changeful notes, and the gay-plumaged paraquet had caroled and flitted, the melancholy owl "greeted the moon with demoniac laughter," while sterile winds whistled around him.

In keeping with the unusual season had been the life of Isabelle Conere. For many weeks after the death of her father, she raved in a delirious fever, and it was months before she left her room. When, late in the spring, she walked through the paths of Rillwood, saw the ravages of winter as she had never before witnessed them, and thought of the struggles nature was everywhere making to recover from her forbidding aspect, a lesson of resignation was taught her; but she could not feel otherwise than that the snows of sorrow that had fallen on her heart, had left it as the frosts of the winter had left the tenderest fruit trees, never to have life and beauty again, that would be sweet to look in upon, imparting joy to others.

She had but one token of her father, which, in connection with his dreadful death, left her the slightest consolation. That was a letter, found on his person by those who prepared the body for the tomb:

"MY DEAR DAUGHTER:—When you get this note, your father will be beyond the reach of human laws or enemies. I formed a determination when I was first arrested, that I should never go upon the gallows, let what would be the result of my trial; and when your project for my deliverance was about to succeed, I had no reason to change a determination that would quiet fears with which, to me, this world is filled. A fatal poison, known to the Indians, I have long kept secretly upon my person, has done its work.

"My life has been almost one continued deceit. I cannot die without making a frank confession to you of all the circumstances which rendered me a villain—for when I was young I was not more wicked than other men.

"I was the captain of the 'Everglade Heroes,' and I murdered Major Bertram. I was at one time a soldier under him. He became acquainted with my sister—made honorable proposals to her, and seduced her. I challenged him to meet me. He spurned me—struck me. I returned the blow, and deserted, to escape court martial. I vowed revenge ; I took that revenge ; but not until I had long been an outlaw, associated with men whom I could only trust in villainy. But what led to the circumstances which impelled me to revenge? what made me then associate with outlaws? I answer with the deepest contrition—love for a social glass of wine, which grew to be a passion for strong drink.

"My acquaintance with Major Bertram was formed at drinking parties in our camp. When intoxicated, I introduced him to my sister. I encouraged their acquaintance, because I was indebted to him for money borrowed at the gaming table, when I was not myself on account of wine. His intimacy with my sister, and his friendship to me (as I then considered it), was flattering to my pride, because he was much my superior in rank.

"That friendship—the friendship of the bottle—has been the curse of my life, and not to your father as himself, but to your father under the influence of strong drink, may you ascribe the sorrows which carried your mother to a premature grave, and which will sadden the last months of your life. When you remember your father, have charity for his wickedness.

"When I joined the band of outlaws, which for so many years was the terror of Florida, I was so deeply intoxicated I could not sign my name to the compact, and was obliged to make my mark. I say it not to extenuate, but in explanation. When the period of the compact had passed, I broke up the band. Then I was sober. Long before would I have done so ; but by the fear of that which the law has now declared against me, I was restrained. A review of the horrors of my dark career only showed me how vain it would be to seek new society, and hope for peace and safety —and then, drinking deeply to drown remorse, I pursued my villainous course, seeking by energy of purpose to quiet the clamors of a conscience which, in sober hours, has always been active. Oh! that I had hearkened unto those clamors, and met whatever fate was in store for me.

"If you have any influence in this world, exert it in behalf of the victims of that vice which degraded me in my youth—made my manhood a period of crime, and has rendered my last days more bitter than the torments of the damned, unless their punishment bears with it vivid recollections of their ill-spent lives.

"I have been rich in gold, but poverty-stricken in all things else, except yours and your mother's love and devotion, which I did not merit. I had been happy at Rillwood, but for the recollections of deep guilt.

"Who will forgive me for abusing your mother's confidence—for entailing upon you the curse of being the daughter of the captain of the Everglade Heroes?

"God forbid that you should curse me, my daughter. May God bless you. I can write no more. Your mother taught you to pray—pray for your wicked father. CONERE."

CHAPTER XIII.

THE LAST SCENE AT RILLWOOD.

LEDYARD BRINTON had come back from legislative labors at the capital, to his quiet English home, with "blushing honors thick upon him." He had been a "progressive" in the councils and debates, but so adroitly had he managed his movements, that, though the rigid conservatists opposed him, they admired his tact, and honored his devotion. He laid the foundation for a number of educational and internal improvement enterprises, which have since done much towards giving character and wealth to the Peninsular State. His prospects were flattering for the highest office within the gift of that people, but it was not his destiny to receive the reward of his well-earned popularity, through political honors.

His love for Isabelle Conere had suffered no abatement during the trials through which she passed, and he was now ready to offer his heart and his fortune. His visits to Rillwood while she was confined to her room, and ever since she had become able to see company, had afforded him little encouragement that she still reciprocated the affection which had once been his pride. After a critical review of her whole conduct since the period of her father's arrest, the numerous lectures of his considerate aunt had no influence upon him, and he determined to ascertain, definitely, if Isabelle had changed in her regards toward him as much as she had in appearance, and in estimation of the world around her.

Brushing from his feet the dews that had gathered, on a bright morning, along the avenue leading from the Augustine road to the front porch of Rillwood mansion, we see him proceeding, with determined step, to learn, surely, from the mistress of the fair grounds about him, whether he shall ever be their master. He was received by Isabelle, in a manner that gave him encouragement, and he soon brought about a conversation which called up scenes in happier days. They sat near a window commanding a view of a grove of orange trees, which, one year previous, were loaded with the promise of golden fruit, and were the haunt of beautiful and sweetly singing birds, but in which were now to be seen only a few stunted blossoms and meager clusters of leaves, attractive neither to the humming-bird nor to the "housewife-bee." In reply to a remark by Brinton, Isabelle said:

"You remember that grove, when we walked through it last spring. Its desolation is not more striking than that of my heart. I am changed, Brinton, as words cannot tell."

"Not to me, Isabelle. It needs but one word from you to make you all to me, yea, even more than you were on the evening we danced together, when your birth day was celebrated by that Patgoe party, about which so many painful recollections cluster."

"You forget that my name is a reproach—that we were separated. What a volume of painful thoughts crowds upon my mind!" And Isabelle walked away from the window, to a sofa at the opposite side of the room. Hot tears fell upon her attenuated fingers, as she pressed them over her eyes, as if to shut out the visions that Brinton's reference had called up. He followed her, and answered:

"Yes, Isabelle, I *have* forgotten all these things—would that *you* could."

"Would that I could," she repeated, when he continued,

"But I have not forgotten vows breathed in yonder grove, at a season like this, when all was bursting to bloom about us. Can Isabelle think of the luxuriance of that time, and in its recollections forget the winter of sorrows she has passed, and believe that to her mind a spring-time will come, crowned with joys and beauties, as surely as one day, these drear groves around the mansion will 'blossom and bear fruit in due season'?"

"I cannot answer you, Brinton, for I know not what the future has in store for me. But can you command forgiveness as well as forgetfulness? It becomes me to ask it of you."

"Most freely—most freely. You *will* be mine, Isabelle."

"I am desolate hearted and poverty stricken—unworthy of you," she answered.

"What mean you, Isabelle?"

"That the property on which I live will never be improved under my hand. It was bought with crime and blood. I must go far from it—it has a curse upon it."

"Leave it, then, Isabelle. Have not I a fortune, ample, and without incumbrance of *any* kind?"

"And Rillwood must be like it, let my fate be what it may. It was purchased by wrong doing—it shall be spent in doing good. It is my design that the negroes upon it shall all be manumitted, and it shall be sold to provide homes for them, as they choose—in Africa or America—and if then there is a dollar left, it shall go to endow an Orphans' Institute in St. Augustine."

"Nobly spoken—like your beloved mother," cried Brinton. "Let me be your agent for this pleasant business."

Isabelle placed her hand within that of her suitor, and he said to himself—

"We are betrothed."

———

When the summer was ended, a noble ship crossed Mantanzas bar, bound for "the classic shores of Italie." Its most richly furnished and most commodious state-room was occupied by Ledyard and Isabelle Brinton.

Fleet Foot.

A LEGEND OF KENTUCKY.

FLEET FOOT:

A LEGEND OF KENTUCKY.

In 1778 Kentucky was the home of remarkable men. They were men who exceeded the Indian in cunning—who had more enduring powers of resistance to fatigue, and who were as relentless in pursuit of their red foes, as were ever the most savage red men in pursuit of white intruders upon the ancient hunting grounds of their tribes.

There are Indian wigwams now toward the Rocky Mountains, and on the plains sloping from the Sierra Nevada, and there are white men, who dare wrap themselves in their blankets and go to sleep alone in the forest—who are brave and hardy, and who know, from severe experience, the trials and fatigues of a hunter's life, but there are none who may be selected as fair representatives of the Hunters of Kentucky. The fatigues, the dangers and perils of Rocky Mountain life, now-a-days, do not equal those which surrounded the pioneer from Virginia, in 1778.

Among the most exciting traditions of the times of trials to the pioneers in the great valley of the West, those belonging to Kentucky have preëminent interest. Her pioneers were compelled to teach a horde of desperate Indians (not before disturbed) that they must retreat from the valley or the hill-side where the white man chose to build his cabin.

Bold and brave, stout and determined men alone, were fitted to carry the rifle and swing the axe in the forests to be felled, for the cabin and the corn field in "old Kaintuck."

Our legend is about such men. Two of them were in the depths of a dense forest on an autumn morning, when, though the earlier harbingers of dawn had given place to roseate tints, which glowed upon hill-tops touching the eastern horizon, it was so dark in the wooded valleys that the hunters with difficulty groped their way. They had not traveled all night, but they had gathered up their blankets, when it was yet an hour before day-break, and were picking their way along slowly — knowing that soon the morning light would break through the thick foliage over them. They had been absent from the Fort, at Harrodsburg, several days; they knew there was anxiety about their fate and they were impatient to relieve it.

It was not light enough for them to see distinctly, when their quick ears detected a footstep stealthily approaching. In an instant each had chosen his ambush and was keenly watchful.

"By powder, its old Martin," cried one of the hunters, and springing from his ambush, he drew his rifle to his shoulder and leveled it at the person thus indicated, who gave a sudden yell, and then in a rough tone said:

"Put down your shootin' iron. I aint fond of such motions, ef they are in fun. Whar's Mac?"

"Ready to pop you ef you'd ben a red skin," answered the individual inquired for, showing himself.

"Well I've got a leetle news for you in partic'lar, but may

be Fleet Foot'll take a sort 'o notion to it too. Sit down on this 'ere log till I tell you, for its a leetle serious, and I'm kinder worked up about it."

The three hunters sat together in earnest conversation until the sun shone broadly on the tree tops, and checkered shadows lay all around them on the fallen leaves.

Old Martin, after reminding the others that he had gone away from the fort at Harrodsburg the day before they left, informed them that he had been working about ten miles distant, where some friends were making a settlement. Mac's sister had gone with him as company for his wife. Four men were at work in the woods, when they heard screams at the cabin. They rushed toward it. Martin's son, one of the four, was shot by an Indian, whom old Martin saw and attacked, while the others continued toward the cabin.

"I put a ball in that red skin who shot Bob," said old Martin, talking to Mac and Fleet Foot, "and then I run for the cabin too. I didn't hear or see any sign of any more Ingins, and when I got to the cabin I found the other boys a debatin' what was to be done. They hadn't seen a red skin, but both the women were gone. I swore a leetle and cussed the Ingins right smart, but poor Bob was in the woods and we had to look arter him. So we went, sneakin', and found him dead enough and we carried him to the cabin and then held a council. I swore I'd go to the fort and git a party, and follow them red skins till we had our women and their scalps ef it took us till snow come. We discussed awhile, and the other boys agreed to get on the Ingins' trail and make signs, and I started for the fort. It was jist about sundown, and soon it got dark and I was a leetle excited, and I got a leetle wrong, and I've been a wanderin' and was just beginnin' to get the right bearins' when I saw Fleet Foot a drawin' a sight on me. It was tarnal lucky."

Fleet Foot and his companion had listened attentively while Martin related the particulars of the attack, and when he had concluded, Fleet Foot said:

"Did you notice what sort of a varmint that was you did the bisness for?"

"I couldn't jist exactly tell, 'cause I hadn't time, but I b'lieve he was a Blackfish," answered Martin.

"We can catch 'em then," said Fleet Foot, "I know them varmints. You know what the old chief told Boone — that I beat all his warriors on a fair race last summer, and he was the old 'un who give me my nickname. Ef I could beat his fastest red devils then, and as I did when I had to creep into the fort, when Mac's brother was shot this summer, Mac and I kin overtake the varmints now, *and we will*. We've got a lot of accounts to settle with 'em and now's the time. We'd chase 'em ef they had'nt no women; but, by powder, we'll have them women ef they havn't scalped 'em, and ef they have there shan't be one of old Blackfish's varmints left in old Kaintuck. Now, old man, you go right on straight to the fort and get five or six hunters and send 'em on arter us, and we'll go right off to your cabin, and before night we'll overtake them Ingins, and may-be afore your boys get up with us we'll do the bisness. Tell 'em at the fort that our blood is up, and the sights on our rifles are itchin' to be drawn on them Blackfish."

"That's a fact," cried Mac, "they know us and they can jist calculate that we'll stretch a few of the rascals ef we get a chance, or they'll do our bisness for us right quick. They got one of my folks and that's as many as we mean to let 'em have — Kate shall be rescued or avenged, anyhow we'll give 'em ten to one for cutting off Harry and Bob."

The hunters separated without formality; old Martin hastening with all his energy to execute his mission, and Mac and Fleet Foot striking a bee-line for the cabin.

Fleet Foot had an interest in the success of the enterprise, about which he did not speak. It was venturesome for two hunters to start from the cabin on the night previous, to follow, they knew not how many Indians, but they went only as spies. It was much more venturesome — heroic if not desperate, for Fleet Foot and his companion to undertake what they threatened. They went not only as spies; unless the party of Indians was very large they determined to rescue the women, if they were alive — if not, to avenge their massacre terribly. Both were daring and experienced hunters. Fleet Foot was one of the bravest and shrewdest of Kentucky pioneers. He was young, but athletic, watchful and quick at expedients, besides he possessed extraordinary fleetness. No Indian could out-run him. He had several opportunities of testing his powers as a runner in saving his own and others' lives. He alluded to some of them in his conversation with old Martin.

On one occasion he was chopping, with his brother and another pioneer, about four miles from the fort, when a large party of Indians, led by the renowned chief Blackfish, suddenly attacked them, shot Fleet Foot's brother, and took the other chopper prisoner. Fleet Foot dashed through the woods, at the top of his speed, with half a dozen warriors straining every muscle to overtake him. It was their design to attack the fort. They were earnestly anxious to prevent an alarm being given, but the young hunter was too fleet for them all. He reached the fort in safety, and the garrison prepared at once to meet the foe. When the Indians made the attack they were repelled with considerable loss.

On another occasion Fleet Foot was shooting at a mark, near the fort, with a brother of his present companion. They were suddenly surrounded by Indians. The other marksman was shot. Balls aimed at Fleet Foot missed him. He ran with all his energy toward the fort, several Indians in full chase after him — others firing at him. He was within seven paces of the fort when he saw that the door was not open. In an instant the thought struck him that it dare not be opened for fear the Indians would rush in. He threw himself flat on the ground between a large stump and the fort. There were numerous guns aimed at the Indians from the fort, and they dare not come within reach of the balls. They amused themselves by firing at Fleet Foot. There he lay, his mother looking down upon him and praying that he might be saved — his friends urging him to lie close and not lose courage — while the balls of the savage warriors, thirsting for his blood, were striking close to him, often throwing upon him the dirt which they plowed up. It was a most perilous and painful position. He conversed with his friends about opening the door of the fort. He said he could rush through it in an instant. They answered him that they dare not risk the lives of the women and children. The Indians might reach the door before it could be securely fastened again. There were not men enough in the fort to fight the large body of Indians in close combat.

The balls from the rifles of the Indians continued to strike around him. A moment the young hunter was engaged in deep thought — then he cried:

"For God's sake dig a hole under the fort, and I'll creep through it."

Immediately his request was complied with, and the brave hunter reached this curious avenue to safety without injury, and was caught in his mother's arms, and wept over as one rescued who had been given up as lost. The baffled Indians retired with savage yells.

When Fleet Foot and companion reached the cabin, they had no difficulty in finding the "signs" made by the hunters who had followed the Indians as spies. They pushed forward on the trail with a speed which only experienced hunters could attain.

It was yet early in the day when old Martin showed a party of five hunters where he had killed the Indian who shot his son Bob. This party immediately followed in pursuit of Fleet Foot and Mac.

It was between mid-day and sun-down when Fleet Foot declared that the Indians could not be much in advance, and he and Mac began to consider what they should do when the savages were overtaken. They conversed a few minutes when Fleet Foot said:

"It's no use — we don't know how we'll find 'em. It'll be time to fix how we shall give it to 'em when we've got a sight of the varmints."

Again the hunters pushed forward zealously. They had not yet met the two hunters who left the cabin the night previous. They began to have serious surmises about their fate. As they hastened on they frequently conversed in low tones about their forerunners. Lengthened shadows were creeping in the forest, indicating that soon it would be impossible for the hunters to keep trace of the signs which had led them on during the day. Fleet Foot observed a small piece of linen on a bush. He grasped it eagerly, and showing it to Mac, said:

"That's a leetle encouraging. It shows the women are yet alive, anyhow, but its tarnal strange we hav'nt ketched them other boys; I 'bleeve they've been a leetle careless and the Ingins have got 'em."

He had gone but a few steps, after he made these remarks, when Fleet Foot cried:

"Jist as I expected. Here's one on 'em anyhow. Them Ingins 'll roast the other, by powder, if we don't get him out of their hands."

"That they will," answered Mac, who looked upon the dead body of a hunter, with whom he had been well acquainted, lying directly in their path. He had been shot and his scalp taken.

"Last year old Blackfish said he'd roast the first hunter he could get into his camp, and if they've got the other fellow a prisoner, I'll bet they mean to give him a taste of what we give young pigs on Christmas, but we won't let 'em, by powder, as you say, Fleet Foot."

"No, by powder, we won't," cried Fleet Foot.

The hunters did not stand over the body of their dead friend even long enough for this conversation. Their duties to the living were too pressing. They talked cautiously as they proceeded. Experienced as they were in detecting Indian "signs," they knew that the savages could not be far in advance, and they hoped to overtake them before it was dark.

While the hunters were hastening in the pursuit under this impression, the Indians were encamped upon a small stream, in a spot which afforded no particular advantages to them in case of an attack.

It was late in the afternoon when the female prisoners, from over-fatigue, began to grow tardy in their march. Both fell behind the main party of savages and were guarded by a brawny warrior who delighted in torturing them. The spies on their trail came in sight of the women and this warrior, who, except an Indian boy, was, at the moment, the only savage in sight. Supposing this to be the whole of the party, the young men, with a reckless impulse, rushed to the attack. They saw their error too late. The brawny warrior was severely wounded by a ball from the rifle of one of the spies, but no sooner had the report of his gun rang through the woods, than the white men were surrounded. One was shot and scalped; the other taken prisoner.

While Fleet Foot and his companion were groping their way by starlight, the Indians were holding a council upon the fate of their prisoners.

The spies had found much difficulty in tracing the path of the Indians, but they left behind them signs which clearly indicated to their followers the path to be pursued. The savages had pushed forward with much speed and caution till they had been attacked; when, supposing that all danger from immediate watch over their movements had been averted, they relaxed their speed, and soon encamped.

Losing the aid of their forerunners, from the time they left the corpse of their unfortunate friend, Fleet Foot and Mac were obliged to exercise their keenest powers, in order to keep the Indian trail.

Twilight was gone, and though the hunters could clearly see the leaves on the tree tops, it had become quite dark around their path. They were about to seek a camping place, and give over the pursuit till another day dawned, when Fleet Foot, stooping forward, looked for several moments intently through the thickening gloom, then he whispered to Mac:

"Somebody's makin' a little fire out yonder about a mile, and I'll bet my ammunition it's them tarnal varmints."

The fire grew brighter; Mac saw it distinctly. The hunters slowly and stealthily turned their footsteps toward the feeble flame. It became more and more distinct, till at length they could see its smoke curling among the leaves of the trees under which it snapped and glowed. A dark form stood between the fire and the hunters; they recognized the outline to be that of an Indian; creeping onward with cat-like caution, both grasped their rifles closer, and put their left hands on their hunting knives. They were impatient to know where were the prisoners, and what was the strength of the Indian party. Presently the fire blazed so brightly that it illuminated three forms which the hunters, with great joy, recognized as those of the women and the captured spy; but with all their skill and all their caution the hunters could not ascertain the number of savages. An old Indian came to the fire and lit his pipe; another roasted a piece of meat, and both joined a party at such a distance from the fire that Fleet Foot was puzzled to tell how many foes he must fight before the prisoners could be rescued. He longed to shoot the "varmints," who exposed themselves at the fire, but prudence forbade him. He instructed Mac to keep his place, and watch closely while he went around the camp and reconnoitered.

Watchfully and noiselessly he stole through the woods, till the Indian council was between him and the fire; then he could count the number of Indians, but he was not satisfied; he desired to communicate to the prisoners the cheering news, that they had friends as well as foes, around them. With this intention, he continued his noiseless course until he stood within a few feet of the prisoners. The young woman was nearest him. He whispered her name. She did not hear him, or if she heard, conceived the voice to be one her active imagination had conjured. Again Fleet Foot whispered that name which was dear to him, and fell sweetly from his lips. The young woman started and looked about her. An Indian on the watch, saw her startled movement, and came near her. The fire shone brightly on him; Fleet Foot was sorely tempted to shoot him, but the risk was too great. The bold hunter's position was one of great trial. Another word from him might alarm the young woman, and her agitation defeat the whole scheme of rescue. Shielded from the view of the Indians by a large tree, Fleet Foot crept nearer the prisoners. He was rejoiced to see the Indian whose suspicions had been excited, return among his companions, and take his seat in the council. Fleet Foot was now within a few feet of the prisoners — he saw them as distinctly as if it were daylight, and he could see, seated upon the ground not many yards beyond the prisoners, a little body of desperate savages, apparently consulting about the fate of three pale-faces, toward whom, the full light of a bright fire blazing on them, more than one Indian eye was continually cast. Again Fleet Foot whispered. To his great joy he saw that the young woman heard and recognized a friendly voice, but having been warned by the conduct of the savage watching her, was shrewd enough to make no movement that would again rouse his suspicions. She dare not answer the voice, and Fleet Foot was left to conjecture whether she knew it was he so near her. He would have run many risks to have known how wildly her heart beat, for it told her that he who was risking so much for her sake could be none other than Fleet Foot.

The hunter was determined not to be in doubt as to whether she knew him, and he whispered:

"I'm Fleet Foot, and Mac's not far off; and old Martin's a comin' with a party of sharp shooters, and afore morning we'll give them varmints what'll keep 'em from killin' any more white folks, or stealin' any more wimen. When you git a chance, whisper to the old woman, and tell her not to go to sleep, and to tell that chap tied up near her to be on the look-out for a fight."

The young woman dropped her head as if it had fallen upon her breast with a nod in sleep, and Fleet Foot understood that his message and warning were distinctly known.

A considerable length of time had elapsed while the hunter was engaged in his dangerous enterprise of reconnoitering, and of communicating glad tidings to the prisoners, and the night was far advanced. He had for more than an hour expected that the Indians would appoint a watch for the prisoners, and break up their council. It must have been near midnight when he was gratified with a sight of preparations on the part of the savages, for a couple of hour's repose before they started on the march of the coming day. The hunter cautiously retreated from his proximity to the camp Two savages left the main body, and approached their prisoners — the others wrapped themselves in their blankets, and stretched themselves upon the ground to sleep. The savages had secured their prisoners by tying their hands tightly behind large trees. They stood in this painful position several yards distant from each other. The two warriors left to guard them, manifested no disposition to allow them any position more favorable to rest or repose. Fleet Foot was a thoughtful observer of this neglect, and it did not auger well in his mind for the safety of the prisoners on the morrow. He was impressed that the council which had just broken up, had decided on bloody deeds. He dare not act alone under such trying circumstances, and he determined to see Mac. It would have been no easy task for an inexperienced woodsman to find his companion under such circumstances, but Fleet Foot had calculated well what were his chances of return to his friend, and he found but little difficulty in tracing his way to the vicinity where he left Mac. A signal, well understood between the hunters, and not calculated to alarm the savages, had they heard it, was given and answered, and in a few moments the brother and lover were earnestly consulting what was to be done to rescue Kate and her fellow prisoners.

"There are ten or a dozen of 'em," said Fleet Foot, "I can't exactly tell which, but any how, there's too many of 'em for us to fight; but, by powder, Ingins or no Ingins, them wimen shall be out of their clutches afore the varmints leave this camp, or I'm a dead hunter."

"That's my mind to a har," answered Mac, grasping Fleet Foot's hand.

"It's tarnal queer old Martin haint come up, but may be he has seen this fire, jist as we did, and there's half a dozen other fellows sneakin' about here now."

"May be," said Mac, "but we can't find 'em, and daresn't make any signal or we'll have all them Ingins up in a minit, and no tellin' what might happen. We must calculate without 'em, and ef we git into a fight and old Martin's about here, we'll have him on our side quick enough."

"Well," returned Fleet Foot, "there's only one way to do it — that fire's gittin' low — it wouldn't be queer if them Ingins on the watch went to sleep, 'cause they know the prisoners can't get away; and I'm certain they don't suspect any body's on the track of 'em. Ef they did they wouldn't a kept up sich a fire. Now, you follow me, and we'll go over there and watch the varmints, and whenever they shut their eyes, you take one and I'll take the other so quick he shant give even an Ingin grunt, and then it'll be an easy matter to cut the prisoners loose."

Mac agreed to this arrangement. Daylight was now drawing near. Whatever plans were calculated on, must be executed without delay. The hunters knew that if they succeeded in releasing the prisoners, as soon as the Indians discovered their loss, they would put forth every exertion, and exercise all their cunning to retake them; but with all this hazard before them, they were resolved to release them if it was in their power, and trust to luck, shrewdness, and the probability of assistance from Martin's party. They were convinced that one or more of the prisoners would be killed on the morrow, and bravely and generously they thought it was worth while to risk their two lives to save three, one of which was particularly valuable to both hunters, but peculiarly so to one.

While the two Indian guards were growing weary and sleepy, they had no suspicion that two hunters, with drawn knives, were ready, if they slumbered, to make that their last sleep.

Fleet Foot began to fear that daylight would dawn before

the savages nodded, and that the others would awaken and all would be lost. Every moment increased the danger and narrowed the probabilities of rescue and escape. At length he brought himself to believe that the moment for action had arrived. He gave the concerted signal, and approached his victim, who stood erect against a tree. He was successful, and drove his knife to the heart of the savage, who may have been dreaming, perhaps, of a wigwam far away, where children, of whom he was proud, awaited his return. The savage fell in his last sleep, heavily to the ground. That one which Mac was to have attacked, was startled by the fall. He was sitting upon the ground, nodding, but was not sound asleep. He sprang to his feet when Mac was not yet near enough to strike him. In an instant he would have been away from the dim light of the fire and out of sight of the hunter, but Mac rushed upon and grappled with him. Fleet Foot sprang to cut the bands which confined the prisoners. Meantime Mac struggled with the savage; both were powerful men—for a moment the savage was confused, and did not employ his strength and agility as he might have done under ordinary circumstances — of this confusion, the hunter took advantage, and was quick enough to plunge his knife into the red man's breast — he fell with a cry which aroused his fellow-warriors, who had slumbered in confidence that his watchfulness protected them.

Ten Indians were on their feet, with their rifles in their hands, before the death cry of their guard had died in the woods. The fire, which they had left brightly burning, had nearly gone out. The brands were scattered. They could neither see their prisoners nor any foes. They did not rush forward to ascertain the fate of their sentinels, nor did they flee hastily from the spot where they had been sleeping. Each individual quietly skulked around a tree. No foe could see them. Not one of them could either see or hear a foe, but nevertheless there were very dangerous foes quite near them.

When Fleet Foot rushed to release the prisoners, he found the good work accomplished. A rough hand grasped his arm, and a voice which he knew well, said:

"We've been watchin' the varmints most all night. They're skeered now, but they won't run nor show themselves yet awhile; our boys understand. We must lay low with our guns cocked till it's day, and we'll all git a blaze at 'em. How many?"

"Ten, I guess," said Fleet Foot.

"Take care o' this woman," said old Martin.

It was Kate. Fleet Foot said not a word, but put his arm around the girl as if he had a special right to protect her.

There was no wind stirring. It was as quiet in the deep woods, as if there had been no Indian camp — no desperate adventure — no struggle — no scene of death. Softly the morning light began to steal through the dense foliage — it searched its way among the green leaves, and slowly dissipated the gloom which hung tenaciously around the trunks of the trees — among the low bushes, and in the wooded ravines. The fox went snuffing to his hole — the rabbit hopped timidly from one moss bed or grass tuft to another — the birds left their nests and sang sweetly on twigs, which overhung fallen leaves stained with blood — the squirrel left its nest, and sat securely chirping on boughs that bent toward ashes, which were the result of a flame that had given light for the planning and executing of bold and daring designs.

Many an animal was, no doubt, watching in that fresh light of morning for an opportunity to secure such prey as he was wont to satisfy his hunger upon; and there were other eyes watching an opportunity to satisfy a passion which will lead men often to more desperate deeds than ordinary hunger suggests. The quiet, beautiful scene, a lover of nature would have rejoiced in, was to be disturbed by other conflicts than those between cruel animals and their victims.

It was scarcely broad day light, when one of the Indian warriors thought he saw a movement in a clump of bushes, a dozen rods or more distant from him. He watched intently. He was not mistaken; other Indians had their suspicions excited; knowing glances were exchanged. The suspicious bush became more attractive to the savages. Presently, what was apparently a woman's bonnet, was to be seen cautiously elevated nearly to the top of the bushes; slowly it turned around as if there were eyes within, sharply looking out to ascertain if there were foes, or suspicious signs of foes, in view. A rifle report rang through the forest, and the exposed bonnet disappeared. Again the forest was free from unusual sounds. It was not long before Indians skulked from one tree to another. They were at first very cautious, but they saw nothing to awaken suspicion, and they became more bold. Now, one left his ambuscade, then another. It was not long before eight warriors stood near the spot where the fire of the night previous had gleamed on both exulting and hopeless faces. They talked rapidly, and seemed desciding upon the course they should pursue; suddenly their council was brought to a violent conclusion, by the unerring aim of half a dozen invisible rifles, and as many savages springing into the air, fell dead; four others — two of them from the council, and two others from an ambush, they were about leaving to join the council — bounded away through the woods with an energy which indicated that each knew he who was the fleetest, stood the first chance of escape. The hindmost Indian had not gone many rods before a ball arrested his career.

Fleet Foot had his eye upon one who distanced all the others. He recognized him by peculiar marks as the savage who had well nigh overtaken him on the two trying occasions previously mentioned, when his fleetness saved his life. The Indian had no weapon but his hunting-knife. Fleet Foot dropped his unloaded rifle, and bounded swiftly in pursuit. Shouts rang after him as he sped on his way. The Indian, glancing behind him, saw what danger threatened. He redoubled his energies, yet Fleet Foot gained on him, cheered as he was in the daring race by Mac, who followed with all his speed, but was barely able to keep in sight.

Away went the savage, bounding over logs, leaping ravines, and climbing steep banks; and after him came Fleet Foot, straining every muscle to its utmost tension. The hunters were all excited about the chase, and several were endeavoring to keep in sight of those who had already lost sight of Fleet Foot. There was one person who could not join in the chase, who had deeper interest in his fate than all the hunters—an interest which was confessed in soft whispers, when Fleet Foot was taking care of her, as old Martin had directed him, in that hour of great suspense both to the hunters and to the Indians, which they had passed before daylight. She would have endeavored to restrain Fleet Foot from his mad chase, but she did not know that such a race was to be run, until her lover was nearly out of her sight.

Fleet Foot was gaining faster and faster on the savage, who redoubled his energies; he took wild leaps and sudden turns, but the white man was equal to him in agility, and, at length, when there was a clear piece of woods before him, the savage found that he must soon be overtaken. Too brave to allow himself to be struck or taken prisoner when in flight, he turned and awaited his pursuer. Nothing daunted, Fleet Foot pressed forward. The Indian had the advantage, should he rush upon him, and the hunter checked his career when within a few paces of the savage. A moment the foes glanced at each other. Three times had Fleet Foot distanced this Indian: thrice to save his own life—the last time—the present one, to take the life of the red man. Each knew the other. Now was to come a struggle severer than any previously decided between them. The Indian was the larger man, and he was, perhaps, better skilled in the use of the knife.

The savage did not wait for his foe to recover from his long chase, but when his eye had run over the frame of his antagonist and taken in the distance between them, he sprang toward him fiercely, aiming a violent blow with his knife. Fleet Foot dexterously parried it, almost at the same moment giving the savage a left-handed blow which staggered him. Following up his advantage, Fleet Foot made a thrust at the Indian's breast; the red man caught the arm which bore a knife swiftly toward his heart, and then followed a tight wrestle—a moment, two knives gleamed in the air—then both fell upon the ground, and the Indian and the hunter were each struggling to escape the other's grasp.

Fleet Foot was borne to the earth, and the Indian, striving to keep him there, exerted himself also to the utmost to reach one of the knives. He was a stronger man than the hunter — he had a great advantage over him, yet the hunter held him so firmly, he could not reach a knife. He dare not release his hold the slightest, lest the hunter should spring to his feet.

His powerful knees were crushing the hunter's breast — his brawny hands were clenched around Fleet Foot's neck — a gleam of triumph danced in his savage eyes, which glared upon Fleet Foot's blackening face. The savage felt sure of his victim — his fleet and daring foe: this wicked joy expressed itself in every feature of his tawny countenance, and broke upon the air in a wild, fiendish laugh. That laugh was meant to be a knell for the hunter, but it nerved him to one great struggle — a struggle in which all his energy was concentrated — in which every muscle was strained — every nerve stretched; he rose partly from the ground, bearing up the athletic savage, who lost the dangerous grasp by which he had for a few moments been almost forcing the hunter's eyes from their sockets; but Fleet Foot only wasted his strength in that struggle — he fell back upon the earth completely in the power of the infuriated savage, who was swift to perceive the surest and quickest mode of wreaking his passion. He clenched in his right hand one of the knives which had fallen in the early part of the affray — he brandished it over his head — and from its polished blade bright reflections were a moment cast, as it hung in the air.

A low, shrill whistle might have been heard near the savage; the gleaming knife fell, but the savage fell with it, his features fixed in death, with that fiendish exultation stamped upon them, which had nerved Fleet Foot to his last effort. That whistle was from the swift passage of a rifle ball that lodged in the Indian's breast. With the report which rang after the ball, there came a shout that lifted Fleet Foot from his prostrated position.

Mac had come within rifle shot, just in time to save his friend's life.

Fleet Foot had been nearly strangled, and was much exhausted; but he soon rallied, and looking at the form of his foe, which was lying beside him, he said:

"It was a tight scuffle, Mac, by powder, and I'd been in kingdom come now, ef it hadn't been for you."

"That's oncomfortable true," answered Mac. "You brag about runnin', but it liked to lost your scalp for you this time. That fellow was enough for you on a race, and a leetle too much in a fight."

Fleet Foot and Mac, on retracing their steps, were met by the other hunters; then were joyful meetings which need not be described—nor scarcely need it be told, that when the party reached the fort (which it did early the following day), there were immediate preparations for a backwoods wedding, which was not long afterward celebrated in a rude, but for the period, distinguished style.

Fleet Foot figured prominently in the later annals of Kentucky, and was subsequently known as General ———. He left a posterity which has been engaged in modern politics as warmly as was ever their brave ancestor in pioneer enterprise.

Hunter Birty;

OR THE

HALF-BREED COLONY OF ILLINOIS.

8

CHAPTER I.

THE MOUNTAIN HOME.

From the eastern bank of one of those swiftly flowing streams that water the mountains of Western Virginia, there stretched, many years ago, a narrow path, that had once been a highway for the deer, the bear and the Indian, but which, at the time of the opening of our story, was the trail leading to a hunter's cabin, from which, rising with the sun every morning, might be faintly seen, far up on the mountain, a thin column of blue smoke.

I would not assert that neither the moccasin of the Indian, the hoof of the deer, nor the ponderous paw of the bear, tracked this path at the period of which I write; but I record the fact, that upon the haunts, where perhaps they had ranged for centuries, unmolested except by each other, there was now a watchfulness exercised, which led, almost every day, to the thinning of their numbers. To the hunter they were all "varmin."

The cabin was built partly in the rocks, the situation having been selected for its advantages, in the event of an attack upon it by Indians, because there was treasure in it which the hunter knew needed strong defense, and to protect which he would sacrifice his life.

He was a man whose hair had been thinned and whitened by long exposure and severe hardship; and he was a woodsman practiced in all the arts of watchfulness, dexterity and intrigue, by which his forest foes were to be detected, attacked, or retreated from.

His cabin treasure was an Indian wife, whom he had stolen from a powerful tribe that occupied a district of country south-west from his retreat, in what is now geographically defined as the State of Kentucky. For nearly ten years, hunted from fortress to fortress, he eluded the pursuit of his enemies—the relatives of his captive. The love of the hunter and his wild-wood wife was romantic in its origin, but was true, and time only served to increase their mutual trust and confidence.

The hunter, upon an expedition of observation and discovery, had been captured by a party of Indians, after a desperate resistance. He was taken to their camp severely wounded, and placed under the care of the chief's daughter, that he might be restored to health and strength, as a victim of torture at their annual war-dance.

The incantations of the "medicine man" of the tribe served only to annoy the hunter; but the kind attentions of his tawny hostess were not bestowed in vain. He endeavored to learn her language, and soon they were able to converse otherwise than by signs. Then he was informed of his impending fate, and then he learned that the care bestowed upon him by the chief's daughter sprang more from the inclinations of her heart than from the commands of the warriors, who had confided their expected victim of triumph to her skill in the use and knowledge of the virtues of roots and herbs.

The hunter encouraged the Indian maiden's love, and when he was confident that the ties which bound her to him were strong enough, he planned an escape. The plan was successfully executed.

No marriage ceremonies united the hunter and the young squaw. He simply gave her his word that she should dwell in his wigwam; and he would be her protector. She was content, believing herself what civilized society understands by the term wife; and as a wife she should be regarded, for the hunter's promise was to him law.

Three children had been born in the hunter's cabin, yet at the period I have introduced it, it had but two inmates—the father and mother.

The hunter had visited a settlement lying eastward of the retreat he then occupied, about one hundred miles. The mother was, one afternoon during his absence, gathering mountain berries with her children. Two of them happened to stray a short distance from her, when she was startled by violent screams. With a mother's instinct and energy, she rushed in the direction whence proceeded the sounds, and saw her two children—her two youngest children—borne into the dark forest from an opening where they had been gathering fruit. She knew pursuit would be idle, and she employed her knowledge of Indian habits in endeavoring to protect her remaining child, the eldest son, who had observed the stealthy approach of his enemies, and was shrewd enough to elude them.

For many days the disconsolate mother sat trembling in her wigwam, fearing to build a fire, lest the ascending smoke might guide some foe to her retreat, and thus be the means of depriving her of the only solace left her. She had recognized the Indians that had stolen the children for whom she mourned; they belonged to the tribe she had deserted, and she presumed them to be agents of her father, who would not destroy *her* life, but would rob her of her children, in hopes of recalling her to his campfire and wigwam. She had therefore no fears for her own safety, but she had lively fears for the safety of her husband and the child that wept with her in her desolate home. Every unusual sound that reached her in her solitude, she feared might be the stealthy step of some foe, or she hoped might prove the signal of the hunter's near approach. Yet with this hope was mingled chilling fear, for the hunter loved his children, and she knew his burst of passion, at finding two of them gone, would be terrible.

He returned at an hour when the wife least expected him. It was early morn. He had traveled all night, in his eagerness to reach home, as if, by some mysterious agency, he had been informed of the misfortune that had befallen him. But the backwoodsman of that day knew the dangers to which his home was always exposed, and whenever long absent, his heart beat with thrilling emotion on his return, in dread that he should find, where had been his cabin or his wigwam, but smouldering embers, in which whitened the bones of all who were dear to him on earth.

The hunter gave a signal as he approached within a few yards of his cabin. It was unanswered. It had never before failed to bring forth his wife and children to bid him welcome. They could not be in the woods, beyond hearing, at that early hour. His steps quickened and his breath grew shorter; he felt that the fears which almost unmanned him were well grounded. He burst open the cabin door—

there sat his wife—crouching from view, with her child beside her—the very picture of dread and despair. She had not heard the hunter's signal, and little expecting him at that hour, had been surprised; she knew his footstep, but dared not meet his glance.

The hunter seemed to comprehend, from his wife's appearance, that his children had been torn from their home, for well knew he that thus would his Indian foes wreak vengeance upon him at the first opportunity. Demanding, in mingled backwoods English and mongrel Indian, an explanation from the mother, he rushed into the forest, with a terrible oath of vengeance upon his lip. He struck off through the pathless woods, in the direction which he supposed would lead him to the principal camp of the tribe of which his squaw's father was chief. It was distant several day's journey. He took no rest, and partook of no food but some dried meat, which he carried in a pouch by his side.

He reached a camp the second day, near nightfall. An inexperienced woodsman would have supposed it deserted, but the practiced hunter knew better. He discovered evidences of recent occupation, and he believed it to be the rendezvous of a small party of Indians—perhaps the party that had stolen his children. He determined to watch.

When gloom began to gather thickly in the forest, the hunter was secreted where, with his rifle, he commanded a complete view of the Indian camp. The night had advanced several hours, and yet the hunter watched without token of the return of the savages.

The anxious father was about to take up his eager march through the woods, when the snapping of a twig arrested his attention. Presently he discovered objects moving, and in a few minutes he was satisfied that the camp was that night to be occupied. A fire was built, and by its light he saw four Indians, who belonged to the tribe of which he was in pursuit. He could not restrain manifestations of passion and impatience, but he was too old a hunter to attack four Indians single-handed, let his passion be ever so intense, when there was hope of overcoming them by stratagem.

Nursing his passion for revenge, the hunter waited until the Indians slumbered. When their camp fire burned low, he crept near the Indians, with footsteps as noiseless as those with which the wily panther approaches its destined victim. He was armed in Indian style. With his tomahawk he launched two of his foes into eternity, without waking either from his slumber; the third one made a sudden movement as the hunter aimed a blow at his head, and was only slightly wounded—with a fierce yell he sprang to his feet, but the hunter was prepared for his movement, and dispatched him with his knife before he could discover the number or character of his assailants. The fourth savage, aroused by the yell of his companion, would have fled precipitately, but the hunter confronted him, and a desperate struggle ensued. He was an athletic savage—in ordinary circumstances more than the hunter's equal, but now he was confused and unable to employ his strength to the best advantage, while every nerve and muscle in the hunter's body was at its highest tension, and he hurled his antagonist to the ground as if he had been a child.

The savage knew his fate. He was too proud to plead for mercy, even had he thought such a plea would avail him anything—but the hunter, with his tomahawk suspended over him, offered him his life if he would tell what had become of the children his tribe had stolen a few days previous. At first the savage denied all knowledge of the children, but, at length, informed the hunter that one of the Indians he had murdered stole them—that they had been taken to the camp of the chief, near the mouth of the Ohio, and that it was the design of the party he had that night vanquished, assisted by his wife's brother and a warrior who had aspired to the possession of her master's wigwam, to watch around his cabin until they had an opportunity to carry away with them the hunter's wife and remaining child; or, if not able to accomplish all this, at least get possession of the boy, and join the main body of the tribe at a southern camp, whence they would cross the great river, beyond the pursuit of the hunter or any party he might rally.

Every threat or process of torture the hunter could devise failed to wrest from the Indian any information in regard to the foes the hunter had not met. Knowing the cunning and desperation of the warriors, he had reason to tremble with fear that, during his absence from home, both his wife and child might be wrested from him. He dare not give the Indian, in his power, his liberty, lest he might be pursued by him and treacherously shot; but he had promised to spare his life, and could not violate his word.

With strips of deer-skin, prepared for thongs—always a part of the hunter's equipment—he bound the "red varmint," as he termed him, hand and foot, and leaving him to his fate, retraced his steps towards his cabin with as much eagerness as he had traveled from it.

When he approached within a few miles of his home, such was the fury which seemed to possess him, that he was reckless of consequences, and rushed madly forward, heedless of all those nice observations which would have protected him from savage intrigue. Then would he have fallen an easy prey to a wily redskin, but none crossed his path. Once more he stood before his cabin, impressed with a dreadful sense of outrage and misfortune. The door was fastened—his impatience could brook no restraint—he burst it open—he found his cabin uninhabited.

With one mad yell he rushed back into the forest. Whither he would have gone, what fate would have befallen him, the imagination may not conceive, had not a piercing scream arrested his furious career. The mother at least was not a victim or a captive. The father and mother, tender only in their own love and in the love of their children, met, mingling their tears; with the hunter they were tears of agony rather than tears of simple grief—agony that he had not been able to glut his revenge—that he had not met the relentless savages who had desolated his home.

His suspicions had been realized. The mother's savage brother, and more than savage lover, in his absence had dragged away, to their hidden haunts, his eldest born, and would have dragged the mother with them, but they feared pursuit. They did not murder her, for part of their scheme was to glut revenge by inflicting torment. She had endeavored to follow the ruthless invaders, but dreadful agony and thought of the husband who would return—from pursuit of other foes—for ought she knew, with the children first torn from her, and find his home deserted, chained her to the scene of her sufferings.

From that hour the hunter was a man of silence and sorrow. He nursed a revenge that was consuming his vitality, yet he never seemed more capable of the endurance of hardship—more successful in the taking of valuable game. He dare not absent himself a single night from his cabin, for fear the companion of his deep grief would be torn from him, and he resolved to change the location of his retreat.

His intimate acquaintance with the country enabled him to select a spot advantageously. He chose the site I have described in the opening of this chapter. Thither he immediately emigrated, and labored diligently to construct winter quarters out of bark, poles, and the skins of wild beasts.

His cabin stood at the mouth of a shallow cave, into which, when pursuing a bear, the hunter had once been driven by a violent storm—a storm which bowed the ancient trees on the mountain, and filled the air with branches twisted from their massive trunks.

Hidden by thick foliage and overhanging rocks, the hunter's retreat was one not easily discovered, while it commanded a widely extended view of valleys, rivers and mountains.

Here the hunter, with some assurance of safety, could leave his wife, for he never would consent that she should accompany him on any of his lengthy hunting expeditions. He was absent sometimes many weeks, and he did not often return without numerous scalps at his belt, but he never brought to the mother any satisfactory tidings of her lost children.

Several winters had left their snows on the secret path that led to his retreat, and summer had come again, when, one sultry evening, the hunter toiled up the mountain, after an absence from home of more than a month. He was weary of limb and weary of heart. He had wandered farther than usual, in the hope that he might find some Indian or white man, who could give him tidings of his lost treasure; that hope was not realized, and the wretched man felt that his hold on the things of earth was growing weaker every day—hope alone had thus far sustained him, and hope was dying.

His footsteps that evening were not unobserved. For several days, as he wandered listlessly through the forest, his course had been tracked by a skulking enemy—now the eagle eyes of that enemy were upon his movements.

As the hunter approached his home, his forest instincts became acute again, and he exercised his usual caution in concealing traces of his progress, that no foe might find easy access to his hiding place. The shades of night gathered on the mountain, ere the Indian lost sight of the hunter, but then the gloom gave the hunter opportunities of concealment, which he never failed to embrace when near home; and he was lost to his pursuer.

The hunter reached his cabin, to sit down with a disconsolate companion, and mourn in silence; and the Indian stealthily and swiftly descended the mountain, attended by the doleful howl of numerous wolves, answering each other from thicket to thicket and from rock to rock.

CHAPTER II.

AN EXPECTED ATTACK.

The glories of autumn were on the forest. The valley was in deep shadow, but the rays of the setting sun illuminated the mountain's crest. Light clouds of smoke, which had risen from the hunter's cabin, hung in the tops of the trees, among whose withering foliage the evening wind moved, with a sound like the mournful music of thickly falling rain-drops. The hunter, with his sad wife beside him, looked upon the valley until night stretched her "sable mantle" over it, and far away, where the firmament seemed to hang on a level with his vision, he could see nothing but the bright stars. They led his thoughts to the "hunting grounds" that, according to Indian tradition, are prepared for good Spirits; and there, he knew, if never again on earth, he should surely meet the dear ones that had been so cruelly torn from their home. The father and mother had that night calculated the respective ages of their children. The father said, had the oldest been spared him, he would have been able to chase the bear and the deer; and the mother had dwelt upon the comfort her younger children would have been to her, while assisting her to prepare for winter their clothing of skins and furs. With such thoughts in their minds, both had seated themselves near the hearthstone, on which were a few fading embers, apparently listening to the pensive wailing that seemed to float among the boughs, which, in summer, drooped with clustering leaves over the front of their cabin.

Suddenly the hunter started to his feet, and all his senses seemed to be absorbed in an effort to hear every sound that might be produced within half a mile.

His wife knew that he suspected his Indian foes had discovered his hiding place, and were about to attack it. Taking his rifle from its accustomed place, and examining the priming, he stepped softly across the cabin, in the direction opposite that whence the sounds that alarmed him had proceeded; then he climbed a rude ladder, which he had constructed in a fissure in the rock behind his cabin, and in a few moments he stood, himself shielded from view, even in daylight, where he could look down upon the path leading to his cabin, and upon the very spot where he imagined his supposed enemy had been. The sky was clear and the stars shone brightly; the hunter discovered an object near the cabin door, but whether it was a savage Indian or a savage beast, he could not decide. Cautiously he crept near the object, and, at length, he satisfied himself that it was a human being. Whether friend or foe it was now his task to ascertain. He presumed it a foe, as a matter of course, and with all his backwoods shrewdness he watched and waited to see whether any signals were conveyed to or from the spy. Several hours elapsed, and the hunter had detected nothing. He dare not explore the woods or rocks around his cabin, for fear he might fall a victim to some foe in ambush; but he determined, at all hazard, to know the character of the individual at his door. Returning into the cabin, he described the state of affairs to his wife, armed her with his tomahawk, and taking his unsheathed hunter's knife in his hand, he suddenly drew open the cabin door, grasped the object lying before it, and dragged it within the enclosure, re-fastening the door as he did so. Then arousing his captive from deep slumber, he saw before him, what at first appearance he took for an Indian boy, about twelve years of age; but no sooner did the youth fairly recover from the surprise consequent upon the manner in which he had been treated, than he cried, in the Indian tongue, "You won't kill me, I am not Indian."

The hunter astonished the boy by straining him to his breast, and he cried—

"It is the first one, the biggest boy."

The mother falling upon her knees, beside the father and son, poured forth, in incoherent sentences, a torrent of thanks to the Great Spirit, who had thus mysteriously, and, as she supposed, supernaturally restored her first-born to her.

The first paroxysm of joy over, the hunter's forest instincts became active again, and he demanded the manner in which the youth had reached the cabin. The conversation between father and son was a dramatic one. I cannot give it in the language I write, and must content myself with stating its substance.

The hunter learned that his son, after he was torn from his mother, was dragged many miles south-west, where he was put under the charge of an Indian, whom, by the description, the hunter knew to be the same individual he had left at the camp, where he had killed those who stole his children. The boy roamed with the tribe, but was never allowed to be out of sight of this Indian and his squaw, until a few weeks previous to the time at which he was restored to his home, when the Indian left the camp and did not return for many days. For the first time he then took the boy on a long hunting excursion. They were absent from the main body of the tribe a number of days. Again the Indian commanded the boy to follow him, and he was brought into the vicinity of the mountain on which he had found his father's retreat. The Indian told him that he brought him to this mountain that he might find his father—that he should leave him, return to the camp and report him dead. He had wandered on the mountain many days, but saw no signs of human life, until on the evening we have described; while seeking a place in which to spend the night safely, he discovered a thin wreath of smoke ascending from the tops of the trees; he traveled towards the point from which he supposed it to proceed, until night overtook him, and without knowing that human beings were so near him, he had lain down in the dark and had fallen into the sleep from which his father aroused him. He had lately heard of the children, who were torn from home before him, but he had not seen them since the first week of his captivity.

A great burden was lifted from the hearts of the hunter and his wife. He believed that the kindness shown him by the Indian who had returned his son, was an example of Indian gratitude for which he should be truly thankful, although he could not regard the debt the Indian owed him as a very heavy one, for he left him but a slim chance for life. He could construe the return of his boy in no other manner, however, and he lived in hope that his other children would some day be returned, yet he was determined to relax no effort to recover them. Father and son could now hunt together—he had a companion whom he could take with him in his long marches, or leave to guard his cabin.

The hunter thought often of what his boy had said about the smoke that had served as the beacon to direct him, and he never allowed an evening to pass without kindling fire where its smoke might ascend as it did on the night the boy returned. Summer and winter there was always smoke over the hunter's cabin at sunrise and sunset, for he knew that if he had a friend in the Indian camp, who ever came in the vicinity of the mountain, he would observe this peculiarity, and understand it as a land-mark.

The hunter did not know the true character of this Indian. He was not aware of his reputation as a cunning fellow whose delight was intrigue.

Some reader may think, for a man of wandering life in a country infested with treacherous Indians and savage beasts, in whose blood his hands were often imbued, the hunter manifested unusual affection for his offspring. Not greater for them was his tenderness or concern, than the tenderness or concern of the panther for her cubs.

The keen observer of human motive, well knows, that beneath a cold and rough exterior often beats a warm heart, and it is a matter of reliable history, that many of the early Western Pioneers—the men who drove back the wild beast and the skulking Indian, and turned the wilderness into cultivated fields, were men of the kindest nature, and most benevolent impulses.

While they were valiant in defense of their homes and

relentless in their vengeance upon those who injured their families, they were ever ready to succor the needy — assist the unfortunate—and sympathize with the suffering.

CHAPTER III.

THE VOW.

Snows that had fallen lightly in the valleys, but were deep enough in the mountain glens to afford the hunter paths by which he tracked to their hiding places the animals necessary to his support, had long since melted, and small streams were rushing in mad currents, roaring among the ravines. Birds, as Lamartine says, " the poetry of song—the hymn of air," were picking soft buds from low bushes, while they looked up to the spreading branches above them, and rejoiced in the promise of green leaves and bright flowers. Throughout all nature there was

> "A sense of renovation
> Of freshness and of health."

The hunter, reviewing a season of comparative quiet, cherished a fierce determination to shrink from neither exposure nor toil in his dreary search for tidings of his lost ones. For the first time since the return of his boy, he went upon an expedition which, if pursued according to his plan, would keep him from home several weeks. He had instructed the youth in the mysteries of forest life, and warning him to be watchful, he felt confident that the boy would not unwarily fall into serious difficulty. It was one of the hunter's most impressive injunctions, that he should not wander far from the cabin. The boy had his father's restless disposition, and this was the most difficult command for him to obey, yet such was the spirit the father had infused into him toward the Indians, who at the first opportunity would drag his mother back to the wigwam she had deserted for his father's love, that even this command he seldom disobeyed; indeed such was the mother's anxiety in regard to him, that he was seldom allowed to be out of her sight for many hours in succession. One day he detected traces of a bear near the cabin. They led down the mountain—he followed the track, in hopes of overtaking the animal, but more in the hope of meeting his father, whose return was now daily expected. He lost the track which he had followed, and late in the afternoon sat down near a path he supposed his father would travel on his return. He had watched a short time, when his quick ear detected the approach of some being, but not along the path. Seeking a hiding place he looked anxiously for the friend or foe that was drawing near. Presently he was able to discover that it was an Indian, and soon he saw that it was the Indian who had restored him to his parents. With an impulse of gratitude the boy stepped from his hiding place, and boldly advanced to meet the savage, who sprang behind a tree, as the youth came in sight, but, in a moment, recognizing him, gave him apparently an honest, heartfelt welcome.

Night was approaching, and the youth not forgetting his mother's anxiety at his protracted absence, told his savage companion that he must return home, and, as they wished to converse together, the Indian accompanied him. They had proceeded some distance when the Indian refused to go any farther, for fear they might meet the hunter and a dreadful fray ensue. The boy told the Indian then of his father's absence, and of his feeling toward him, who had been the means of restoring his child. At this information the savage's countenance contracted with a smile which expressed the shrewd deceit of his character, and he walked on without hesitancy until nearly sunset. The boy pointing to a column of smoke rising among the trees around the cabin, related the service it had rendered him in finding home, and told his father's determination in regard to it, on account of that service. The Indian took leave of the boy, assigning as a reason that he had already been too long absent from the party that had accompanied him into the vicinity.

In a few minutes the boy made glad his mother's heart by appearing before her unharmed. While he told his mother about his afternoon adventure, the savage he had met stood in sight of the cabin. He marked well its situation, and not until he felt satisfied that he could approach it in the darkest night, did he retrace his steps. When he had walked half an hour, he stood before a fire, around which, wrapped in their blankets, lay ten others of his tribe. They were immediately aroused. The new comer held an animated conversation with one who was the leader of the band. With the hunter's pretended friend as a guide, in Indian file, the whole party then began to ascend the mountain.

The young hunter slumbered on his rude couch, while the mother waited with sleepless eyes and attentive ears, for the signal which should announce the return of the lord of the cabin. She fancied she heard approaching footsteps, and she arose and went to the door to listen. Immediately she was alarmed by a violent knocking. The young hunter was aroused, and he demanded who was at the door. He was answered in the Indian tongue:

"The friend you left a little while ago in the forest. I have lost my companions. I am faint and weary. You will not refuse me food and rest—I have been wounded by a fall in the dark, and my strength fails me."

"You are alone," said the boy, "and would not deceive us."

"Have I not too often befriended you to be now suspected? Why did I liberate you from captivity, and restore you to your parents, at the risk of the vengeance of my tribe?"

"Do not trust him," said the mother. "We know not that it is the friendly Indian."

"Yes," answered the boy, "I know it is; I know his voice."

"By the Great Spirit I swear I would not deceive you," replied the Indian, as he heard the conversation of the mother and son. "You will not refuse a cup of water! I will sleep at your door till morning—you can see then I have told you no lie."

The youth had confidence in the Indian, and could not resist the benevolent impulse which dictated compliance with the savage's request; still he was determined to be watchful, and arming himself with a huge knife, he removed a portion of the fastenings of the cabin door; instantly it was burst open, and the treacherous red-skin, with his party, rushed into the cabin.

"We have come," said the leader of the Indians, (who was the brother of the hunter's wife, and now the chief of the tribe, his father being dead,) "to take back the fugitive squaw and her papoose to the wigwam she deserted for our enemy. He has slain many of her kindred. His blood shall yet stain the leaves of the forest. You must go."

"You are not my kindred. You are my foes. You may take my body—the Great Spirit will take my spirit;" returned the hunter's wife, brandishing a tomahawk in a manner which showed that she did not speak idle words.

"A squaw defies us!" said the brother of the hunter's wife. "We have no time to waste."

The chief rushed towards the hunter's wife, and the false friend grasped the boy. A struggle ensued. The squaw, with uplifted tomahawk, for a moment kept her savage brother at bay, while the other Indian endeavored to wrest from the boy a large knife, with which he was armed. By a glimmering light from the cabin fire, the dusky forms of the leading Indians, with their allies, grouped at the cabin door, were to be seen for an instant, in the position I have described: in a second all was changed.

"Strike," cried a firm voice, in a language all understood; "kill him as quick as you would a wild-cat."

The hunter stood in his cabin. He had impetuously dashed through the guards at the door. He saw the Indian who menaced his wife, and before he had time fairly to recognize the hunter, gave him a blow which caused him to reel and fall helpless upon the ground; but in that fall the Indian expressed the accumulated savageness of his nature and his passion for revenge. His knife drank the blood of his sister. She fell, with a cry for help, upon the body of her brutal relative.

With a full sense of his situation swelling his heart, quickening his pulses, bracing his nerves and contracting his muscles, the hunter met those who rushed upon him to avenge the death of their chief. He fought for his home, for his children, and for the revenge that had been consuming his life for years, and he fought with remarkable power and desperation. He saw not his boy — he knew not what had been his fate, but he knew that before him lay four Indians whom his powerful arm had slain, and still, though losing blood from a number of severe wounds, he fought on. The Indians, without their leader, without the animating spirit that led them to the hunter's cabin, began to give way. Furiously the hunter pressed upon them, and only two escaped without serious injury. Among the dead were the hunter's chief foes, the false friend and his wife's brother, and among the dead also, as he believed, was that wife, for whom he had fought so valiantly.

The hunter pursued the savages a few steps beyond the cabin door, then staggered back, and, exhausted with the loss of blood, fell across his threshold. He knew that he should die — he had not seen his boy in the fray — how joyful was the hope that he lived and might avenge the wrongs of his father and mother, perhaps be the means of liberating the children so long searched for.

The father, with an effort to collect his failing strength, called his boy. His hopes fell when there was no answer, but again he called, and then his hopes rose again, when there came a firm response. Crawling from a hiding place, where he had lain with a wound on his right arm, which had disabled it, the boy crept towards his father. The dying hunter took the youth's hand, and eloquent, even in the meagre language used between them, told the boy of all the hardships he had suffered on account of his feud with the tribe of Indians to which his mother had belonged, and then he said to him:

"The pale faces are our friends. Soon the red varmints will be driven from these vallies and mountains — the pale faces will dwell in them. Go among the pale faces — join those who would drive back the red-skins—have no mercy for them—avenge your father's and your mother's death—and by the Great Spirit swear you will seek, and if alive, liberate your kindred in bondage — if dead, exterminate their destroyers. Never forget your father's dying command. Swear!"

The boy took the oath as his father administered it to him —and then the hunter said,

"Let me die in my cabin."

With his last energies, he dragged himself into his cabin, near the spot where lay his wife's body. And there with a convulsive clutch of his boy's hand the brave hunter took his last breath.

Scenting blood, a band of wolves came to the cabin, and dolefully howled while the young hunter watched. They glutted their appetites upon the bodies of the Indians which had fallen at the cabin door, yet the boy heeded them not.

When the grey mist of the morning began to gather upon the mountain's summit, the young hunter had secured the cabin, so that he knew the bodies of his parents were safe from the ravages of the animals that would for many nights howl their requiem, and when the sun began to dispel the mists, with his father's rifle, knife and tomahawk and hunter's coat, the boy wound his way down the mountain, at the foot of which he knew a path that would lead him to a settlement where his father had traded, and which had often been described to him.

One of those whom the young hunter believed to have been killed, arose from among the corpses in the ill-fated cabin and sought anxiously for traces of his footsteps. The youth had feared pursuit, and the "signs" of his progress were ingeniously obliterated, until he felt himself safe.

CHAPTER IV.

NEW FRIENDS.

It was a hazardous undertaking for that youth, then not eighteen years of age, with no companions but his rifle, his tomahawk and his knife, to plunge into the unbroken wilderness threatened at every step with foes seeking human blood; but he had no alternative, and he was accustomed to hazardous enterprises—the dangers of the forest were well understood by him, and he feared not to encounter them.

It has often been said that men's characters never develop till they are thrown upon their own resources. The young hunter has yet to develop his character, and in the pathless woods, with no counsellor, no companion, and a solemn vow to fulfill, he was indeed thrown upon his own resources.

He had often heard his father talk of a settlement of whites northeast of their mountain retreat. Thitherward he bent his steps. He had wandered many days along rushing streams and through dense woods, when he rested one evening near a spring gushing from massive and towering rocks. He prepared to render palatable portions of a deer he had shot, and as he stood holding a piece of the meat, hunter fashion, over a brisk fire, was startled by a slight noise behind him. Before he could turn to ascertain its cause he was grasped by two powerful arms, and held in such a manner that he was completely at the mercy of his captor. He struggled violently.

"Keep quiet, little red-skin, I ain't a-goin' to hurt you," said a rough voice. Still the boy struggled, and his captor released him saying,

"You've spilt your dinner, but never mind, I've got a plenty. You ain't all Ingin. What you doin' here? Where'd ye come from?"

The boy felt that he would not be injured by the brawny hunter who had surprised him, and employing what few English words he had picked up, he told truthfully how he had lost his father and mother, and then stated his own present purpose.

"You'll go with me," replied the backwoodsman. "We'll take care o' them red varmints. What'd they call you, little Ingin?"

The youth gave the name he had borne among the Indians, and pronounced it several times, but the hunter could not catch the correct sound, and with a gesture of impatience, he cried—

"Taint no odds—call me Clinker, and I'll call you Birty. I know'd a fellow o' that name once, and a tarnal cunnin' creter he was too."

There was a frankness about this backwoodsman which won the boy's confidence. After they had eaten together, and Birty, as we shall hereafter designate him, had related the principal incidents of his history, Clinker said, "You're just the chap I wanted to scar up. Yer haint no body to look after ye, and over these mountains here, I've got a gal 'bout your size as haint got nobody to take care o' her 'ceptin when she goes to another cabin 'bout ten miles off. Them tarnal red-skins took her mother's scalp one day, when I was a huntin', but I reckon since a few on 'em have paid for that scalp. You an' that gal can look out for the old cabin, an' she needn't trouble her nabors. Agreed, little Ingin?"

Birty offered no objections, but expressed himself glad of the opportunity; provided it should not interfere with his determination to seek out his brothers who were in Indian bondage.

"Haint I got a spite, too, agin them varmints, and won't we hunt 'em for each other," answered Clinker.

On the second day after this conversation, Birty was shown his new home. Its garden spot broke the wilderness, near a small stream which wound through a thickly timbered valley, but which, from the distance he first viewed it, looked only like a dark line stretched across the tops of the trees.

It was a cabin of more pretensions than his father's. It had a chimney, in the solitary window there were a few panes of glass, and it was surrounded by a small corn field. Here Clinker left his adopted son until he should find the girl who was to be his companion. Birty met her on the following morning. She was a tall, athletic, but well formed maiden, with a countenance frank and intelligent, though bronzed to a shade that Kentucky girls of the present day would think most fatal to matrimonial prospects. Her attire was not very similar to that fashionable in our time. Her hair was confined carelessly by a large thorn — her dress consisted of home-made cloth and skins, which hung about her in a manner innocent of art.

Her name was Martha. Her father called her Mat, and he told her she must consider Birty as a brother. He should leave them hereafter to take care of his cabin. Between these young persons, thus thrown together, there sprung up naturally a mutual sympathy which ripened into a friendship as pure as the friendship of a brother and a sister. They were as brother and sister.

Birty was naturally a musician, and sitting at the cabin door on a pleasant evening, he would sing the wild songs he had heard his mother sing. Gradually he learned to whistle, in imitation of the birds that built their nests, and swung in the branches overhanging the cabin. He taught Martha to sing his wild Indian songs, and he instructed her to imitate the varying notes of the wild birds. She was a ready pupil, and soon excelled her master. Many a pleasant hour did the two children of the forest spend together thus employed.

Those were rare concerts in the deep woods, by the glad birds and the rude backwoodsman, with his untutored companion. Willful sportsmen did not then frighten the harmless bird from its nest or from its leafy trysting place, and the charmed songsters were not alarmed when Birty and Martha joined them in their hymns of praise.

Would that more of those who now love music had such respect for the wild songs of the wild birds that they dare not level the murderous barrel at the songsters, and that those who must have sport would all find it elsewhere than in shooting the birds that would make their nests in farm yards, or near our village dwellings.

Birty's life in this valley, for the time and circumstances, was a quiet one, too quiet for his restless nature, and for the fierce passion to revenge the grievous wrongs of his family, which burned within him.

He had grown to be a man in strength and stature, and he was eager to travel towards the Indian hunting-grounds where he hoped to gain tidings of the playmates of his early youth. Day after day his eagerness grew more exciting, and when, by a settler, who spent a night at the cabin, he learned that a party of hunters was about to explore the wilds of the then entirely unsettled Kentucky Territory, he resolved to be one of the number. This resolve he communicated to Clinker.

"You don't do that alone," answered Clinker, to Birty's astonishment. "I'll find them chaps myself. There's nothin' here to keep a feller."

"But ye don't consider," answered Birty, "who'll watch the cabin and look arter Mat."

"She'll go to the settlement—we shan't be gone more'n half the winter. We can lick enough o' them red-skins in that time."

So it was fixed—Clinker and Birty joined the hunters, who were to explore the wild lands of Kentucky, and Clinker's daughter took up her abode in one of the cabins of a settlement about ten miles from the spot she had assisted to cultivate in the wilderness. Birty and Martha parted like brother and sister. When they took leave of each other Clinker, in his rough but honest way, said:

"Thar, I'll be licked by a red-skin, if I didn't know a tarnal sight better, I'd think, Birty, as how you and Mat were some kin. It's astonishing how you've tuck to each other."

Clinker knew not the fate in store for his daughter, or he might have manifested something of the feeling for which he ridiculed Birty.

He had not been absent from the settlement ten days, when a large party of Indians attacked it in the night, burned several cabins, and took a number of women and children prisoners, among whom was Martha.

CHAPTER V.

THE CAPTIVE.

It was late in the month of September, 1775, when Clinker and Birty joined the party that was to explore the Western wilds. The place of rendezvous was Powell's valley. The company consisted, in the language of the times, of "twenty-seven guns," or twenty-seven fighting men. Daniel Boone, the renowned Pioneer, was one of that party, as was also Hugh McGary and several other hardy hunters from the backwoods of North Carolina.

The history of that expedition is a portion of the history of Kentucky; it is known not to have afforded much opportunity for the ambitious to distinguish themselves, but Birty so conducted himself that he elicited the admiration of Boone. That old hunter separated from the rest of the party, at Dick's creek, leaving them to pursue their way to Harrodsburg, then a settlement of four cabins, while he bent his course toward Boonesborough, the site of the first fort erected by the white man in Kentucky. He invited Birty to accompany him. Birty accepted the invitation.

"You're a tarnal fool," said Clinker, when Birty told him of his determination. "Ye better stick to the other chaps."

"We didn't come here to plant corn. I'm for fightin'

Ingins. These fellers aint a goin' to do no fightin'—Boone's the chap what'll make the rascals scarcer."

"Them's facts, Birty—and fightin' Ingins is what we're arter. If you leave this crowd so'll I."

Thus it was agreed upon, and Birty and Clinker, without adventure of note, accompanied Boone and his party to Boonesborough, and took up their abode in the fort. Mann Butler, in his history of Kentucky, says:

"Well might the Indians, could they have anticipated the faintest shadow of the ills in store for them, and their whole race, from this foothold of the white man have contested the fatal lodgement with the last drop of their blood. The genius of their Pontiac, their Turtle and their Tecumseh, did not display itself more gloriously at Detroit against St. Clair, and on the Thames, than it might have done, in preventing the white man from erecting his forts in the great hunting grounds of their tribes.

"A fort in those rude military times, consisted of pieces of timber sharpened at the end, and fairly lodged in the ground; rows of pickets enclosed the desired space, which embraced the cabins of the inhabitants. A block house, of superior care and strength, commanding the sides of the fort, with or without a ditch, completed the fortifications, or stations as they were called; generally the sides of the interior cabins formed the sides of the fort. Slight as this advance was in the art of war, it was more than sufficient against attacks of small arms, in the hands of such desultory warriors, as their irregularities of supplies necessarily rendered the Indians. Such was the nature of the military structures of the Pioneers against their enemies. They were even more formidable in the cane brakes and in the woods than before these imperfect fortifications."

There fairly began young Birty's career as a daring backwoodsman. There he had the first opportunity of associating freely with men and women—joining in their amusements or taking part in their athletic sports.

A certain number of the most active men about the fort, were selected as hunters for the families which there had homes. One of the most fortunate of those hunters was Birty. He was a young man of remarkable muscular development, and his power of endurance was astonishing even to some of the old hunters, whom he met. He was in the habit of making long excursions from the fort, and he would not allow even Clinker to accompany him. On his return from these exhibitions he told often of conflicts with Indians, but he never appeared with a scalp at his belt. Once he related an encounter with a brawny savage, to Clinker, who, as if doubting Birty's word, said:

"Where's your trophy, boy? Show us the critter's har."

"I never scalped an Ingin in my life, and never will. Ye don't 'spose, Clinker, I haint no more respect for myself an' a bear cub, what you couldn't get to touch a dead carcass. Taint in me, Clinker; I hate Ingins, but when they're dead I let 'em alone."

Spring came. Clinker had returned to Virginia, to seek in vain for his cherished Mat. Birty still made the Boonesborough fort his rendezvous, though he was seldom there many days in succession.

Early in the summer of 1776, unmistakable "signs" of Indians, with warlike intentions, were discovered in the neighborhood of the fort. Birty took it upon himself to be a spy upon their movements. The unbroken forest was now his dwelling place, but he often thought of his Virginia home. Numerous birds sang in the branches of the trees forever overhanging him in his wanderings, and his only recreation was whistling such notes as most nearly imitated their varied warblings.

He discovered one afternoon satisfactory evidences of the close proximity of a considerable body of Indians. All of his forest cunning, and his backwoods instincts were awake. Night approached, and still he met none of the enemy; however, he knew a party of them must that night encamp in the vicinity. He watched eagerly for signs of their camp, believing that they intended to make an unexpected attack upon the fort at Boonesborough or at Harrodsburg, and he was determined to thwart their intentions by giving the inhabitants timely warning.

The full round moon rose behind the trees and shone clearly upon the ancient woods. Birty looked up through the foliage and saw distinctly broken patches of the blue sky, but he could detect no curling smoke for which he watched as a sign of the savage camp.

He prepared to take his evening meal and roll himself in his blanket within the sheltering top of a fallen tree, when he fancied he heard a familiar, but for that place and hour, a very strange sound. It grew louder and appeared to come nearer. Birty left his hiding place and cautiously took a position where, without being observed, he could see any object that might approach in the direction of the sounds.

Presently the hunter answered the sounds; then thinking of the exercises he had had at his Virginia home, he imitated those birdwarblings with which he had been familiar.

To his astonishment they were all answered perfectly. His curiosity was now wrought to a pitch, that would have induced him to brave any danger in its gratification. Again he imitated the song of a familiar bird—again it was answered. Now he examined the priming of his rifle—satisfied himself that his knife and tomahawk were safe, and skulking from tree to tree, approached the spot whence he imagined his notes had been answered. Standing at the foot of a venerable tree, he saw a young squaw, who appeared to be listening eagerly for some sound by which she had been startled.

As the hunter watched her she poured forth a gush of melody that could be likened only to the mocking bird's wild music. Birty, when the squaw's voice ceased, echoed those sounds, and the squaw's attention was fixed upon the hunter, as he stood with his rifle leaning against his arm, and his polished knife gleaming from his belt in the moon-light.

Cries of recognition escaped both the hunter and the squaw—Birty and Martha Clinker had again met. Explanations were mutually demanded, and conversing in the Indian tongue, which Birty learned in his youth, and which Martha had learned in her captivity, Birty told how it happened that he was there, and what had befallen him since they parted. Martha related the circumstances of her captivity, and Birty desired she should that night flee with him to Boonesborough, whence she could return to Virginia in quest of her father. Martha refused. Birty urged her to give the reasons. She answered:

"My heart leaped to see you as does the heart of the doe for a lost fawn, and I would greet my father as the fawn would greet the long absent doe, but I cannot go back with you now. Among the Indians at yonder camp is one Birty, as much like you as one fawn is like another, and did I not know that you are not an Indian I should think you were brothers. He took me to his wigwam, when the party that captured me joined the rest of the tribe. At first he was repugnant to me—then I received his attentions because he reminded me of you, and he was so different from what I had been told Indian warriors are like, that I began to love him, and I dare not desert him, if for no other reason, for the sake of a pledge of our love which sleeps in our wigwam, and is yet dependent upon its mother for the life it enjoys."

"Is that Indian older than I am?" inquired Birty eagerly, still speaking in the Indian tongue.

"Many moons younger, I should judge," answered Martha.

Then a hope which had long since died, revived in Birty's breast.

"Can you bring this Indian to meet me to-morrow night?" he said.

"I dare trust you, Birty, but I dare not ask him," she replied.

"Tell me then whither the tribe is traveling."

"Toward the great river, to meet friends. They talk of white foes collecting to drive them from their hunting grounds —they are preparing to meet them."

"I am watching their movements, and have been for several days. You will give me your word that they do not design to attack any of the settlements in this neighborhood?"

"I overheard the warriors in the council last night. I know their march will be secretly continued to a point on the Ohio, where they expect to meet other warriors, who are determined to fight for their hunting grounds. I must go back to the camp—farewell, Birty."

"We shall meet again," said the hunter.

"You will tell my father I am not unhappy in my Indian home," answered Martha.

Birty watched her till she disappeared among the trees. She had forbidden him to follow her, and he obeyed. He resolved to be among those whom the Indians, gathering their forces together, had determined to expel from the cane brakes and forests of Kentucky, but he was not satisfied to leave the party so near him, till he knew more of their numbers and character than Martha had communicated.

On the morrow he stood near the Indian camp when preparations were made for marching, and he saw Martha with the squaws, her papoose in Indian fashion fastened upon her back; but he could see no one whom he could identify as her husband. To look at the Indian that, as Martha said, resembled him, was to Birty an enjoyment for which he was ready to brave dangers that would appall hearts unaccustomed to forest life; and he resolved to follow the Indians until he had satisfied his curiosity in this particular.

When the savages gathered around their camp at night, four of their number were missing. They were vainly looked for. Birty could have told where their bodies were lying. Following the Indian trail he had overtaken these stragglers, and when he had satisfied himself that neither was that one for whom he looked, thoughts of the last scene witnessed in his mountain home, nerved his arm, and the savages fell, and neither could have told what manner of foe was near him. Birty had seen others that day who might as easily have been his victims, but he was not satisfied that they did not answer the description that Martha had given; and they joined their companions unharmed.

The Indians had not suspected foes until the absence of their warriors on the night of which we write. While savages smoked their pipes, Martha heard the wild notes of the forest bird far back in the woods; and then she could have told those around her the fate of the absent, but she dare not; nor dare she go to Birty and warn him of the danger that, on the following day, might threaten him.

Again and again Birty called in bird-like music, that he knew Martha would understand, but he received no answer. Stealthily he crept nearer the camp. He could see the dusky forms of the Indians passing to and fro, but he was not satisfied—with the utmost caution he crept so near that he could almost hear the conversation of a group of warriors in council. He understood their language, and he determined to know the subject of their consultation.

With the shrewdest exercise of his knowledge of Indian habits, he skulked from tree to tree. Moonlight had thus far aided his movements—now it retarded them. Heavy clouds hung in the sky, and he waited for the moon to be obscured by them—then he crept very near the council.

Now he could distinctly hear every word that was uttered, and the report that Martha had given him was confirmed. He suspected that her husband must be one of the warriors in the group before him, and he resolved to run a greater risk in order to satisfy his curiosity. Again he cautiously skulked toward the Indian camp. The risk of detection was great. Birty was full aware of that risk. He had determined to brave it, and he crept on.

There was a deep shadow on the woods, and Birty had reached a clump of bushes so near the council that he was confident, when the moon shown again, he could see the face of every warrior. He had been so intent on watching the difficulties to be overcome immediately around him, that he had not kept himself correctly informed concerning the period when the cloud which obscured the moon would pass from before it, and while he stood exposed to view, its mellow radiance fell on the thin woods where the Indian council sat.

An Indian on guard caught a glimpse of Birty as he dashed into the bushes. That Indian gave the alarm. Instantly the hunter was surrounded.

He sprang from the bushes into the open woods, and, remarkably fleet on foot, would have escaped comparatively unharmed, but his foes were numerous. His first impulse was to fight, reckless of consequences, but in an instant he saw that it was scarcely possible he could escape with his life—then he thought of Martha—of his curiosity in reference to the Indian Martha had described as her husband, and he surrendered. He was securely bound and carefully watched. When day dawned he saw with bitter disappointment that there was no one among the Indians who bore the slightest resemblance to himself.

CHAPTER VI.

A SKIRMISH.

The Indians held a council, and Birty, closely guarded, was confined to a tree near the centre of the camp. The Indians had no suspicion that he understood their language, and they talked freely in his hearing. He learned that they had resolved to make him run the gauntlet, and then torture him to death. They believed him to have been the murderer of those who had recently disappeared from their ranks, and they regarded him with true Indian vengeance. All this must be done within two days—at which time it was expected this party would overtake another, that had gone forward early the night previous as a scouting company. The leader of the scouting party was Martha's husband, as Birty judged from the talk in regard to him.

Birty looked upon the Indian warriors as they sat in council or stood near him, keeping watch, and he had ample opportunity to calculate the dangers of his situation and speculate upon the chances of escape. He knew that he should not be harmed, unless some accident occurred, until another night had passed, and he resolved to conduct himself as if he had no anxiety about his fate. He would be watchful, but submissive. He was watched suspiciously by several of the

Indians, as if they half believed him to be a warrior from some other tribe, who had joined the whites. His half Indian extraction and the peculiar associations of his life, had indeed rendered him very much, in many respects, like original sons of the forest, yet in bearing and intelligence, he was very different from those who now had him in their power. He only asked that the watchfulness of his guard would be withdrawn long enough to allow him a few moment's conversation with Martha. He saw her several times, but she had no opportunity to come near him.

Birty rejoiced when the Indians began to make busy preparations for departure. They had smoked their pipes and taken their hasty morning meal, when they held another council within ear-shot of Birty's position. One who seemed to be a man of authority, said to his fellow savages:

"The pale-faces came to drive us from our ancient hunting grounds. We go to join Indians who will drive back the pale-faces. Our captive can tell us whether the pale-faces are like the leaves of the forest in number, in summer or in winter. He can guide us to their wigwams. We shall offer him his liberty if he will tell us their number, and show us their wigwams. The white squaw can talk with the captive."

The warriors agreed to this speech, and Martha was sent for to interrogate Birty.

The prisoner saw her approach him with no slight emotion. She asked him the questions which the warrior who had been spokesman propounded, and he answered:

"Tell 'em to do their ugliest. I shan't show 'em the first pale-face—but let 'em know the whites are mighty plenty over East, and give 'em to understand that I'm a friend of

Dan Boone's, and if they come any of their Ingin sprees over me they'll have the old chap arter 'em. For yourself, now Martha, I'll tell ye that I'm goin' to leave this place afore another day, and you've got to cut me loose to-night if I don't get a chance to kick over some of them red devils to-day."

Martha dare make no reply to Birty for fear of exciting suspicion, but her face assured him that he would have her aid, if she could give it. When she told the warriors how sternly the captive rejected their proposition, and what he threatened them, the big fellow who had spoken, uttered a significant " Ugh ! " Several followed his example, and then in a few minutes the order was given for a march. In a short time the whole party was under way. A heavy burden was fastened upon Birty's back, and with his hands tied behind him, he was driven before two stout warriors. Birty's proud heart beat indignantly, as he marched that day, a slave to the " varmints " that had so deeply wronged his family. His vows of revenge were deep and earnest.

Night was coming on, and Birty had seen no opportunity of escape. His hopes of freedom were centred on Martha's aid, and the character of the weather. The day had been lowering, and there were tokens of rain. About noon the clouds broke away and the sky became clear; then Birty's hope of liberty was a feeble one, but as afternoon advanced the sky was again overcast. At sunset it was darker in the forest than it was on the previous night, when Birty stood as a spy upon the Indian camp. Birty watched the gathering gloom with most intense interest—it was to aid him in making the escape he had planned. He had been so obedient to the commands laid upon him by the Indians, that his guards had relaxed much of the vigilance they had exercised at the commencement of their march; and the prisoner thought this augured well for the future.

The warriors selected a resting place upon the bank of a small stream; Birty saw that there were low bushes along this bank, and thick woods on the opposite side—he was satisfied with the choice his captors had made. An immense fire was built, whose light flashed up among the ancient trees, revealing the Indians seated upon the ground with their prisoner securely bound in their midst. The previous night he had not been permitted to lie down. He was now ingeniously bound to two warriors who lay on either side of him. They were confident he could not stir without awaking them. The captors slept, but the captive did not. Nearly half the night had passed—the fire gave out fitful flashes as a gentle wind swept through the forest, and Birty felt most painfully that his chance of deliverance was every hour growing narrower.

As he speculated upon his gloomy prospects he felt the cords tighten upon his swollen limbs—he began to grow listless from fatigue and despair—he thought he heard a light foot-fall—presently some one bent over him—it was Martha. She cautiously cut the cords which bound Birty to his guards, and he stood upon his feet. In a moment his limbs were free —he stretched them out as if to ascertain whether the muscles would obey his will—then he looked upon his slumbering foes to find where the one was lying who had taken possession of his rifle, tomahawk and knife.

The apparent leader of the party, the spokesman of the previous morning, had Birty's weapons—the knife and tomahawk were in his belt.

Birty would have felt himself unarmed without the knife, tomahawk and rifle of his father—he knew their metal.

He crept stealthily toward the warrior, whom he was to "*rob.*" He took the rifle in his hand—slipped the knife safely from the savage's belt, and had his hand upon the tomahawk; the Indian moved as if he would awaken—a mad impulse seized Birty, he hastily tore the weapon from its place and struck the warrior a blow which buried the tomahawk in his head. Fatally wounded, the savage in his dying struggles was convulsively thrown forward and fell back upon the warrior lying next to him, who was aroused instantly. He sprang to his feet before Birty could strike him, and uttered a war-cry with furious energy. It was no time for Birty to fight—his safety lay in dexterous dodging and fleetness of foot. All was confusion around the camp fire. Birty had his presence of mind. Quickly the Indians gathered theirs. Several started in swift pursuit of the fugitive. Two warriors were close upon him, one of them had almost overtaken him, when the sharp report of several rifles rang through the forest, and the foremost Indians fell.

Birty knew that friends had most unexpectedly but most opportunely come; yet he relaxed not a muscle in his flight, and well that he did not, for he had advanced but a few steps when he met Martha, who, expecting that Birty would peacefully escape, had gone outside of the camp to meet him and give him some words to bear her father. She was now frantic with fear that the Indians might find her babe, and for revenge, murder it in her absence. She had discovered that friends had come to Birty's rescue. There were quickly successive shots at the camp, and yells and curses. Fear for the safety of her child nerved her, and into the thickest of the conflict she would have rushed had not Birty restrained her.

"Where 'd you leave it?" he said. She described to him a spot which he vowed he could instantly find. He bid her not to go nearer the camp till he returned, and then went in quest of the papoose. The conflict did not wage near the spot where its mother had left it, but it had been aroused from slumber and was screaming with fright. The mother who had stealthily followed Birty, fearing that it was wounded, rushed before him and snatched it from the ground. The hunter heard the child greet its mother with a cry of recognition, then without a word he rushed to the battle-ground, and found it occupied with friends. The savages had been routed—leaving several dead, and taking with them a number of wounded.

"Hello!" said a rough voice.

Birty recognized it, and he answered: "Hello! Clinker, where'd you come from?"

"Birty! sure as I ever killed a red devil," replied Clinker, rushing towards the spot where Birty stood.

It was a joyful meeting, but Birty felt that there would soon be a more joyful one.

"You aint the chap what was running from them Ingins, Birty?" said Clinker.

"Are you the chap what cut 'em down?" replied Birty.

"I'm one of 'em," answered Clinker. "There's a dozen of us, all the right grit. How'd you get in that trap?"

"I'll tell you arter a while. How'd you happen here?"

"Why you see, Birty, when I left you at the fort and went home, I found the devil'd been to pay—the tarnal Ingins had been down on the settlement, and they'd carried off Mat. I owed 'em an old grudge, and I cum back to Kaintuck to fight 'em—some of these boys cum from the settlement and some we picked up. We got on track of the Ingins, at this camp, jist by accident, yesterday, and we followed 'em till last night, and it was dark. We know'd we was close on 'em, and we thought we'd take 'em afore mornin', but it got tarnal dark. I was a watchin' a while ago when them clouds broke away, and I give the boys the word, and we started. We arriv, Birty, jist right, didn't we?"

"You did that," answered Birty, "to keep the red devils from killing me, and to catch one of their handsomest squaws."

"Where is she, Birty?"

"I'll fetch her."

Birty went in pursuit of Martha, and Clinker's men sat down around the fire, from which they had driven the savages.

Birty had some difficulty in finding Martha, but at length he succeeded, and returned to the camp with her. Martha was in a most gloomy state of mind in reference to her separation from her husband, for she knew her disappearance would be reported to him in the most unfavorable light—that she would either be considered dead or as a fugitive from his protection. Strange as it may appear, there was something about that Indian which had so endeared him to her, that for his society she willingly relinquished all hope of return to the settlements of the whites, unless peace should be declared between them and the Indians. In condolence to Martha, Birty said to her in his rough language, but in a cheerful tone of voice:

"Don't take on so—you'll feel better arter a while, I'm certain."

When they came near camp, Martha dared not look at those she considered her foes. Clinker heard them approach, and went forward to meet Birty—when he saw what he supposed to be the squaw, he cried:

"She needn't be afeard of us. We aint Ingins what burns women."

Martha recognized the voice. She suddenly raised her head, and cried:

"Father!"

Clinker caught her to his bosom, and exclaimed:

"It's my Mat, sure as I'm a Clinker! I'm cussed if this aint luck! I haint got as big a grudge agin them red devils as I was trying to make out. Whar have you been, Mat? How'd you get here? What on airth is this?"

Clinker had just discovered the papoose Martha bore in her arms. She held it up before him.

"A little Ingin, eh?—Whar'd ye get the critter, Mat?"

She dare not answer, and Birty said:

"It's her'n, old fellow."

"Her'n?" returned Clinker in surprise—"Her'n? how the devil d'ye make that out?"

"One o' them Ingins belongin' to the party you just licked made her his squaw," answered Birty.

"Lightnin', I'd liked to catched him at it—I'd a sent him whar Ingins don't mix with white folks—but 'taint no use makin' a fuss when the game's gone. Them red varmints don't get Mat agin, as long as old Clinker's got a rifle."

These were harsh words to Martha's ear—she had often wondered how her father would receive the intelligence of her maternal relations among the Indians, and she had always pictured him more disturbed in regard to it than he appeared. In this she had cause for congratulation, yet she could not consider herself in any other light than as a prisoner, and her heart was indeed sad.

The clouds which had overspread the sky had nearly all disappeared, and daylight approached. Birty informed Clinker that he had learned, from the Indians, of another party of warriors, a day's journey in advance, and it was thought politic not to linger around the old camp of the savages longger than was necessary.

When the earliest rays of the sun robed the tops of the trees with dew-drop rain bows, Clinker's men were all under march. Their progress through the woods was rapid but cautious. They did not intend to be surprised by any party of Indians, large or small.

They were all experienced hunters, and they were mostly men from whose families the Indians had taken victims, or whose homes had been destroyed by the torch of the red man.

CHAPTER VII.

THE PURSUIT.

It was late at night when a few straggling Indians entered a camp where all was quiet—where warriors lay slumbering around the camp fire, while the silver moonlight, falling between the leaves of closely-standing trees, faintly revealed their sombre forms. This was a place of appointed rendezvous for two parties of Indians—the advanced party commanded by the husband of Martha; and the party which had been beaten and dispersed by Clinker's men.

Sad was the news which the stragglers brought, and when a wild shout was given, known as a signal of ill fortune, in the camp which had all been repose, commotion was general.

The brave who appeared to command the warriors, was a model of rage and desperation. He cursed those who had brought the sad news, as cowardly squaws, and he ordered immediate preparations for a march. Those preparations were swiftly made. It was but a short time before the savages were all marching with quick step toward the site of the camp where Clinker's men had seen friend meet friend—and where a daughter, mourned as dead, had been restored to a father who fought those among whom she was a voluntary captive, and who, had he met him, would have slain the being she best loved on earth, with as little compunction as he would have shot a panther crouching to spring upon him.

Meanwhile Clinker and Birty, with the captives they had liberated, were marching through the forest on their way toward Boonesborough. Their march was conducted with extreme caution, because they expected to meet other parties of Indians, and both had dire vengeance to wreak on the red men. There was a great difference between these two men. Clinker was brutal, even savage in his nature—Birty was rough-spoken, and rough-mannered, yet all who knew him acknowledged that he had a kind heart. He would never shoot a wild beast unless he had need of food or clothing, and although he killed every Indian on whom he could surely draw his rifle sights, he was never known to take a scalp. Clinker always had one or more scalps dangling from his belt. Birty often talked with him about this savage propensity, and sometimes Clinker would answer:

"Them red devils shan't git ahead o' old Clinker. Ef they'd catch him his har'd be off quicker an' ye could say Ingin. I want to know how much sarvice I do my country."

"You don't fight Ingins jist because they ain't white?" said Birty in reply one day.

"I'd shoot 'em any how," answered Clinker; "but you know I've got a big spite agin 'em, an' I shan't guv up 'till every moccasin's druv out o' this country."

"I've got a bigger spite agin 'em than you have, Clinker, but ef they'd jist let wimmin and children alone, and let me go among 'em to hunt them little chaps I told you about once, I'd make friends with 'em quicker'n you could shoot your old rifle," said Birty, with deep feeling, as he strode away from his companion, scarcely hearing his taunt.

"Ef ye git a cuttin up sich shines, Birty, you won't be fit to hunt Ingins any more. You'll haf to stay at the settlement and take care o' the wimmin."

The hunters had traveled two days, and were drawing near the settlements. Clinker, who, on account of Martha's sadness at her separation from the father of her papoose, had watched her as if he was afraid she would desert him and return to his enemies, relaxed, in a great degree, his close attention to her, and she was quite at liberty on the third night to roam whither she would.

She secretly left the camp with her papoose, and wandered into the woods in the hope that she might meet some of the Indians among whom she was known, and by them be restored to her husband. She had faint hope that she might meet her husband, for she knew that he would pursue the whites as soon as he heard of her captivity, and it was her determination to keep him from attacking them if she should meet him or any of his followers before the affray began. Her affections were divided between the parties. She would desert her father for her husband, but she must prevent her husband from making war upon her father. In this mood she watched until it was nearly morning. She dared not leave the camp altogether, for fear she might fall into the hands of some band of Indians that would carry her farther from her husband than the whites, and not be so lenient to her as her father and Birty. Her footsteps were heavy when she turned them in disappointment towards her father's camp.

The Indian leader pursued the party that had captured his white squaw in vain. He supposed they would hasten to Boonesborough. He struck across the country to meet them, and on the third day he would have encountered them; but, meeting a small company of hunters, Clinker was informed that a party of Virginians had recently come into the country, and was then at Harrodsburgh. He determined to visit the Fort. Birty had no objections, and the rest of the band were not particular whither they were led. Their course had therefore been changed. By this maneuver the pursuing Indians were somewhat baffled, but when Martha was going back from her search in the forest, her husband was nearer than she supposed. At the head of a small party of tired warriors he was about to attack the hunters, when he saw Martha as she passed between him and the camp-fire. He gave a signal known only between them, which, though heard by the hunters, caused no alarm. Martha, hoping yet fearing, drew near him—so near that he spoke to her. Her heart bounded as she recognized his voice, and in a moment she was leading him far away from her father's men.

"Stop," he said, "I must lead my men against the pale faces who shot our warriors. They will have revenge—"

"My father is there," answered Martha, "and he whom I have spoken of as a brother. I have deserted them to go back with you. You must not attack them. I love you, but I love them, and I will protect them. They are many—they are brave—they might kill you and all your warriors. If you attack them, kill me, for I will go back to them if I am alive."

The warrior bowed his head, and muttered stern Indian oaths, but Martha was firm, and with a signal he led his warriors away.

They were surprised that he did not attack the hunters,

but had confidence in their leader and dare not question his orders or his motives.

Clinker, who had been wandering about the woods for sometime, called Birty to one side and said:

"Mat's gone as sure as shootin', papoose and all. I've been huntin' her for half an hour, an' I can't git trail of her. There's been red devils, or she's run off expectin' to find that varmint you say's her papoose's daddy. I'm goin' arter her, and you must go along."

"To-night?" said Birty.

"Yes, right off," answered Clinker.

"You're mad," returned Birty. "Somethin's turned your head. What'd you do in the woods now, findin' Ingins, when you could'nt see one two rods off. 'Taint no use, Clinker. Wait for daylight, then we can track the varmints, and we'll git 'em afore night."

Clinker was obliged to yield to Birty, but was restless and impatient.

He was inclined to believe that Martha had voluntarily fled, but Birty said he supposed the White Eagle, as she called her warrior, had overtaken their party and with a signal called her away. If so the hunters might guard for an attack. Birty's advice was acted upon. Clinker was the most watchful of the guards. He started at every sound, and often grasped his rifle tightly, and felt for his knife and tomahawk, as if he had detected foes stealthily approaching, but no cause for real alarm existed. At each of these outbursts the hunter would renew his vows of hostility to the red man with increased bitterness, and when the soft light of morning began to come down on the hills, he was almost in a frenzy of rage and desperation.

It was a misty morning, and as day advanced a gentle rain fell, which early in the forenoon was diversified with brisk showers. The hunters held a council and instituted a shrewd search for Indian "signs" around their camp. They found enough to convince them that Birty's opinion concerning Martha's disappearance was correct, but on account of the rain they could not surely follow the savages.

Clinker was desperate, and urged his companions to a pursuit at all hazards. They were determined to pursue their march to Harrodsburg, unless plain Indian "signs" could be discovered, and Clinker was obliged to relinquish the hope of immediate revenge and rescue. He consoled himself with a promise that after a few days spent at the Fort in preparing ammunition and clothing, Birty would accompany him, with such volunteers as could be raised, on an expedition across the Ohio into the western country, where, as Birty had reported, the Indians were collecting for the purpose of attacking the people of "Kaintuck" in a body.

CHAPTER VIII.

AN OFFICIAL EXPEDITION.

The spring of 1778 had come. In the spring of 1776, George Rogers Clark, (a name ever to be mentioned with honor and respect in the eventful history of Kentucky,) a second time visited those vast and enticing hunting grounds—that "favorite theatre of romantic adventure." By his nobleness and valor he gained the confidence of the people who had settlements in that wild region. He saw, with statesman-like foresight, the value of those lands to Virginia as a frontier, and he assembled the people at Harrodsburg to devise means of public defense. At this meeting, Clark and Gabriel Jones were chosen members of the Assembly of Virginia. This choice could not give the gentlemen elect seats in the Assembly, but they resolved at all events to visit the seat of Government, then at Williamsburg. They found that the Legislature had adjourned; but Clark would not relinquish the object of his mission, and he obtained from the Executive Council an order for five hundred weight of powder, for the defense of the Kentucky stations. This order was received on the 23d of August, 1776. Patrick Henry, then Governor of Virginia, assisted Clark greatly in his efforts for the protection of Kentucky. At the next session of the Legislature, held in the fall of 1776, a petition from Jones and Clark was received, and the "county of Kentucky," embracing the limits of the present State, was created. Owing mainly to the excellent management and judicious watchfulness of Clark, the powder for which he had received an order, was safely conveyed from Pittsburgh to Harrodsburg. In the spring of 1777, the Kentucky militia was organized, and the whites were then prepared to repel the invasions of the Indians upon their settlements. Hitherto the Indians had only met small bands of the backwoodsmen, fighting generally in their own defense, or in protection of their homes and families.

In the fall of 1777, Clark again left Kentucky for Virginia. He returned as Colonel George Rogers Clark, with two sets of instructions—one public, for the defense of Kentucky; the other secret, ordering an attack upon the British post Kaskaskia. On the 4th of February, 1778, Colonel Clark, as he himself expressed it, "clothed with all the authority he could wish," left Virginia to carry out his secret instructions.

It is not necessary to our story that we should follow Clark's career minutely. It is a part of the History of Kentucky, familiar to her sons and daughters. They know his adventures on the Ohio, from Fort Pitt to the Falls, where he fixed a post by fortifying Corn Island, opposite Louisville. There he disclosed to his troops their real destination, and was assured that he had their confidence. All ardently concurred in the plan, excepting one company, a part of which fled from the post, and many of them succeeded in reaching Harrodsburg, but on account of their dastardly conduct, were refused admittance to the fort.

It was a gloomy day when Colonel Clark's men, in their shallow boats, passed the Falls of the Ohio. The sun was in a total eclipse, and the darkness of night was upon the water. Some of the superstitious thought this an omen of ill-luck, but none dare mention their fears except to a few friends, in their especial confidence. No adventure worthy of record, however, occurred, until the troops were landed on an island near the mouth of the Tennessee river.

There Clark had rested but a few hours, when he was informed that a party of hunters had encamped within a short distance of his troops. He ordered that they be invited to visit him. Several accepted his invitation. They proved to be a company from Kentucky settlements. One of the hunters was acquainted with a number of the men in Clark's command. The Colonel observing this, desired to speak with him. When the individual was brought into his presence he said: "I understand that you are a Virginian."

"Yes, sir, I'm one o' the Big Knifes, but all the chaps whar I've been didn't know it, or 'praps I hadn't been here 'mong friends agin."

"May I inquire your name?" said Clark.

"The people what know me, sir, call me Tom Clinker."

"You say you have recently visited Kaskaskia."

"I went up that way a couple of months or so ago, after a daughter I'm trying to git from the Ingins."

"Can you tell me who is the commander?"

"I've heard the name, but its worse an' Ingin, an' I aint good at twistin' out such fellows. But I can tell you, sir, he aint no fool. He's a wide awake chap, an' he keeps a sharp look out. He tells the Ingins and the hunters that Virginia boys are worse than savages. They call 'em Big Knife out here, and the're as feared as death on 'em."

"That will not be to our disadvantage," answered Clark. "Now, tell me what you think about the number of men I have being able to take Kaskaskia."

"You could do it jist as easy as I'd take an old bear, but you must do it a leetle in the same style—take the critter when he don't know what's goin' to happen him."

"I understand you" said Clark and am obliged to you for the information you have given."

"Well, look here, Colonel, some of us fellows thought we'd jist like to go back there and help drive them Britishers off our ground. Ef you want any of our help, jist let me know it, an' we're ready to start."

"Where are the men who would join us?" inquired Clark.

"I'll fotch a few of 'em," answered Clinker, as he started in quest of Birty and his companions."

Clark followed him, and soon met the most of the hunters in a body. They composed the party that had gone out according to Birty's promise when Clinker consented to return to Harrodsburg. They were all willing to accompany Clark. The information which Clinker had given him was confirmed. He learned that the name of the commander at Kaskaskia was M. Rocheblane, and hearing more detailed accounts of the dread in which the Virginians were held by the British and their allies, he determined, as Mann Butler says in his History of Kentucky, " to enlist this national apprehension in his service, and employ it as an auxiliary to his diminutive force." As important aids in the furtherance of this plan, Clark gladly accepted the offer of the hunters to join his brave band.

After this accession to his forces, Clark ordered the boats to be prepared, and the whole party dropped down the river a few miles. A short distance above what was then known as Fort Massac, the boats were concealed, and with their commander sharing, as one of them, all the fatigues and privations of a march through the wilderness, the Kentuckians and Virginians traveled across the present State of Illinois toward the ancient French village of Kaskaskia. Clark understood well the manner of conducting a forest expedition, and no adventure of importance happened to his company until the third day. The principal guide then became bewildered.

Suspicion was immediately excited among the wily Kentuckians, and a general cry arose against the unfortunate hunter. Birty knew this man well, and he knew he was no traitor, and when others clamored against him, he said:

"Give the feller a chance. He'll fotch things straight. I'll see the Colonel."

Hastening where Clark was consulting about the guide's conduct, Birty made bold to say,

"Tain't fair to make a fellow out meaner than an Ingin till you've give him a chance. He's only a little stuck just now. He's true as my old rifle, an' when he gets the cobwebs out of his head, he'll tell whar we are just as easy as I can tell whar a red skin is when I get a fair sight on him."

The guide begged that he might have a chance to establish his innocence. Clark was not a man to condemn a fellow soldier without good reason. He said to the guide:

"You have told us that you have often traveled this route, that you know this country well. I will give you a fair opportunity to recover yourself, but then, if you do not conduct the detachment into the hunter's road leading to Kaskaskia, you shall be hung."

Accompanied by Birty, Clinker and one or two soldiers, the guide went into the prairie in full view, and after about an hour's examination, found a place which he recollected; he then knew his whereabouts precisely, and had no fears that his innocence would not be established. When he had again gained the confidence of his commander and his fellow soldiers, Birty said to some of those who had clamored against him,

"Now you see, don't you, how you'd strung a poor fellow up afore he had a chance to say his prayers—all for nothin', too. I'd think myself tarnal mean, ef I'd treat the ugliest red-skin arter that fashion. Ef the Colonel hadn't know'd more'n you possum heads, we'd all been up a stump now, unless 'praps some o' the rest o' our chaps could 've told whar this trail was."

Such was the rough but noble character of the true Kentucky hunter of those days.

On the evening of the 4th of July, 1778, the soldiers and hunters encamped within a few miles of the town their commander designed to attack.

It was the second anniversary of the Declaration of American Independence, and it was talked of that night as the hunters and soldiers gathered in groups, with a spirit which showed that the men were all ready to sell their lives in its defense. No guns were fired in its honor, but many resolves were formed under its influence.

If the men of our day had the chivalrous respect for that instrument which those rude hunters and soldiers felt, and were ready to manifest it at the cannon's mouth, the observance of the national holiday would be more general and appropriate. It would not be observed merely by the firing of squibs, in the streets of our villages and cities, and by the booming of cannon, and by rhetorical speeches in our groves, but all the people with thoughtful hearts would remember and do honor to the valiant men who declared our independence —and at each return of its anniversary the bonds of our Union would be strengthened.

CHAPTER IX.

THE SURPRISE.

The shades of night had fallen upon the forest, when the order to prepare for march was communicated to the different companies of Clark's detachment. The Colonel, recognizing the intelligence and trustworthiness of Birty, had consulted him frequently. The hunter had been a close observer, during his brief visit with Clinker, to Kaskaskia, and he advised extreme caution in approaching the town. He assured Clark that its means of defense were not formidable, but a large body of Indians might lurk in or near it.

The Colonel accordingly arranged his plans for a complete surprise, and for such a display of his forces as would make the "Long Knifes" appear quite as terrible as the Kaskaskians had been led to believe them. In boats which had been secretly procured, the Virginians and Kentuckians were all safely transported across the river Cahokia, which flows past the town. Clark, with the third division of the detachment, proceeded to the fort within point blank shot of the town, while the other divisions prepared to make simultaneous attacks upon different quarters of the village. Clark was successful, and when an appointed signal was given, the inhabitants of Kaskaskia, reposing in fancied security, found themselves suddenly surrounded by foes they had been taught to dread more than the most wily and cruel Indians.

With mad shouts and terrible yells, in the Indian style, Clark's men rushed through the streets, and those who could speak French cried at the top of their voices that every man of the enemy who entered the street would be instantly shot. The town, consisting of about two hundred and fifty houses, was completely surrounded, and in less than two hours, the inhabitants were disarmed, and without the shedding of a drop of blood, Kaskaskia fell into the hands of the shrewd and valorous Clark.

When the troops first entered the village, Birty led a small party to the Governor's house. Their design was to seize upon the public papers, it being supposed that many of them would be highly important to the Americans. The Governor was taken prisoner without difficulty, but no papers of importance could be found. Every part of the house was diligently searched, except the private apartments of the Governor's wife. When the diligent search had proved fruitless, one soldier proposed that the lady's trunks be broken open. Birty heard this proposition, and with a nobleness which characterized him on all such occasions, he chivalrously stepped forward and cried:

"Thar ain't a Kaintuck here dare do that. None 'o you would insult that lady for all the documents in creation."

Immediately headed by Birty, the men withdrew, and the public property, if any had been secreted by Madame Rocheblane, was saved.

During the whole night Clark's men patrolled the town in true Indian fashion, keeping up the utmost tumult by whooping and yelling as the Kaskaskians never before heard white men whoop and yell, and the people thought that, indeed, their enemy was as barbarous as had been represented.

On the following day Clark withdrew his troops from the town, and stationed them at various commanding positions in the vicinity. No intercourse with each other or with the soldiers had been allowed the inhabitants, and their anticipations were of the most gloomy character; it is therefore not strange that when the troops were removed, and they found themselves free to walk the streets, they gathered together and had animated conversation in regard to the destruction that threatened them. Perceiving these movements, Clark had a number of the prominent citizens arrested. A priest of the village having witnessed Birty's noble conduct at the Governor's house, sought the hunter and desired that he request permission for a deputation of citizens to wait on the American commander. Birty hastened to Clark's quarters, and obtained this permission.

Pitiful indeed was the sight presented to the chief citizens of Kaskaskia, and great was their astonishment when, in their best array, they waited upon their conquerer and his fellow officers. Dirty and ragged, the appearance of the Virginians was indeed frightful to the deputation of refined and delicate Frenchmen. They were unable to tell the commander-in-chief from those around him, and they looked upon the whole band as if convinced by observation that they were as savage as they had been represented.

Clark demanded their business, and when they had learned that he was commander, the priest said,

" You have conquered our village, and our people are to be separated, perhaps never to meet again on earth. We desire that you will grant us the privilege of assembling in our house of worship, there to take leave of each other."

Clark knew that these people thought their religion obnoxious to the Americans, and like a true American, he replied,

"We leave every man's conscience with his God. We have no quarrel with you because of your religion, and you are at liberty to assemble at the church, but not a single individual must attempt to leave the town."

The gentlemen of Kaskaskia endeavored to prolong the conversation, but Clark dismissed them cavalierly, in order to heighten their alarm. The entire people left their houses and assembled at their church, where the priests celebrated mass. A deputation then waited upon Clark to thank him for his indulgence, and the people returned to their houses, and found them as they were left. No soldier had attempted to rob or pillage.

When the deputation that waited upon Clark had returned thanks to him for the indulgence he had granted, they begged leave, at the request of the inhabitants, to address their conquerer. Clark having signified his willingness to hear the address, one chosen as spokesman said,

"We are prisoners of war, and we submit to the loss of our property, but we pray that we may not be separated from our wives and our children. Our conduct has been influenced by the commandants whom we had. Our position is not favorable to the reception of accurate knowledge, and we do not know the real merits of the war between Great Britain and your people. Many of us have, however, been inclined to favor the Americans, but we ask not our property. We only ask that we may be left free to take care of our wives and children."

Clark now fairly saw the dread in which his little army was held, and he resolved, in a spirit of honorable chivalry, to carry out the lenient views it had from the first been his purpose to make known, when the opportune moment came. He conceived that the period for this stroke of policy had arrived, and turning abruptly toward the speaker who had addressed him, said :

"Do you take us for savages? I am almost certain you do, from your language. Do you think that we intend to strip innocent women and children, or take the bread out of their mouths? My countrymen disdain to make war upon helpless innocence. It is to prevent Indian butcheries that we are here. The King of France has united his arms to those of our people against the British, and the war will soon be over; but you are at liberty to take whatever side you please. We have no disagreement with you on account of your religion. You are at liberty to conduct yourselves as you please, without apprehension from my troops. Your friends in confinement shall be immediately released."

The deputation was more astonished and agitated at this chivalrous speech than they had been in the midst of their greatest terrors. An apology for considering the Virginians and Kentuckians barbarians was offered, but Clark refused to hearken to explanation, and said:

"Relieve the anxieties of your people, and inform them that I only ask of them to comply with the terms of a proclamation which I shall shortly issue."

Birty, with an order from Clark, flew to the relief of the prisoners. In a few moments they were all at their homes, and the sad dejection of the village was changed into most tumultuous joy. All the bells of the town were rung—the people shouted in the streets—women wept for joy—prayers of thankfulness were offered in the houses, and the church was crowded with rejoicing people, who joined the priests most fervently in offerings of praise and prayer.

Colonel Clark had determined upon the taking of the little town of Cahokia, situated about sixty miles from Kaskaskia. When the people of Kaskaskia heard of this expedition, many desired the privilege of accompanying the Virginians. They said the people of Cahokia were their friends and relatives, and, at their advice, would surrender without bloodshed. Clark allowed such as desired, to accompany his soldiers. Birty and Clinker were among the Americans.

Clinker learned that, about sixty miles up the Mississippi, there was a large body of Indians, and he determined as soon as it was practicable to pursue them, under the belief that his daughter might be among them.

The people of Kaskaskia did not misrepresent those of Cahokia. The town fell into the hands of the Americans without the firing of a gun, or the shedding of a drop of blood—a manner of warfare most exemplary for that day, and even for this.

Clinker and Birty had permission from Clark to scout, with a small party, in the vicinity of Cahokia, and they did not let the opportunity pass unimproved. They reconnoitered the camp of Indians, of which they had word, but failed to discover anything which gave them reason to believe that the object of their search was among the savages. Birty knew the characteristics of the tribe to which Martha's husband, who was called White Eagle, belonged, and he saw none of them there.

The Indians were in too large a body to be attacked by

the scouts, and they dare not harass the small bands that went into the woods, lest the main body be alarmed, pursue them, and make sad havoc in their ranks. The time for which they were empowered to act as scouts having nearly expired, Clinker consented to give up the pursuit of his daughter in that direction. The hunters set their faces toward Kaskaskia. They had traveled about half the distance between Cahokia and Kaskaskia, when they surprised a band of Indians, killed three, and took one prisoner.

That prisoner was a young squaw, and the most beautiful one the hunters had ever seen. They endeavored to learn from her the destination of the Indians, and the tribe to which she belonged. Birty spoke to her in the Indian tongue, but she answered him not. She did not seem to hear him, but stood before him as mute and immovable as a statue. Again and again Birty endeavored to call her attention, but he received no more intimation from her that he was heard than he did from the trunks of the trees around him. Her head was bent forward upon her breast, and her eyes were not lifted from the ground.

"She's a dumb Ingin, I reckon," said Clinker. "Who ever heard of one afore? We'll take her to Kaskaskia as a curiosity."

"Don't be fooled by a possum," said one of the men in answer to Clinker. He replied:

"I reckon if we keep our eyes on her, she can't do much harm if she does play possum—but I don't believe the critter can either hear or talk. She's about han'some enough, though, an' it's a great pity if she don't know it, when sich rough chaps as we are tell her so."

The captive was given into Birty's care. She walked by

his side—made no attempts to escape, and was willing in all respects to be directed by him; but she seldom lifted her dark eyes from the ground, and gave no heed to the words of kindness which he addressed to her.

CHAPTER X.

A TREACHEROUS PLOT.

The latter part of the month of August had come; the fruits of the glorious summer were passing away before the rapid approach of the sad but beautiful season, when

> "Mid autumn's purple sunsets,
> A dirge note swells the blast,
> And tells that soon the brightness
> Of the year will all be past."

Colonel Clark was shrewdly watching the movements of the Indians, and was about to form treaties with the different tribes. Several bands had assembled at Kaskaskia to smoke the calumet. It was not his policy to invite the red men to a treaty, but to wait a request for peace from them. He understood Indian character, and when he had concluded a treaty, the Indians had confidence that the Virginians, or "Big Knives, had but one heart, and did not speak with forked tongues," as one of the chiefs emphatically declared at the first council with him.

When Clark had concluded amicable arrangements with several of the principal tribes of the then populous Indian country, Birty and Clinker, who, week after week, with a small party of hunters, had traversed the Illinois forests and prairies, returned to the camp of the Big Knife. They wandered freely among the savages, Birty in the hope of meeting that countenance which Martha had described to him, when he met her in the Kentucky forest, and Clinker in the hope of gaining some definite tidings of his lost daughter.

Industriously each had pursued his search for several days, without the slightest clue to its object, when, returning to the village late one evening, Birty discovered that a small party of Indians he had not before seen, had encamped upon the opposite bank of the little creek of Cahokia. Secreted in a clump of bushes near the water's edge, he warbled those notes which he had learned from the forest birds. Those were strange sounds for that region, when the sun had gone to shed light upon another hemisphere, and the pale stars twinkled in the firmament. They blended with the whisperings of the night breeze, and with the gentle murmuring of the stream that flowed at the musician's feet, and died away in the distance without echo. Again those wild-bird notes rose upon the balmy air, and when the musician listened to hear them die away, a faint echo, with softened cadence, was borne to his ear. He uttered one shrill note. It was echoed, not faintly, but quite distinctly—again he uttered it, and again it was answered. He was confident, then, that one object of his search was in this Indian camp. He watched the opposite shore of the creek for an hour eagerly, and was about to turn toward the village and take the chance of meeting the white squaw on the morrow, when he heard a shrill note, coming, as it were, from the bank directly opposite. Presently a canoe shot out into the stream, and in a few minutes Birty sat with Martha Clinker, talking over the adventures she had met since she deserted her father's camp in Kentucky. Through her influence White Eagle had brought his braves to Kaskaskia to ascertain what terms of peace the Big Knives proposed.

When Martha concluded her narrative, she said:

"You know where my father is?"

"Among the whites in the village," answered Birty. "He has been seeking you ever since you left him."

"I wish I could see him," Martha answered; "but you must not tell him I am here. I will not live among the white people unless my husband goes with me."

"Shall I tell him that I have seen you?"

"Not until we meet again. I must return now. I shall be missed, and it may not be well for us to be watched."

"Shall I hear the wild-bird to-morrow night?" said Birty.

"If I am not watched," answered Martha.

The light canoe shot out into the current, and the hunter turned his steps toward the village. He did not neglect to inform an officer in Clark's confidence, of the addition to the Indian forces.

On the morrow Clinker visited the new Indian camp. He mingled freely with the savages, and looked eagerly at every squaw, but he did not see his daughter. She saw him, however, but dare not meet him. She pointed him out to the White Eagle, and said:

"I know you are a warrior of honor. You know I fled from my father to dwell with you in the wigwam. Promise me, that let you meet him where you may, you will protect him for my sake."

The Indian regarded his companion with emotion, and he promised all she asked.

Squaws have not often an influence of this character over

the warriors, in whose wigwams they dwell; but Martha Clinker had been reared under influences differing widely from those which had surrounded the youth of her female companions, and he who had her love was no common Indian.

His fellow-warriors often amused themselves by laughing with each other about his being the squaw, and Martha the warrior; but no one who valued his life was rash enough to utter such a taunt in his hearing.

According to appointment, Birty, who had been in Clark's employ during the day, stood on the bank of the creek opposite the Indian camp, as soon as the stars were mirrored in its waters. He had no sooner given the concerted signal than a canoe shot out from the opposite bank, and it was but a few minutes before he met Martha at the water's edge, where she waited. She was much agitated, and told him she could remain but a moment.

They talked together rapidly not over five minutes, when Birty suddenly took leave of her, and walked briskly back to Colonel Clark's quarters, avoiding the camp of a party of Indians from various tribes, who had pitched their tents within a hundred yards of the fort, on the same side of the creek. Those Indians had manifested great friendliness to the whites, but had been regarded by Clark with considerable suspicion.

The Colonel was absent, and Birty could not see him. He would confide his business to no one, and he wandered again away from the fort. He walked toward the camp of the suspicious Indians, and watched their movements narrowly. Midnight came, and still Birty watched; but the noon of night had scarcely passed, when he saw a number of warriors in complete battle array, sneak out of their camp, and march toward the creek. He followed them stealthily. They waded into the creek, and were soon on its opposite bank, out of his sight; then he turned his footsteps toward the fort again. He knew Clinker was on guard that night. He sought him and said:

"Now, old chap, afore long you'll have a lot of darned red skins what'll try to get under your protection, and ef you let 'em, there'll be a tarnel fuss in this ere camp."

"Jist you trust old Clinker," was the answer. "I'll give 'em my protection — that's it," stamping his rifle on the ground.

Birty went with Clinker to warn other soldiers on guard, and while he talked with one of them, several guns were fired on the opposite side of the creek, and Birty cried:

"Now watch 'em, boys."

It was but a few moments before a number of Indians rushed toward the American quarters; and when they approached the guard, demanded protection, alleging that they had been fired upon in their camp, by the Indians on the opposite side of the creek. They attempted to press within the American lines, but were repulsed and obliged to return to their own quarters. They had scarcely gone when Birty hastened to Clark's room, and found him, even at that late hour, at his desk, writing. The hunter was excited, and he proceeded to announce the object of his untimely haste without ceremony.

"There's treachery stirrin' out here, Colonel," he said. "You know them tarnal suspicious red devils down here on our side o' the creek? A lot of 'em laid a plan to get your head, but they wasn't quite smart enough."

"Where are the treacherous villains?" interrupted Clark.

"The guard druv 'em home," replied Birty. "I can find every rascal of 'em."

It was no time for compliments. In a few minutes the whole garrison was aroused, and Birty headed a company which hastened to the Indian quarters and arrested the individuals he designated. When brought into Clark's presence, they stoutly denied the charges made against them, but Birty said:

"Look at the red liars' leggins and moccasins—that'll tell the story."

Examination was made as the hunter desired, and the lie that the assassins had been fired at by friendly Indians, put at rest.

Clark was determined that the traitors should be made an example of. He ordered them to be loaded with chains and closely guarded until the following day. The Colonel did not dismiss his followers that night until he had said to Birty:

"Your services in detecting this plot shall not be forgotten."

Birty owed his good fortune entirely to Martha. She had told him that among the Indians on the bank of the river, near the fort, was one who was like a brother to the White Eagle. He had made her husband a visit that day, and she had overheard him reveal a plot to kill Colonel Clark, and murder his garrison. This plot, whose fulfillment Birty had witnessed as far as the savages were permitted to carry it, Martha minutely detailed, and to acquaint Colonel Clark of the threatened danger, Birty had visited his quarters early in the evening, as described.

CHAPTER XI.

THE COUNCIL.

The Indians who had been detected in their base conspiracy, were known as Meadow Indians. Their tribe, as before remarked, was composed of stragglers from various tribes, so that they had friends among all the savages assembled at Kaskaskia; and their arrest created a great excitement, yet none dared to question the propriety of Clark's conduct toward them.

In order to show the amity existing between the Americans and the French, Clark let it be understood that the latter should decide the fate of the would-be assassins.

On the day following their arrest, they were brought into the council-room, but were not allowed to speak until all other business had been transacted; then Clark ordered their manacles to be removed, and when they were free, he said to them:

"Everybody says you ought to die for your treacherous attempt upon my life during the sacred deliberations of the council, and I had determined that death should be inflicted upon you. You must know that you have justly forfeited your lives, but on considering the meanness of watching a bear and catching him asleep, I have found that you are not warriors. You are like old women, and are too mean to be killed by the Big Knife. But you must be punished for putting on breech-cloths like men; they shall be taken away from you. I will give you plenty of provisions for your journey home, because women don't know how to hunt, and while you stay, you shall be treated as squaws in every respect."

When Clark had concluded this speech, he began to converse with persons around him, as if there was no further business for the council. The offending Indians were much agitated. The treatment they had received was very different from what they had been led to expect, and their natural pride was deeply wounded.

One of their chiefs arose and made a speech, offering Clark a pipe and a belt of peace. Clark would not allow the speech to be interpreted, and taking up a sword lying on his table, he broke the offering of peace indignantly, saying:

"Big Knife never treats with women."

Chiefs of other tribes now interfered in behalf of the Meadow Indians, and among those who spoke was one whom Birty watched with intense interest. He supposed him to be White Eagle. This Indian said:

"The Big Knife knows that these men have wives and papooses; for their sakes he will grant them peace."

But the American officer was not ready to acquit the offenders so easily, and he said:

"The Big Knife never made war upon these Indians. Whenever we come across such people in the woods, we shoot them as we do wolves, to keep them from eating deer."

The excitement was intense among the Indians. They conversed among each other, and among their friends, in a manner which showed that they felt keenly the contempt with which they had been treated. The Meadow Indians appeared to feel that the tomahawk threatened their whole tribe, and peace with the Big Knife could alone save them. Suddenly two young men advanced from the crowd, and to the astonishment of the whole assembly, sat down in the middle of the floor, throwing their blankets over their heads, in token of entire submission.

Birty watched the Indian whom he supposed to be White Eagle, and saw that he appeared deeply interested in the youngest of the warriors upon the floor. The hunter judged that he was the Indian from whom Martha learned what she had communicated. Birty became as intensely interested in the scene, as he would have done had he known the search of his life was to be ended—the solemn vow he made to his father fulfilled. He could not satisfy himself why this feeling was fastened upon him, and he was unable to shake it off. He was struck with the nobleness of the Indians who had offered themselves as a sacrifice for peace with their tribe. He knew they had taken no part in the attempted assassination. He stood near Clark—he stepped nearer and whispered:

"Give 'em a fair chance, Colonel, for my sake. Them chaps was'nt in the scrape; one of 'em's the fellow who told the trick, so I got wind of it."

The Colonel turned toward Birty and smiled, but said nothing. At this moment two chiefs arose, and one said:

"The warriors you call squaws, have families—these young men have none. They give their lives for the sake of those families, to atone for the offense of their brothers. Is the Big Knife satisfied?"

Again the pipe of peace was offered. Clark was embarrassed. He had intended to give the offenders their liberty, but in a manner and with a reluctance that should enhance its value, and have an influence upon all the Indians who heard the circumstances. For a few moments all was silence in the council—suspense and anxiety held many of the spectators breathless. The noble youths sat more unconcerned, apparently, than those who contemplated them, only occasionally looking out from under their blankets to see what was passing around them.

Clark regarded them with emotion, evident to all who understood his character. At length he advanced toward them, ordered them to arise and uncover themselves. They stood before him, expecting to receive their sentence of death, while the assembly of Indians, French and Americans, listened with deep anxiety to see what the Colonel would order to be done with them. Birty was puzzled; he did not believe Clark would sacrifice the noble young warriors, but was at a loss to conjecture what would be their fate. Clark summoned him as an interpreter, and said:

"The Big Knife rejoices to find that there are men in all nations. These two young warriors who have offered themselves, are at least proof for their tribe. Such warriors are alone fit to be chiefs. With such Big Knife will treat. Through them peace is granted to the tribe, and I take them by the hand as chiefs."

He took the warriors by the hand, and when Birty had interpreted his speech, the young warriors were introduced with proper ceremonies, as chiefs, to the whites present and the other Indians; the result of the council was communicated from mouth to mouth, and whoops and yells of the liveliest character resounded about the fort.

A council was now held, peace was formally granted to the Meadow Indians, and presents bestowed upon them to distribute among their friends. Birty rejoiced to see the Indian he judged to be the White Eagle, and the youngest of the recently created chiefs, meet with a cordiality that betokened deep sympathy between them. He was about to step forward and address them, and make himself known to him whom he supposed to be the lord of Martha's wigwam, when he felt some one pull his coat. He turned and saw beside him an old and wretched looking squaw, who beckoned him to follow her. He instinctively granted her wish, and she led him out of the fort, when, taking him by the arm, she said, in the Indian tongue:

"You pale face?"

"What do you want to know for?" said Birty.

"You pale face?" was the squaw's only reply.

"My mother was an Indian," answered Birty, for he was never ashamed of his descent, but was at first reluctant to tell the squaw, because he doubted her right to question him. She was peremptory, however, and having no fears, he yielded, as the best way to escape from her.

"You ever live among Indians?" she said.

"When I was a little boy," he answered.

"You run away?"

"I did."

"One big Indian take you to hunt with him,—you never came back?"

"That's the fact—how do you know?" said Birty in some surprise.

"You are my boy—my boy," answered the squaw, as she attempted to embrace him; but he stepped back and demanded,

"What do you mean?—I don't know you."

"I was your mother's friend—you live in my wigwam. Warrior went to find you—killed your father and brought your mother home—warrior never came back—other warriors say your father killed him. Your mother killed too. Warriors say all killed. You know this?"

"You speak of the murder of my father and my mother—I do not remember you. How do you know me?"

"White squaw yonder tell me you are not Indian," (pointing toward the camp of the White Eagle;) "I ask her who you are—she told me I know you—your mother my friend."

"Then you know that white squaw's husband—you know whether he is an Indian?—tell me if he is," cried Birty.

At that moment a crowd of Indians rushed from the fort. They pressed around Birty and the squaw. She was separated from him, and when he looked for her she had gone. Her information had most deeply interested him. He felt that, through her, he could get the information he had so long sought. He determined to find her again at all hazards.

CHAPTER XII.

A REVELATION.

BIRTY pursued his search for the aged squaw until nightfall. He obtained no tidings of her. He crossed the creek and visited the camp where he supposed he should find Martha. She was absent; her companions had not seen her that afternoon: the White Eagle had come to his wigwam expecting to meet her, but was disappointed, and had returned to the village. Birty had not seen Clinker during the day. He suspected there was mischief brewing, and he hurried back to the fort. There he inquired for Clinker, but could hear nothing of his probable whereabouts. He gave up his search for the squaw, and determined to find his friend. He was about to leave the fort, when he met the White Eagle. For a moment the Indian and hunter looked at each other in silence. The Indian was the first to speak. He said:

"My squaw was this afternoon taken from my wigwam by the Big Knife who is her father. She will not live with him She must return. You know where she is; tell me, that I may take her back—you are her friend."

Then this Indian knew Birty. That was news to the hunter. He answered:

"I am her friend; she shall return to your wigwam. I go

now to hunt her father. There is an old squaw in your camp who has secrets she would tell me. You saw her speak to me to-day. Bring her to the fort in an hour, and you shall see your squaw."

"She shall come," said the Indian, and he parted from the hunter.

Birty now hastened in pursuit of Clinker. He visited the house of a citizen with whom he had formed an acquaintance, and learned that Martha, having come to the village, had sent for her father—that they had met—and the old man had told her she should never go back to the Indian's wigwam. She resisted him, but in vain. She secretly sent a message to the White Eagle, and he was on his way to complain to Colonel Clark and demand the release of his squaw, when Birty met him. He preferred Birty's offer to Clark's interference. Birty was directed to the house where Clinker had Martha a close prisoner. When they met Birty expostulated with Clinker, but the old man was deaf to advice. He had determined that his daughter should not be among the savages another day. If White Eagle chose to leave his tribe and live with him, he could do so, but Martha should not roam the forest with him any longer. She begged her father to go with her, but he answered:

"I'm agin every one o' the red devils. My wife's scalp hangs in some o' their wigwams. Who knows but I might sit down to eat under it? I'll never go among 'em—you needn't ask me."

Birty saw that he would waste time to argue the matter with the old man, and he knew he must meet the Indian at the fort, according to promise. He hastened on this mission. The warrior waited for him with the squaw.

"Come with me," said Birty, "and you shall see your squaw."

White Eagle and the aged squaw followed Birty. He led them to the house where Clinker had Martha a prisoner. The old man admitted them; and Birty promised that no force should be used to wrest his daughter from him. Happy was the meeting between Martha and the warrior. Clinker was touched by it, and he regarded the finely formed, noble looking Indian with deep interest, when he seated himself upon the floor beside his squaw, took their papoose upon his knees, and played with it until it laughed and crowed in great glee. This was a scene the hunter had not expected to see among Indians, but as we have before said, White Eagle was no common Indian.

Birty was impatient to know what the aged squaw, who claimed to have been his mother's friend, had to say about him, and whether she knew anything of his relatives who had been lost among the Indians. He said to Martha, in the Indian language:

"Did you tell this squaw my history?"

She answered in the affirmative. Then Birty said, pointing to the White Eagle:

"Does he know who I am, and that we have often met?"

Martha answered:

"He knows that you are my friend, but he does not know your history. The squaw saw us conversing together. She told me that she knew you; and she told me of your captivity among the Indians, as you had told it to me, but she warned me not to let my husband know it. I obeyed her warning, on the promise that she would tell me all she knew of you. She will tell you what that is."

Birty turned to the squaw and begged her to comply with Martha's request. She had no reluctance about so doing, and she said to Birty, in the Indian language:

"You were taken among the Indians when a small boy. You were stolen by your mother's brother, and a warrior who would have made her his squaw, had not your father stolen her. His brother was found by them bound in the forest. He said your father left him a prisoner. He vowed revenge. He carried you back to your father. He got your confidence. He was the means of his death and the death of your father, and your mother, and I believed of you, until I saw you speak to this young squaw (pointing to Martha), near her wigwam, when you came there the other day."

"But my mother had other children among the Indians. Do you know what became of them?" cried Birty, eagerly. "Do they live?"

"They do," answered the aged squaw.

"Where?" said Birty, in a tone which fixed the attention of all in the room upon him. The warrior upon the floor was by no means an unconcerned spectator of the scene before him.

"There were two of those children," said the squaw. "When the chief of the tribe did not return from his attempt to take you and your mother prisoners, the Indians were divided. One of the children was taken across the great river, far away into this forest; the other was kept by a warrior, who remained at the old hunting-grounds of his tribe. They never knew that the Indians among whom they lived were not their parents. They now believe themselves warriors; they are warriors—not squaws."

"I will find them," cried Birty, "unless I lose my life in the search; and if you have deceived me, your life, old as you are, shall pay the forfeit."

At these words the squaw stepped back, and pointing her attenuated finger at Birty, said, in a shrill voice:

"Look at that pale-face. You all know him."

All eyes were upon Birty, and all were anxious that the squaw should explain why she wished their gaze thus fixed. In a moment she turned with a statuesque effect, pointed to the warrior upon the floor, and continued:

"Look at that Indian. You all know him. See you not that both might have been born of the same woman?"

The suspicion which had long dwelt in Birty's mind was resolved into a conviction, but for a moment he could not utter a word. The Indian started to his feet and cried:

"The squaw dare not lie. Thou art my brother."

Birty rushed toward the speaker, and the brothers met in an embrace, of which Martha in a moment shared; then Clinker, who had regarded the whole scene in silence, cried:

"Tarnal good luck, arter all. There's some white blood in that fellow my gal's been mad arter three or four years. I allers thought 'twas strange she'd take arter a whole Injun that way."

The old squaw shouted with glee, and she was receiving the congratulations of Clinker, although she understood not a word, when Birty addressed her:

"You said both my brothers lived. Tell us where the other is, and our joy will be complete."

"You saw him to-day," replied the squaw.

"Is he among the Indians who were at the fort?"

"He belongs to the tribe the Big Knife called squaws—

but he was not one of the squaws. He was the first to offer himself as sacrifice to appease Big Knife. That warrior knows—"

"It is the tall chief. We have been like brothers since I first knew him. We will seek him at the camp of the Meadows," said White Eagle.

"No you won't," cried Clinker. "You hold on where you are, an' I'll fotch him."

Birty, the long-lost brother, and Martha, sat down to converse together, and Clinker hastened on his mission. He returned in half an hour, bringing the tall chief. He had not been informed of the joy that awaited him. He had followed Clinker because he had been told that White Eagle wanted him. When he entered the room all were silent, and the aged squaw who had thus far controlled the ceremonies of re-union, met him and said:

"Thou hast been like the lone buffalo on the prairie. Now thou shalt be like the beaver at his dam. Thou hast been like the bird that has lost its mate. Thou shalt be like that bird when its mate is found. Thou hast believed thyself without kindred. Thou hast believed a lie."

"What mockery is this?" cried the young chief.

No one answered him till the squaw said:

"Did I ever deceive thee? When I took care of thee, after thou hadst been wounded in battle, did I not love thee? I tell thee that thou hast kindred, and they are here."

"Where?" cried the warrior, looking about him.

"Yonder," answered the squaw, pointing her thin finger at Birty and White Eagle.

"One I know is my brother," replied the chief; "the

other is a pale-face. He too is my brother, but the same blood does not flow in our veins."

This remark having been interpreted by Martha, Clinker impatiently exclaimed—

"If to be born of the same woman makes you of the same blood, that you are, or this old squaw's a tarnal liar."

White Eagle now stepped forward and said:

"We have long been brothers at heart. I believe the squaw, that we are brothers in blood. She was our mother's friend; our father was a pale-face; our oldest brother here (pointing to Birty) dwelt among the pale-faces. We have dwelt among the Indians. Hereafter we will live together." The tall chief was satisfied; the Indian brothers embraced, and then Birty was acknowledged by the Meadow.

The squaw, who had been the instrument of this happy re-union of the long separated, walked up to Birty and said:

"Thy mother's friend has no wigwam. She was once a chief's daughter. Now she's an outcast. Shall she have a home?"

"As long as I have one," answered Birty. His brothers joined him in that declaration.

The brothers talked long and anxiously about their varied fortunes, while Martha listened with thrilling interest, and the venerable squaw sat silent; but often her care-worn countenance lighted up with a gleam of inward satisfaction.

Clinker saw her smile several times, and he cried:

"Well may you grin. You've done a nice job. That you have."

The squaw heard his voice, but did not understand the import of his words; she did not even turn her eyes toward him in reply. It was all the same to Clinker; he had not seen so happy an hour since he lost his wife far away in the valleys of Virginia; and he shook and jostled his little grand-papoose till the child, wearied with his rude caresses, cried lustily for its mother's soothing care.

The child's cries, to soothe which Martha had taken it, attracted the attention of the whole company, and an interval of silence between the brothers ensued. The aged squaw started suddenly to her feet:

"Thou didst believe my story," she cried in a shrill voice. The gaze of all in the room was fixed upon her, but her countenance wore an expression none could divine.

"Thou hast believed words as false as the warrior tells the pale face when they ask him for the hunting grounds of his tribe," continued the squaw in the same shrill voice, which trembled with emotion, while she returned the stern gaze of those she had brought together as brothers.

The Meadow chief advanced toward her with a quick step, and in a voice expressing deep passion, cried:

"If thou art false, thy serpent tongue shall never speak after this night. I have loved thee as if thou hast been my mother, but if thou hast brought me here to deceive me, I will kill thee as quick as I would a wolf in my wigwam."

The squaw blanched not before the stern gaze of the young chief, nor did she change expression when Birty, with White Eagle, came forward and stood beside him. Birty was in a maze of doubt and vexation, but he did not interfere with the examination the tall chief had instituted. The squaw answered him who threatened her, in a tone and with a look undaunted:

"When didst thou first know me?"

"Many years ago, when I was learning to be a warrior,"

answered the Indian. "Thou wast brought to our camp by a warrior, who said he found you wandering in the woods. Thou wert kind to me, and I loved thee as a mother, and then thou didst tell me I was not without friends—that I had two brothers, and thou wast acquainted with my father and my mother."

"When didst thou first meet me?" said the squaw, turning toward White Eagle.

"Many years ago, when our camp was across the big river, thou didst come there and beg our protection. Thou wast like a mother to me, and I loved thee. One day when the warriors sought thee, thou wast gone. Thou didst tell me the same story my brother the Meadow has told."

Then the squaw said:

"When I was gone from that camp, I went where this warrior dwelt," pointing to the Meadow chief. "I had been told where those who once belonged to your tribe were, and I sought them. Thou didst not see me again until two moons ago. When didst thou first see me?" turning to Birty.

"Never till my coat was pulled by you at the Fort, after the council to-day," said the hunter.

"Thou hast all answered well but he," pointing her thin finger at Birty. Then she laid her hands on the Indians and continued:

"Thou couldst not know me, but he might. Thou didst believe that I was thy mother's friend. Wilt thou believe that I am thy mother?"

"Thou hast spoken false," said the Meadow chief. He had no opportunity to finish his sentence.

"I can tell," cried Birty, as he grasped the squaw, and tore a piece of deer skin, in the form of a cape, from her neck.

In an instant he threw his arms around the squaw, and mother and son were locked in an embrace more ardent than the embraces exchanged by those who had met as brothers.

"It is my mother—OUR mother," cried the hunter in a voice subdued with emotion. "I thought she was killed with my father, at our cabin, on the mountain in Virginia. Now I know she was not. We are brothers, and we have found our mother."

Confidence was restored. The squaw was received in her true character, with demonstrations of joy, which were not feigned, but were from the heart, for as a woman, the brothers who lived among the Indians had long loved her.

"This is a tarnal queer affair," cried Clinker, when Birty had explained to him what the squaw said; "I'd like to know how it all happens. This tarnal old critter tells two stories. I don't know which to believe yet. I'd like to know how she found out all about these fellers, to know they are her boys."

Clinker's curiosity was a natural one—one which all the party felt, and which the squaw proceeded to explain. Her story was a long one. It need not be given in detail.

She related that on the night of the affray at the cabin on the mountain, she was severely wounded, but not killed, only stunned and weakened by loss of blood. She crept to the cabin window, and called her boy, but in vain; she saw that the hunter's rifle, knife and tomahawk were taken, and she concluded that her boy had gone forth with them, as she could not find his body. She was too weak to leave the cabin for several days. When she did leave, she attempted to follow her boy, but was unable to do so for any distance, and she wandered about the woods until she fell into the hands of a party of Indians traveling south. She was taken into the mountains of North Carolina, where she remained several years. Then the tribe with which she lived wandered into Kentucky. She heard the warriors describe Indians with whom they had a skirmish, when away from their camp on a certain day. From the description she believed those Indians to be a remnant of the tribe her father once governed. She fled from the Indians among whom she had lived, and sought their enemies. Her conjectures proved correct, and she was kindly received. She kept her own secrets. She learned that the tribe had been divided. Among those she had found, she met a boy whom she knew, and whom she watched with a mother's care, but who had no suspicion why this care was exercised over him. Often she was tempted to reveal herself to him, but was restrained from so doing by a previous determination that she would never make herself known to one till she was satisfied that all her children would never be brought together. When she learned where the other portion of the tribe was encamped, she sought it; there she found another boy. She soon adopted him as her own; and she longed to return to the other, but she waited in hope of some day finding the eldest. The two Indian brothers had often met on hunting expeditions, but the mother knew this not. The youngest boy had separated from his tribe and become one of the Meadow Indians. When they came to Kaskaskia, and the squaw saw the two brothers meet as acquaintances, her determination to reveal herself was fixed. She went to the camp of the White Eagle for this purpose, when she saw Birty conversing with Martha. She was struck with his appearance. She watched his movements, and when her suspicions had become convictions, she went to Martha, told the history of her oldest boy, and Martha acknowledged that it corresponded with what she knew of Birty. Then the venerable squaw's plans were soon laid. She adopted the deception, which she practiced, to bring all her children together, satisfy herself that they would be as brothers, and that they had love for her as a friend. It required Indian fortitude of the most intense character to support this stratagem.

For a few minutes after their mother had finished her explanation, the brothers were silent. White Eagle caressed his child, and as the Meadow Chief watched him, a shade passed over his countenance, which did not escape the notice of his brother. He said:

"Thou art sad, my brother. Has any harm befallen thy betrothed?"

"She is lost to me," answered the other. "She was captured many days ago by a party of pale-faces, and she has gone, I fear, to the Great Spirit."

"Where was she captured?" inquired Birty.

"One who fought the pale-faces, told me near the Cahokia, which flows past our camp — between this and the great river."

"Describe her," said Birty.

"Her head hung upon her breast as the flower droops upon its stem — her hair was heavier than the moss which hangs on the trees of the Southern forest in the winter season — her eyes were blacker than those of the buffalo in the heat of the chase — her teeth were whiter than the beaver's — and her brow was so fair you would have thought her a pale-face. She was called the Silent Maiden. Often, when separated from me, she would, for many days, be as silent as the summer stream, which has emptied itself into the great river."

At these words Birty started to his feet and rushed from the room. In less than a quarter of an hour he returned to explain his sudden departure, leading an Indian maiden, whose "head hung upon her breast as the flower droops upon its stem," and who had been "silent as the summer stream that has emptied itself into the great river."

She uttered a wild scream, as her eyes fell upon the young Meadow Chief; then was Birty conscious, for the first time, that she had a voice. Wildly fervent was the embrace with which the Silent Maiden and the tall chief met. The beautiful squaw was then presented to her friends.

The sounds of rude revelry did not die out in Clinker's log hut, till the bright stars lost their lustre in the spreading gray of morning.

All in that hut were happy, in a love deeper than that which brother feels for brother, but Birty. He had no betrothed.

The particular friends of Clinker and Birty were early informed of the re-union of the long separated brothers, and Colonel Clark congratulated Birty in person, for having been so fortunate as to find his brother to be the noble Meadow Indian; and he assured the hunter that his words in behalf of the Indians, under arrest, had weight upon his mind in favor of clemency. As the romantic meeting of the three brothers became known in the fort, many of the soldiers sought their society.

The woodsmen of 1778, though chivalrous, were not versed in those petty arts devised to disguise emotion, and make impulse appear like settled intention—they were plain, blunt men, rude of speech, and honest.

CHAPTER XIII.

THE LAST.

The Indians, assembled at Kaskaskia to bury the hatchet, and make treaties with the Big Knife, began to depart on their autumn hunting excursions.

The three brothers—who were each called Birty by the whites, one, Hunter Birty; the second, Indian Birty; and the third, Meadow Birty—assembled in council with their mother, Clinker, Martha, and the Silent Maiden, to decide upon their future course of life.

Hunter Birty was emphatically opposed to an identification with the Indians, because, he argued, that there were few of them the right kind of people—that the whites would, in a few years, drive them all from their hunting grounds—that game would become scarce, and therefore the plan which the brothers should adopt, was to select a rich piece of land, build cabins upon it, and farm and hunt together.

Clinker and Martha gave this plan the weight of their influence, and finally Indian Birty and Meadow Birty consented to part from their old companions, and adopt a semi-civilized mode of life. Martha besought Hunter Birty to select a companion from among the French or Indian maidens at

Kaskaskia, but he would not hearken a moment to her counsel. He said:

"I'm Hunter Birty—it don't suit hunters to have wives and papooses."

When the spring of 1779 opened, a colony of half-breed Indians had established a "station" upon the borders of one of the richest prairies of Northern Illinois. The land subsequently came into their hands lawfully, and for many years their descendants held it.

The county of Illinois had been created by the Virginia House of Delegates, and Colonel Clark, having in a great measure accomplished the object of his march among the British possessions, received the thanks and warm eulogiums of his countrymen.

Before the Colonel left Kaskaskia he bestowed upon Hunter Birty a substantial token of his regard—a rifle, which, until the days of his death, was Birty's constant companion—which was to him wife and children. His father's rifle was bestowed upon Meadow Birty, and with the tomahawk and knife, so long the weapons of Hunter Birty, are now cherished heir-looms among the decendants of the Half-Breed Colony of Illinois.

Golden Bird of Menominee.

GOLDEN BIRD OF MENOMINEE.

FIRST love, and the constancy of woman, have been favorite themes with the poets and romance-writers of all ages. Mainly, however, examples, upon which to found touching verses or eloquent paragraphs, have been taken from civilized society. Let me select one from rude forest life.

At the head-waters of the Red Cedar River, in the northern part of Wisconsin, is a beautiful lake, which the Indians called Menominee. There often the white man went to join his red brethren in the athletic sports of the hunting grounds, or in the quiet enjoyment of the fishing party.

One spring-time it happened that a young man wandered to the banks of Lake Menominee, and, after striking his tent in the forest, constructed a raft on which to explore the beautiful sheet of water he had discovered.

At sunset, on a pleasant evening, he sat upon the bank of Menominee, when a light foot startled him. He arose to his feet cautiously, and, looking about him, perceived an Indian maiden, who carried a heavy bark basket, filled with roots and herbs which she had been gathering. Her full dark eye met that of the young hunter, when she halted a moment, then fearlessly stepped within a few feet of him. The hunter had a handsome face and a noble form, and the maiden gazed upon him with mute but eloquent admiration. She sat down her basket and pointed across the lake. The hunter understood her gesture, and bowing, showed her his raft, moored a few yards distant. Taking up her basket, the maiden proceeded to the rude vessel, and the hunter followed. He knew the language of her actions, and in half an hour had landed her on the opposite side of the lake. Swinging her basket on her arm, the maiden sprang upon the shore and disappeared in the forest.

On the morrow, when the hunter emerged from his tent, he found, at the rustic door, an offering of roots and fruits, prepared as Indian luxuries. He supposed that they were left as a reward for his gallantry to the young squaw; and when, during his hunt in the forest that day, he met a party of friendly Indians, he described to them the appearance of the maiden, and learned that she was the daughter of a chief, and the most beautiful squaw of the tribe. She was known as Golden Bird.

When the hunter returned to his camp, he found Golden Bird waiting for him with a present of choice game. Her smiles welcomed his appearance, and her manner, when she tendered him the present, told the hunter plainly, that the forest girl sought him as a lover; but he remembered one beyond the confines of the forest, with whom his troth was plighted, and, too honorable to deceive the trusting maiden, he endeavored to make her understand that he could not return her affection. In the trusting innocence of her love, she mistook this kindness, and interpreted his attentions as she wished him to interpret the offerings she had made. The forest near the hunter's tent was that night the Golden

Bird's chamber, and on the morrow, while he roamed near the Menominee, she gathered for him a handful of precious stones, and when he refused them, she wept. Laying them at the door of his tent, she wandered into the woods, disconsolate. When absent from him, she was ever gloomy and depressed, but when in his presence, especially if he gave her the slightest attention, was as gay and glad-hearted as any other beautiful bird of the forest.

She abandoned the wigwam of her fathers—refused the counsel of her friends—forsook her kindred and followed the pale-faced hunter. Her attentions were a burthen to him, and he resolved to change his camp.

One day she was absent for a few hours, and his raft was rowed to the outlet of the lake, and slowly it floated down the stream. When it was moored at night, the hunter congratulated himself that the Golden Bird had been eluded, but to his great surprise, before nightfall, the maiden appeared before him with an exclamation of joy, and tendered him a bundle of herbs ingeniously arranged.

Every look and gesture told him that, with her, the affair had become one of life and death; that his smile was, to her, heaven. Had not his heart been wedded to another, he could never have chosen for his bride one of the rude, untutored children of the forest, and he thought that if he could escape her attentions, in a few days she would forget him, return to her father's wigwam, and accept the love of one of the braves of her tribe. Alas, he knew not the strength of Golden Bird's affection. The bluffs were high and abrupt along the river. She could not follow the raft. The hunter refused to take her with him. Standing upon a high rock, as the paleface, whom she had wooed, but who had rejected her love, faded from her view, she watched his raft with streaming eyeballs, and when he could no longer be seen, still she looked; and when the sun sunk at night behind the hills lining the river, still Golden Bird gazed intently into the dim distance; and when, on the following morning, light gilded the tops of the rocks, it shown on her disheveled hair and disorded robe, and still her eyes, spell-bound, were fixed on the point at which the hunter had disappeared from view.

Three days afterward, when her friends, after diligent search, found her, she was leaning against a shelving rock, and her gaze was yet on the stream which had borne away the object of her devotion. An Indian lover was there, and he sought to recall her attention, but she heard not the tones of a voice with which she had been familiar from childhood. When they bore her away tenderly from the spot where she had the last view of the hunter, her eyes closed in despair. She was too weak to tell them her heart had gone after the pale-face, and her spirit would soon roam in the hunting grounds to which the spirits of the brave warriors of the tribe had departed; but they saw that her life was fast fading, and they watched with her, in the depths of the forest, until it went out. Her spirit withdrew from the body as peacefully as dies out the day on a calm summer evening.

No tales of the times of chivalry—no romances of heroic deeds in Oriental lands, portray constancy purer than that of this Indian maiden—ill-fated Golden Bird of Menominee.

THE
Counterfeiters of the Cuyahoga.

A BUCKEYE ROMANCE.

CHAPTER I.

THE STORY OPENS.

THROUGH northern Ohio, toward Lake Erie, flows a winding stream, which the Indians named Cuyahoga—or crooked water. It is the principal river of several counties which lie in what is now known as the Western Reserve, but which in the early history of the West was called New Connecticut, comprising a large tract of land ceded by the General Government to the State of Connecticut. It was settled mainly by active, enterprising Yankees, who, if they were not as laborious farmers as the Pennsylvania emigrants, had generally more intelligence and public spirit, erected more tasteful dwellings, gave more skillful attention to mechanics, constructed better roads, and more rapidly developed whatever mineral resources were hidden beneath the soil on which their clearings were made.

A little settlement, began at the mouth of the Cuyahoga, increased rapidly in importance, and to its vicinity immigrants were attracted. Following, back into the forest, the winding course of the stream, they made settlements along its banks, and in a few years the town, situated where the river cast itself into the Lake, became a port of considerable commerce. It is now a principal city of the West. It bears the name of the first official surveyor of the Reserve. The country is rolling, and the Cuyahoga, winding around hills and through ravines, tumbles over many little cascades of romantic as well as practical interest. Yankee ingenuity very soon discovered this practical interest, and turned it to good account. Mills and factories were erected, and little villages sprang up around them.

Enterprise had so far developed and enriched the region round about the Cuyahoga, that a canal was required to convey its productions to the Lake shore, and this canal had been several years a source of convenience and profit, when a young man, fresh from the city of Boston, made himself known in a village situated at the principal falls of the river. He engaged workmen for the construction of a cottage in the place of a rude cabin, belonging to a farm which stretched away from the river at one of its most romantic points.

A village—especially in a new country—is the center, if not of universal sympathy, of universal curiosity. There was something more than curiosity—there was anxiety to know all about the proprietor of the new cottage. Was it for his father?—was he an agent for some western capitalist?—was he about to be, or had he just been married? He was rather young for the last conjecture to gain credence, because no one supposed him to be more than twenty years old. Gossip was confounded. The young man was discreet. He kept his own secrets. Even the landlord of the village inn, with whom he boarded, could only tell that he was from Boston—that is, could only tell so much about him in connection with his business designs; but of the young man, individually, he knew something more. He knew that he was a sharp enemy of such practices as were common in his bar-room.

The rubicund boniface had been cut to the quick of anger, if not repentance, on several occasions, by pictures which his young guest had drawn of the results of the drinking customs he encouraged. Two or three times the Bostonian had held discussions with the frequenters of the bar-room, and he had not made friends by the faithful expositions he gave of the bondage which drew them to the tavern, morning, noon and night.

Gossip concentrates at a village tavern. While one set of influences gravitates always toward the church, another just as surely gravitates toward the tavern. During the hour between service, on several Sabbaths, there was gossip concerning the cottage-builder, in the village churchyard. He had sat one morning in the deacon's pew—that was the only time he had been seen at church. It must be confessed that he had then given marked attentions to the pastor's discourse, but why did he not come again? Why? Nobody had ever heard him swear; he was upright, even liberal in his dealings. Why? The same question was put often at the tavern. The landlord said he was "more agin drinkin', and more like a Christian, so far as he could see, than many of them that went to church regularly, but then it was queer, and for his part he didn't like the fellow anyhow. He'd nothing particular agin him, but it *was* queer."

What *was* queer, the landlord did not definitely explain, but the expression was taken up by several of the faithful subjects of his dominion, and it became public opinion that about the new cottage some remarkable mystery hung.

Meantime the cottage was finished, and in a few days it was furnished with rich, antique furniture, which had been sent from Boston to one of the village warehouses.

The tavern commanded a view of the canal. The men who had come there to get their drinks, before engaging in the occupations of the day, saw the young man, who had for a number of weeks been the subject of their gossip, go one Monday morning directly from the bar-room porch to a packet, on which was a sign-board, saying "For Cleveland."

Here was additional subject-matter for gossip. Whither could he be going, and what for? The most satisfactory conjecture was, naturally enough, that he must be on an errand for the family that would occupy Brome Cottage—that was the name he had given it: therefore during his absence tongues were not idle concerning it and its mystery.

It was a handsome cottage, handsomely situated. It commanded a view of rough water and rougher rocks—of overhanging trees, which, gnarled and scraggy, grew out from the steep craggy banks of the river; and it commanded also a wide view of fair fields and deep woods—woods for miles unbroken—fields blackened with many large stumps, but lying beautifully, and to the farmer possessing rich promise.

In all its parts the cottage was not completed; the design, drafted evidently by an experienced architect, was not fully carried out, and except that some forest trees had been removed and others left, in fulfillment of a purpose which contemplated surrounding adornment, there had yet been no attempt made to lay out a yard or a garden.

On the Saturday morning succeeding young Brome's departure on the canal-boat, there was bustle and activity at the cottage. The villagers soon learned that it was occupied by an elderly lady and two young persons. One of these was the youth with whom they had become somewhat acquainted, and the other was his sister. So much mystery was unraveled. But what was the family, and where did it come from, and what would it do? It was not poor; it was respectable, but not very rich. There village gossip could safely go, but it could go no farther without launching into boundless speculation—fathomless conjecture.

Martha Brome, the mother of Harry and Alice Brome, was a widow lady, who had spent the hopeful period of her life in the city of Boston. Her husband had been an enterprising merchant. When about to retire from business with a competency, the failure of several large houses brought on a commercial crisis in his circle, by which his prospects of ease and quiet, in mature age, were crushed. He was a heart-broken as well as a fortune-broken merchant, and he died in a few months after his business prospects had been blasted. He was not, however, a bankrupt. He had speculated largely in western lands, and when his affairs were settled, it was ascertained that his wife and chilren controlled an excellent young farm, near an Ohio village, and that they had, besides, several thousand dollars with which to improve their property.

Mrs. Brome was a "strong-minded woman"—a woman who could calmly meet stern realities. When she understood the condition of her pecuniary affairs, she calculated practically for herself and family. She determined to relinquish the society of her friends—sunder the ties which, throughout her life, had been gathering in the city of her birth, and for the sake of her children emigrate to the West.

Harry had been his father's doting pride. He had been liberally educated, and he was an upright, thoughtful young man. His mother hoped that in a new country he might become a man of distinction.

Alice was a slender but healthful girl, with her mother's spirit and pride. Brother and sister concurred cheerfully in their mother's plans, and while the mother and Alice visited some near relatives, Harry was sent West to prepare their farm for their reception. They had carefully estimated their resources, and what could be commanded with them, and young Brome was prepared to make the most of the funds at his disposal. When his mother had closely examined the result of his agency, and the manner in which his trust had been executed, she was well satisfied, and so frankly told him.

Saturday was the first day the Brome family spent at their cottage, and consequently Sunday was the second. The village gossips had calculated somewhat on this Sunday. There was preaching at but one church. Across the valley rang the solemn tones of the bell, and the people with staid step and sober mien turned their faces toward the spire which should lead the minds of the devout from earth heavenward; but it must be confessed that, on the particular occasion concerning which we write, many of the church-goers had more curiosity about what they should see at church than what they would hear from the preacher.

Whether this be a more common error among country than among city people, we would not pretend to decide. We are writing a history—not speculating on human frailties in the abstract.

But the Brome family did not hear the village pastor's sermon. Those eyes turned away from the preacher's desk, when steps were heard in the aisles, saw only faces that were familiar. It was not until the succeeding Sabbath that any representative of Brome Cottage appeared in the deacon's pew.

The Deacon and the Pastor! What potent names in the Yankee village! Parson Humiston was a steady, good old man, beloved by all his congregation, and respected by the chiefest of the village sinners. His sermons were safe and solid, if not eloquent; he could tell the children pleasant little pious stories, and he had a meek and winning way of administering practical counsel and spiritual encouragement to the maidens, old or young—to the mothers, sad or gay—among whom he visited. Shakspeare said a sweet, low voice is a beautiful thing in woman; he might have added, a meek and winning way of administering counsel is a beautiful thing in a pastor.

Deacon Anstey was a contrast to the parson. One was of ample form, good-natured, genial; the other was thin, spare, hard-hearted and sharp. He was liberal to the church—never anywhere else. In his business dealings he was even miserly; but he was an enterprising merchant, and controlled a profitable business. Sometimes there were bitter stories told about him—sometimes he was called a hypocrite—sometimes a sleek scoundrel; but he was always regular at church meetings—he had bought the only bell there was in the village—he paid a considerable portion of the parson's meager salary, and, by hook and by crook, he was a deacon.

Harry Brome had carried a letter of introduction from a Boston merchant to Deacon Anstey, and the deacon had been quite civil to him; but Harry was not attracted by his sharp, thin voice, to seek frequent consultation, and between him and this important personage the coldness and reserve of a first acquaintance had not been broken, up to the period when, with his mother and sister, he was, from the deacon's pew, the chief attraction in Parson Humiston's congregation, on the second Sabbath after their arrival at Cuyahoga village. The week which ended with the coming in of this Sabbath had witnessed only one event which demands record in this history. Harry Brome had registered his name in the office of a village lawyer as a student at law.

During a "quarterly occasion," the Methodist minister of the circuit made an effort to organize a Temperance Society in the village, and Harry assisted him energetically. When the preliminary meeting was called he spoke earnestly and pointedly, and rather intimated that, among citizens who should be moral exemplars, he saw need of temperance reform. This was bold if not impudent for so young a man and so new a citizen.

Deacon Anstey was quite incensed. "The upstart," he said, "a sprig of the law, who wants to make himself talked about!"

"Not altogether," said the landlord, who knew Harry; "I reckon he's pretty strong temperance, 'cause he used to lecture the fellows at my house, but then I agree with you, Deacon, it's rather sassy."

So the gossip ran. The temperance enterprise signally failed, and young Brome came out of the contest with a few warm friends, but many bitter enemies. He was impetuous and by no means conciliating, and when he had opportunity criticised opponents, on whatever question of which he had the better side, with unrelenting severity, pursuing, with caustic irony, any advantage he might gain.

CHAPTER II.

THE PLOT OPENS.

"Harry Brome, Attorney and Counselor at Law." These words, plainly painted upon the window shutter of a small office, told a story in which the occupant of that office had a life-interest. Some of his enemies had said, "What does he try to domineer over a hired man for on his mother's farm—why don't he go to work himself?" but Harry had studiously pursued his own and his mother's purpose, during two years, and had been admitted to the bar, with warm commendations from the lawyers who reported to the court upon his fitness. During those two years many small revolutions had transpired in the village. From a number of households, lights had gone out and in others stars had risen. Barton, the landlord, had several mortgages on property which was free when Harry Brome first knew its owners; the general business of the town had increased, but Deacon Anstey had not been as successful as in former years. He had reached too far and grasped too tightly. He had found it convenient to request permission to resign his deaconship, which permission had been granted. He and young Brome were no better friends than when they were first acquainted.

Brome Cottage had become an inviting home. It was a

"remarkable place" in the new country—a place travelers stopped to admire, and a place travelers talked about when they had journeyed far from it. When the jessamine and honeysuckle crept over its trellised arbors, and vines with beautiful flowers entwined the latticed windows—when roses bloomed along graveled walks that were shaded by young trees, beneath which, in prepared plats, rare plants, flowers and shrubs grew, it appeared in delightful contrast with the rough fields and massive forests by which it was environed.

Each morning, when the birds were lively, and prodigal of songs, the Brome family was gathered in the garden. Harry and Alice industriously assisted their mother in the labor of making such improvements as she did not choose to intrust to their gardener. Mrs. Brome was the same calm thoughtful woman. In appearance she had but slightly changed during the two years of her western life, and what change could be observed was the result of improved health. It was remarked by a shrewd observer of human nature that " sorrow and suffering are essential to the rich development of female character." The trials and cares which had been imposed upon Mrs. Brome had only served to develop a character fitted for distinction in a wide sphere of action. This character was faintly understood at Cuyahoga village.

Mrs. Brome had not been neighborly according to the definition her neighbors attached to this phrase. She had never given a party. Parson Humiston had been with his daughter to take tea at the cottage many times, and he always spoke highly of Mrs. Brome, of Harry and Alice. A few of his parishoners could not understand why he was so favorably inclined toward a family which did not regularly sit under his preaching. Very rarely did Mrs. Brome attend his church, and Harry and Alice were oftener students of nature in some quiet glen or shady nook, or of books at home, than of the pastor and his people at church. Besides Parson Humiston and his daughter, there were a few persons in the village who appreciated the Brome family; and though they thought Harry a little harsh in his opinions, and somewhat indiscreet in the sternness of his disputes with those whom he considered vulgar or hypocritical, though they deemed Alice quite too retired in her taste and manners, they were satisfied that Mrs. Brome understood her duties and obligations, and would not fail to lead her children aright. Napoleon, with profound conviction, said—"The fate of a child is always the work of a mother." Mrs. Brome was assiduous in her care and thoughtful in her instructions, and she indulged visions of bright promise for her children. It is for this history to tell whether she experienced that

> ——"there is nothing upon earth
> More miserable than she that has a son
> And sees him err."

Northern Ohio was "flooded" with counterfeit money. Much of the "spurious currency" was so faithfully executed that the best judges were often deceived. It was a common rumor that somewhere in the vicinity of Cuyahoga village, was the head-quarters of the counterfeiters; and it was whispered that persons of honorable standing before the community had secret cognizance of the counterfeiters and their haunts. Where these rumors originated no person could tell. The village landlord, who was supposed to occupy the chief post among newsmongers, was often interrogated concerning them, and he invariably answered:

"It's a tarnal lie, the whole of it. Nobody who knows

anything would suppose that, if counterfeiters were in this region, they'd be peddling their trash about here thick as huckleberries. Them fellows is sharp. They don't sell their wares where they make 'em."

There was some philosophy in Barton's opinion, but in spite of it, the suspicion that the counterfeiters were hidden in or near Cuyahoga village, acquired force and currency. Frequently men of undoubted honesty found themselves in possession of considerable sums of money, which better judges than they pronounced counterfeit. They could not always remember from whom it was received, and there was general complaint of swindling, and business confidence was much disturbed. Harry Brome, on several occasions, was victimized, and, once or twice, under such circumstances as gave his prejudiced enemies opportunity to mutter indefinite whispers and make mysterious allusions.

He one day pursued a man named Sandys, who had given him several bills, which a friend pronounced counterfeit; when he found him, he talked hastily and bitterly about the circulation of such stuff. High words had passed between them, when Brome said:

"This is the second time that I have had bad money from you. You are either a very poor judge, or you don't care whether I am cheated or not."

"And s'pose I don't," answered Sandys, coolly, "what'll you do about it?"

"I'll tell you what I'd do. If I could prove that you gave this to me knowingly, I'd send you to the penitentiary, where there are many men who have done less harm in the world than you."

Sandys was a grocer and liquor merchant, and there had never been cordiality between him and Brome.

"You talk well," retorted Sandys, "but *pre*-haps we'd be in company. Some folks is a little suspicious that you know how to get rags with picters on 'em."

"What, Sir," demanded Harry, "do you mean to insinuate that I have ever dealt in counterfeit money?"

"Insinuate," said Sandys with a cold sneer, "I don't know what that is."

"Well, Sir, I'll make you know, if you dare to hint a suspicion that I have any knowledge of the counterfeiters which would implicate me in their rascality. I believe that some of them are not far from this spot. I only wish I could get a clue to them. This place would soon be too hot for them or any of their accomplices."

This threat was uttered in a manner which impressed Sandys that it was aimed at him. He stepped toward young Brome with a clenched fist, muttering an oath between his teeth, when a stranger addressed them:

"I wish the direction to Brome Cottage, and would be obliged to either of you gentlemen for it," said the stranger.

"Here's a puppy can take you there," cried Sandys, turning on his heel, and leaving young Brome to explain the circumstances under which he was found.

Harry at once recognized the stranger as the son of a merchant in Boston, with whom his father had been associated in business.

"You do not know me?" said Harry; "country air has improved my complexion."

"I did not, but now I *do* know my old friend and school-mate," returned the stranger, extending his hand, which was cordially grasped.

Exchanging sketches of adventure since they had been at school, the young men walked slowly toward Brome Cottage.

When Harry introduced his companion as Joseph Etherege, of Boston, Mrs. Brome distinctly remembered him, and gave him a high-bred but not cold welcome, which caused him to feel that he had found a home.

Etherege had known Alice Brome only as a giddy school-girl. He was delighted to meet her a young woman of education and spirit, delicate, but not fragile, polite, but not affected. Alice was not beautiful in that sense which requires symmetry of features, but she had an expressive countenance and a graceful form; her mother's fair complexion and deep blue eyes, with the same winning grace of manner, the same dignified repose in her deportment.

CHAPTER III.

THE COUNTERFEITERS DISCOVERED.

Harry Brome was a capital sportsman. He knew well every glen and dell and vale in which game was abundant, within a circuit of many miles around his mother's cottage; and he could tell where an experienced fisherman was certain, if "the sign was right," to take from the river a string of choice fish. Etherege was as fond of forest sports as Harry, and he had been a guest at Brome Cottage but a few days when he could describe all of Harry's favorite haunts. The places of romantic interest along the river having been visited, the deepest woods and wildest ravines having been explored, Harry determined to interest his companion in geological speculations concerning a cave which he had discovered, on one of his hunting expeditions. It was near the opening of a deep ravine, in an unfrequented forest, which crowned a range of low hills along the river, about three miles below the village.

It was a pleasant autumn afternoon when the young friends set out on their expedition. There was promise of good shooting, and each had his gun. They had no sooner entered the forest than they became more interested in the pursuit of game than in geological investigations or speculations, and they were led away from the path Brome had designed to follow. In endeavoring to retrace his steps he temporarily lost his reckoning, and Etherege joked him about being bewildered.

"Here's a faint trail, suppose we try that?" said Etherege.

"I have no objection," answered Harry, "because we cannot be very far out of the way, and have time enough to get home before dark, if we take another day for the cave."

"I am inclined to think we'll be compelled to take another day. Your luck is bad to-day. I've got more game than you have, and you are lost."

"Of course *you* know the way," returned Harry, laughing, "lead on."

Etherege walked on briskly, and Harry followed. They had only proceeded a few steps when a squirrel ran across their path, a few rods in front of them. Etherege gave him chase, and Harry watched the race. The nimble creature did not take to a tree, as the sportsman had expected, and Etherege continued to pursue it. Harry now joined him, and both exerted themselves to get a shot. They were disappointed. The game escaped; and when they gave up the chase, they found themselves on the brink of a ravine which Harry declared to be that in which the cave he sought was to be found.

"But we'll not explore it to-day," he said; "we'll not lose ourselves another time, and shall not waste the day chasing squirrels which we cannot shoot."

"That's very cool," returned Etherege; "but now if you'll kill that woodpecker, getting his supper out of the top branch of yon old tree across the ravine, I'll say no more about your bewilderment."

"Protection from your wit is easily purchased," cried Harry; "here goes."

He raised his gun to his shoulder and was about to discharge it, when suddenly he rested the barrel across his left arm and listened.

"What's up?" asked Etherege.

"Hish!" answered Harry.

Watchfully and noislessly he moved a few steps along the brow of the ravine, then stopped and listened again: then he proceeded a few rods farther, when he turned and beckoned Etherege toward him, who came forward as cautiously as his companion.

"You know, Joseph, I told you about the counterfeit money in this country and my suspicions, on the day you inquired for our cottage in the village. Well, I have often met suspicious fellows in these woods. Just as I was going to shoot, I heard my name mentioned down here in the ravine by a voice I believe I know, and it belongs to a man who bears me no good will. Now I'm going to see what he's doing."

Harry crept forward, and Etherege followed him. Presently Harry stopped where the bank of the ravine was precipitous, and swinging himself around an overhanging tree, he gazed intently into the hollow below him.

"By Jupiter! the game's up," he whispered, turning to Etherege. "This is a capital day's shooting. Look yonder."

Etherege looked as directed, and saw three men sitting under a tree, apparently intently occupied in a game of euchre.

"They're playing euchre," he said, "and it don't strike me that the game *is* up."

"I'll show you what kind of euchre it is," answered Harry; "come this way—I am going to euchre them."

Harry crept to a point where he could closely observe the persons he had discovered, then he said to Etherege:

"One is Tom Darwin, a noted scoundrel, the other is Deacon Anstey, and the other is that man Sandys with whom I had the dispute, on the day you came to Cuyahoga. As sure as fate they have a lot of 'coney' between them."

"And what is 'coney'?" whispered Etherege.

"That's the counterfeiters' technical name for spurious notes. These scoundrels are preparing to circulate a 'batch' of them. I see through the scheme. Sandys and Anstey provide the money, and employ Darwin to put it off. If I don't get them in limbo, my name's not Brome," said Harry with energy.

"Hark!" said Etherege.

The friends listened, and, from the conversation of the counterfeiters, learned that Sandys was telling them about his dispute at the village with Harry.

"We must look out for that fellow," said Anstey. "He and I have always been enemies. I tried to conciliate him when he first came to the village, but he scorned my advances, and I've hated him ever since."

"He's got grit," said Sandys, "and if he could get a clue to our operations he'd never sleep till he tracked us. We've got to watch him, now, I tell you."

"Gammon," said Darwin in his coarse rough way; "you fellers never will get along, if you're afraid of a sassy little

Yankee lawyer. You keep your eyes open and *pre*haps we can get *him* in a scrape."

The counterfeiters now conversed in so low a tone that Brome and Etherege could not understand them.

Harry had seen enough, and he told Etherege that it was time to proceed homeward. In retracing their steps, the young men were not so cautious as they had been when seeking the counterfeiters, and when they were passing an open spot on the brow of the ravine, Tom Darwin caught a glimpse of them.

"The devil and his imps," cried he; "by the Lord Harry, yonder is that infernal Yankee lawyer now!"

"He's seen us—he's followed us," cried Anstey, quaking, "and you've made a pretty muss of it by getting in this place, Tom."

"You're an old woman if you were a deacon once," answered Tom, angrily; "if I can run my risk I guess you can your'n, and you'll have to, that's all, *Deacon* Anstey."

"Never mind, Tom," said Sandys, who was more collected than Anstey. "It's all right. It's not likely them fellows saw us, but we must find out whether they did or not, and you and I can do that."

"Suppose they did see us and know we had 'coney' here to-day, what's to be done then?" inquired Anstey, not yet assured that he was safe.

"We'll have to leave this country sudden, that's all," answered Sandys.

"Not as you knows on," said Tom Darwin, impudently.

"What then, Tom?" asked Sandys.

"We'll put the sneakin' spies out of the way first," answered Darwin, between his teeth.

Neither Sandys nor Anstey made any reply to this threat. It was more than they were prepared for, but what they could or *would* do, were it certain that young Brome had discovered them, neither could answer.

The business of the "council" in the forest having been transacted, the counterfeiters separated and proceeded to the village in different directions, where they assembled another "council" to decide what was to be done in the event that Harry Brome should take any step which indicated that he had clue to their rascality.

Meantime Harry and Etherege had safely reached home, unconscious that they had been seen by the counterfciters.

CHAPTER IV.

CONSPIRACY DEVELOPED.

JOSEPH ETHEREGE was a fortune-hunter. He had received a liberal education; he had traveled in Europe—and this at the period of which we write, was an important fact in the education of a young gentleman; he had graduated from a medical school of high standing, and with money enough to purchase a large tract of land in a new country, he had emigrated westward for the purpose of "locating." Harry Brome was quite anxious that Etherege should "settle down" at Cuyahoga village, but the young doctor would make him no definite promise. Whenever he talked of visiting other counties or towns in the State, Brome was eloquent on the prospects of the Cuyahoga valley, and Etherege hesitated to take leave of his good friends at Brome Cottage. Perhaps one reason why he hesitated was, because he began to have an interest in the Brome family; an interest more enlivening than the sports of the field, and quite as engrossing as money-making—indeed, it was embraced in the plan of "fortune-hunting" which the young man had arranged.

Walks and drives, readings and talkings, in and around Brome Cottage, were not altogether objectless, and their object was something more than time-killing.

Alice Brome was a charming girl; fitted especcially was she to charm an enterprising, enthusiastic young man, who, resolved upon an earnest effort in a new country to become a citizen of influence and usefulness, wished a helpmate competent to understand his strivings, and appreciate the spirit which animated them.

Alice was one evening reading a new novel, when she threw it aside with a slight scornfulness in her manner. Etherege took it up and discovered that she had been perusing a scene between lovers who were lack-a-daisically tender —whose love was of the whimpering, lachrymose character —which is an emotion of "fancy"—a victim of whim and caprice—the love which animates flirts, male or female— which finds wedlock irksome, and which deliberately souring, for the sake of appearances, expresses itself in "my dear," but never sings :

> "Home, sweet home. Be it ever so humble,
> There's no place like Home."

Etherege could have no other opinion than that Alice was a worshiper of the sensible and the truthful. He was pleased with her quiet, dignified expression of contempt for such silly "scenes" as the novel depicted. He did not then reveal the satisfaction he enjoyed, but determined, on the first fitting occasion, to suggest the "scene" to the remembrance of Alice.

One morning she invited him to go with her into the garden and assist in the care of some flowers, which needed protection from the winds of early autumn, that had already tipped with yellow the leaves of the maple trees in the forest.

Etherege watched for an opportunity to recall to Alice's

mind the sentiment the novel which he had seen her read awakened, without arousing a suspicion that he had divined the cause of the scorn with which she had thrown the book aside.

"It is quite natural," said he, "to associate summer flowers, which the frosts of winter kill, with the friendship good fortune attracts, but which bad luck drives away. I am not surprised that many poets and many romancers have perplexed their wits to find a new expression for the thought."

"But after all, Mr. Etherege," said Alice, "it is hardly fair to the flowers. They are not false. They leave no duties undischarged. They bloom and are beautiful for us until their allotted time to die."

"A beautiful defense," exclaimed Etherege; "I judge from it that you have less even than the usual slender confidence in friendships which are made when the sun of fortune is warm."

"We may find good and true friends, Mr. Etherege, in the height of prosperity, but we cannot always tell on whom we may rely till misfortune reverses our obligations, and makes them valuable to us. But I am talking what is very commonplace, and you cannot be interested."

"You are quite mistaken. I think your words have meanings which do not at first appear in them, and I am interested to know whether your thoughts are not led away from common friendships, to obligations and relations dearer and more important."

"You are not gallant, Mr. Etherege, to give my words meanings of your own, and then ask confession of me; but I am not reluctant to tell you that I have been thinking of a book I read not long ago, in which "real life" was depicted as the silly pastime of coquetting boys and girls. Holding marriage to be a solemn and thoughtful step, I was indignant that such books should be popular, among women who are expected to teach children what is expected of them, and what they may well accomplish in the world."

"You are quite utilitarian," said Etherege, designing to elicit further expressions of the train of thought in which Alice had fallen, but she answered him:

"Only a little practical, as my mother says, Mr. Etherege. But here comes Harry; I will appeal to him."

"And why appeal?" said Etherege, smiling. "I have not disputed you." Alice looked a mischievous response, but spoke none; for Harry, swinging his gun with one hand and grasping Etherege with the other, said:

"Come, I have harnessed the horse for a ride. A gentleman at the village yesterday described to me a desirable tract of land which is for sale on reasonable terms, and I propose that we take a look at it. If it is what he represented it to be, there is a speculation in it."

"There will be no harm in taking a look at it," answered Etherege, "and I am at your service."

"The ride at all events will be pleasant," said Harry, "and as on our return home we may drive near that cave, above the falls in our river, which we did *not* visit the other day, we may derive pleasure as well as profit from the trip."

Harry led his friend from the garden, and placing his rifle in a safe place beneath the wagon seat, said:

"We may meet some adventure that will require it. I always take it along."

"Perhaps you'll come across the counterfeiters again," returned Etherege.

"I should not probably have occasion to shoot one of them if I did, but when we get into the woods, if we can do nothing more, I'll beat you shooting at a mark so handsomely, that you will never dare to say another word about my having been lost."

"I take the banter," said Etherege.

The property Brome designed to visit was situated about ten miles from Cuyahoga village. When the friends had talked with its owner, learned the price and terms of sale, and had acquainted themselves with the character of the soil and other advantages possessed by the farm, Etherege was well pleased, and, somewhat influenced perhaps by the conversation of the morning, determined to make an investment. He told the farmer that Mr. Brome was his banker, and that if he would meet him in the village on the following Saturday, he would receive a deed for the property and make the required payment.

"The business of our ride is over; now for the pleasure," said Harry.

"It is afternoon, you observe," returned Etherge, "and if we visit the cave you must drive briskly."

Harry cracked his whip, and his smart horse whirled the light wagon rapidly toward the village. In half an hour Harry checked the speed of the animal, and turning him from the main road into a dim track stretching through a dense forest, drove slowly and cautiously for about another half hour, and then reining up, bid Etherege alight.

The horse was detached from the wagon and securely fastened; Harry took his gun from its resting place, and was leading the way toward a narrow ridge which could be discerned between the trees, when Etherege said:

"If these woods are haunted by counterfeiters, I should be a little afraid to leave my horse in them."

"Pshaw," returned Harry, "I've left him many a time. There's more risk in stealing a horse than in making spurious money, and the fellows we saw out here are sly rogues, I assure you."

"Do you suppose they can have any suspicion that you know their rascality?" said Etherege.

"They know that I have been watching for the counterfeiters, and that I would send them to the penitentiary if I could detect them; knowing their own guilt, of course they are a little afraid of me. They would not hesitate to injure me if they could do so safely to themselves."

"It becomes you then to be cautious."

"I know it does; I thought of that when I brought out my rifle to-day."

Conversing about the counterfeiters and what was to be expected and what feared of them, the two friends approached the high and rocky "bluffs," into which the cave they sought opened. They were in the vicinity of the place where they had discovered Darwin and his confederates in council during their previous search for the cave, and Brome proposed that Etherege should seat himself at the foot of one of the hemlock trees which crowned the ledge of rocks, while he reconnoitered the ravine beyond. Etherege was not suspicious that harm would befall himself or his companion, and he consented, upon condition that Harry would not be absent more than fifteen minutes.

Brome had not skulked along the brow of the ledge overhanging the river more than five minutes, when he caught a glimpse of some one dodging among the trees before him.

He glanced at his gun as if to inquire whether he could rely on it, and followed the shadow which had attracted his attention. It led him down the ledge and toward the place where his horse and wagon stood. He had an opportunity to see the man whom he followed, but could not recognize him. He thought of what Etherege had said about horse-stealing, and, neglecting his engagement to return to his friend, in a quarter of an hour, continued the pursuit. Presently the suspected horse-thief no longer endeavored to disguise his progress, but walked forward boldly, and striking into the path which led into the public road, pushed forward toward it.

Then Brome regretted his suspicions, and hastened to retrace his footsteps. He walked rapidly to the brow of the ledge and proceeded to the spot where he had taken leave of Etherege. The young man was gone. Brome whistled, and anxiously expected a response. None came. He hallooed. His voice echoed among the trees, but the echoes brought no other answer than their own. He began to feel solicitude, if not alarm. He closely examined the ground around the tree where Etherege had sat, to ascertain if any footsteps were imprinted on it. He could discover none. Then he looked along and down the ledge for some trace of his departure; he observed a handkerchief lying some distance below him. He hastened to pick it up. There were drops of blood on it, and it belonged to Etherege.

Brome's fears were now intensely excited. He suspected that Etherege had been attacked and had fled toward the wagon. He ran through the woods with nervous haste, and when he reached his wagon could discover no sign of his friend, but when he looked for his horse, he saw that the strap, with which he was hitched to a tree, had been cut. Between the tree and the road there were deep hoof-marks, as if the horse had been urged swiftly away.

Brome was in a maze of doubt and conjecture. Again and again he hallooed. No answer came. Already the sun threw lengthened shadows, and, convinced that Etherege must have been pursued by some foe or foes and had fled to the horse, cut him loose and escaped, Brome at once determined to follow.

If his conjectures were well founded, he should soon meet his friend, with company returning in quest of him; if not, he could alarm the village and search for Etherege.

Brome had not traveled far on the public road, when he met a man with whom he was acquainted. Then he learned that his horse, riderless, had been seen dashing at full speed toward the village. Harry dare not idly indulge conjectures as to the fate of his friend, but he hastened to the nearest farm-house, and engaging a horse, galloped home to assure his mother and sister that he was not harmed; inform them of the circumstances of his friend's disappearance, and make arrangements for a thorough search of the woods in which he had been lost, or—murdered!

CHAPTER V.

THE SEARCH.

BROME halted at the cottage door only long enough to inform his mother and Alice that Etherege was mysteriously missing. Leaving them to painful surmise and perplexing conjecture, he rode to the village for the purpose of securing aid for a thorough search of the woods in which his friend had disappeared. His impetuosity, his nervous anxiety, declared to the loungers at the tavern, before he alighted from his horse, that he had exciting news to communicate. They gathered around him, eagerly repeating to each other the words in which he told how he had lost Etherege.

Concerning what might have been the fate of the stranger Brome had conflicting suspicions, and he expressed none of them; but Barton, the landlord, said:

"Murdered for his money—that's what he's been—I'll bet a treat for the town."

"He had no money with him," answered Brome quickly.

"But he had money somewhere, hadn't he?" returned Barton, "and the fellow who took him off knows how to get it. You must look out for him, Mr. Brome."

Harry was about to reply, when he saw Sandys walk

away from the tavern steps, muttering. He could not hear the grocer's words, but a friend of Harry's did.

"Likely the fellow who took him off, *does* know where the money is, and if he don't be watched it's 'cause I'm blind. It's lucky Barton thought of that."

While Sandys was muttering and plotting, Brome had said:

"Never mind, Mr. Barton, about speculations now. We must scour the woods, and I am here to raise a party of volunteers."

Sandys heard those words and hastened to find Anstey.

When Harry led a party of villagers in quest of Etherege, the grocer and the ex-deacon were with it.

All night shout answered shout—fires gleamed and torches flickered in the woods to which Brome had conducted Etherege. When the light of morning came, and the fires and the torches died out, hope died in the minds of the searchers, and they went home weary and unhappy, bearing tidings which increased the excitement in the village.

It was Sabbath morning, a beautiful Sabbath morning; a purple haze hung on the hills, and the air in the valleys was calm, and sweet, and exhilarating. The Sabbath bell had a softened sound, and it seemed as if the sexton rang it slowly, so slowly indeed, that to many its notes were knell-like—to the family at Brome Cottage they were doleful.

Parson Humiston had a thin congregation and an inattentive one. In his last prayer for the morning service, he remembered the missing Etherege and prayed that, in the providence of God, he might safely be restored to his sad friends. The church attendants remembered the burden of this petition more vividly than they did the lessons of the sermon, when they went out among the villagers to talk of the minister's eloquence.

In a new country, in a young village, the people know each other much better than they do in developed towns or thriving cities. They have more interest in each other's welfare, and more sympathy for each other's misfortunes. A severe affliction in one family throws a pensive influence into every other family. Therefore it was that the people of Cuyahoga village were sympathetically absorbed in emotions of curiosity, conjecture, and sympathy.

At Brome Cottage there was no rest, no peace. The search of Saturday night had satisfied Harry Brome that Etherege could not be found in the woods, and he was convinced that Tom Darwin was answerable for his disappearance. Upon consultation he determined to hazard the arrest of the outlaw. Having ascertained where he was most likely to be discovered, Harry, late on Sunday evening, took the village constable into his buggy, and secretly departed on the desperate venture of arresting, upon vague suspicion, a man who was known to be bold, reckless, and revengeful.

When Brome and the constable went away from Cuyahoga village to hunt Darwin, he was skulking about its streets, seeking Sandys and Anstey.

In the rear of Sandys' grocery there was a low, dark room, in which many a scene of villainy had been planned, and thither the outlaw wended his way.

The grocer was at home. He received Darwin with a show of cordiality and gave him a seat in the council-room, then he went out, locking the door and bolting it on the outside, leaving Darwin to meditate on his past life—its schemes of villainy and its scenes of cruelty, or to plot new conspiracies. He knew that for the present he was a prisoner, but he was confident that Sandys would soon return, and that with him would come Anstey and others who were in the secrets of the Counterfeiters of the Cuyahoga.

The outlaw thought often of young Brome. He feared him more than he did any of the village officers. He was satisfied that Brome knew him to be a "counterfeiter," and that he would arrest him as soon as he could get evidence enough to hold him. He had plotted to circumvent Brome, but the plot had failed of execution, and now the outlaw wanted to report progress to his confederates and consult on the next steps to be taken for the safety of the band.

"I'll watch 'em to-night," said Darwin. "I'll let 'em know it all. I'll get 'em in the fix. They've got to come in, and just about daybreak I'll leave 'em in the lurch. This town's not quite the place for me. It's a little too warm here, and afore the folks know just what grocery-keeper Sandys and *Deacon* Anstey really are, I'd better be off. I've had one experience in striped trowsers, and I wouldn't like another."

While Darwin thus plotted for himself and against others of the counterfeiters, he had no suspicion that Harry Brome was already watchfully employed in guarding against his emigration from the valley of the Cuyahoga, at least until they had met.

Brome, though confident that Darwin was responsible for Etherege's disappearance, trusted that his friend was not murdered, and, guarding against Darwin's secret escape, he had determined to confront the outlaw, tell him what he knew about the counterfeiters, what he suspected concerning Etherege, and assure him that if he would restore the young man to his friends, he should be permitted to elude the clutches of the law.

The constable with whom he searched was but partially in Brome's confidence. He was not yet certain how far he dare trust him. He was a resolute and careful man, but he was neither very active nor very shrewd.

CHAPTER VI.

THE COUNCIL.

DARWIN was walking his prison when Sandys returned. The grocer was accompanied by Anstey, and a man named Tickell, whom Darwin had only met in council once before.

The counterfeiters were not very cordial in their greetings, and with a heavy frown on his brow, Darwin said:

"Well, *Deacon*, it's a little scarey, aint it?"

"That depends on what you have been doing," returned Anstey.

"What do you suppose?" angrily cried Darwin.

"Keep quiet, Tom," interposed Sandys, "we want your head cool to-night."

"I *am* cool," said Tom, "I'm going to keep cool, and now I'll just ask Deacon Anstey, in a quiet way, what he *supposes* I've been doin'."

"No offense, Darwin," said Anstey, with submission, "but there's big excitement in the village, and it's a little suspected that you know what has become of that fellow, Etherege, the friend of that little devil, Brome."

"I do know just that," answered Darwin, "and that little devil knows too."

"I'm afraid he does," said Sandys.

"I know it, I tell you. I saw it done."

"Saw what done, Darwin?" cried Anstey.

"Now, Deacon, *you* keep cool," answered Darwin, "and I'll tell you. I made up my mind about a week ago that them fellows did see us in the ravine, and that that sassy little lawyer was laying his traps to catch us. I didn't say nothing to you fellows, but I determined to catch *him*. Do you understand that?—to put him out of the way, Deacon Anstey."

"You'd kill him, Tom Darwin. You did kill that Etherege. I wash my hands of it. Oh God! I never thought of this," cried Anstey.

"Bah, you chicken!" returned Darwin. "Now I tell you I did not kill him; I haven't said he was dead."

"Look here, Tom," said Sandys, who was fully as anxious as Anstey, but had more prudence, "you're trying to put a riddle on us. Talk it out, and let us know what's up."

"Who's that fellow?" said Darwin, pointing to Tickell.

"He's safe," answered Sandys. "I'll go bail for him."

"If he leaks," said Tom, "or shows signs of leaking, he knows where a ball will go."

"He aint afraid of you, Tom Darwin. He knows you, and you ought to know him. If you can't trust him, he'll go out," returned Tickell.

"There's a little grit in you," answered Tom, "and you've heard too much to go now. I'll trust you. Deacon Anstey, I'm going to give you what you wanted to know when you first came in here."

Anstey made no reply, and Darwin continued:

"I was at the cave where our manufactory is, on Saturday, and as I was crossing the hill, I caught a glimpse of the sassy lawyer and the Yankee he takes about with him. I took a notion to get our necks out of a scrape by getting the Yankee's in. I thought if I could catch the lawyer, I might keep him safe a couple of days, and get the Yankee suspected for having made away with him, or compel Brome to hush up about us."

"The Lord, Darwin, you have been playing a *nice* game," sighed Anstey, striding across the council-room.

Darwin looked at the ex-deacon with a sardonic smile, and went on :

"That plan wouldn't work, because the lawyer had a rifle and the Yankee didn't, and I was a calculatin' what might be done, when, by the powers, the lawyer—"

"A trumped-up story, a trumped-up story," cried Anstey, taking courage from the desperate character of the trap into which he saw the counterfeiters falling. "You've killed that Etherege, and you'll be found out—you'll go to the gallows, and we'll go to the peni—"

Anstey had not time to finish the word; Darwin sprang upon him, crying :

"Do you call me a liar, you hypocritical old villain?"

A knife gleamed in the outlaw's hand, and he might have plunged it into Anstey's breast, but a quick thought that such an act would prevent the flight he had planned, restrained him. He hurled Anstey to the ground, declaring with an oath,

"You're too mean a coward to strike. You'll go to the penitentiary as true as ever you were a deacon, mind that. I know what's become of that Etherege, and unless something comes to that Brome, my neck goes it too. But something *will* come to him. That's all I've got to say. I'm mum, Deacon Anstey, till I get you into a worse scrape than you're in now. But I'll watch you—mind you, Deacon Anstey, I'll watch you sharp."

Sandys tried all his arts to induce Darwin to reveal what he knew of the fate of Etherege, but the outlaw was obdurate.

"I'm going out of this hole," said he, "and Deacon Anstey may as well go home. It's no use to coax me. I tell you I won't say another word this night. Let me alone. Don't vex me now, and maybe the next time that I am here I'll be talkative."

Sandys conducted the counterfeiters into the street, and they separated in darkness, each plotting to shield himself from the retribution which he feared.

Tickell thanked his stars that he had accidently been admitted to the council. He was every where considered a vagabond sort of a fellow, but he had once been a respectable and prosperous citizen, and no one suspected that he had any part or lot with the counterfeiters.

He was the tool, the slave, the victim of Barton, the landlord, but his family would have been the landlord's victims more bitterly than language can describe, had it not been for many kind words and many little offices, many needful gifts, which came to them from Brome Cottage.

Tickell was not wholly corrupted, and he thought he saw in Darwin's partial revelations a deep plot to bring trouble upon the Brome family—he reflected on the kindness of that family to his own, and he deliberately considered whether the counterfeiters had stronger claims upon him than Harry Brome, and his mother and sister. He might run perilous risks, but he determined to watch for an opportunity to befriend his benefactors.

CHAPTER VII.

A CONFLICT.

THERE were yet no signs of dawn when Tom Darwin skulked away from Cuyahoga village. He followed the street nearest the river until he had reached a bridge which crossed it, half a mile below the town. Half way over the bridge, the outlaw sat down as if to soothe a disturbed spirit by the roar of the waters which dashed over huge rocks in the bed of the river. He was not a man who analyzed quiet emotions—he did not clearly inquire into motives for actions which involved no apparent danger, but instinctively, no doubt, chose the bridge as a place for meditation, because he could think more keenly and plan more sharply, where the roar of the river answered to the tumult of conflicting dreads, fears and resolves, which disturbed his mental repose.

The banks of the river were high where the bridge spanned it, and they were precipitous and craggy. The narrow bed of the stream was broken by a number of low but clearly defined precipices, and the water, rushing in eddies and counter-eddies around the rocks which resisted its current, then plunging over cascades, roared with a force which bore the stunning sound to a considerable distance on either side.

Amid the deafening roar of the Cuyahoga falls, in the

darkness of the hour which precedes day-break, the outlaw sought to reconcile the conflicting fears and purposes which influenced him, and to shape a satisfactory course of action. Had Sandys or Anstey suspected that he had the remotest intention of fleeing from that part of the country, they would have taken sure means to check him; but his intentions were known only to himself, and he chuckled quietly when he thought of the perplexing rage that would overcome Deacon Anstey, when it was certain that Darwin had fled, and taken the secret of Etherege's disappearance with him.

The mist which morning had lifted from the valleys, upon the hill-tops began to assume a roseate glow, when Darwin walked rapidly from Cuyahoga bridge, and turning into a path that led down the bank of the river, pursued it a few rods; then crossing a field, he entered a strip of dense woods. He did not follow a path, but walked in nearly a straight line until he reached a natural opening where a spring bubbled up, creating a small marsh, in which tall grass grew.

There the outlaw halted, and after taking a "refreshing" drink from a pocket cup, in which there was a very little water, he gave a shrill whistle. For a moment he listened attentively. His signal was not answered, and he exclaimed with nervous impatience:

"Curse the fool, I told him to be here at day-break. I'ts half an hour after that time. I'll blow him up if he aint more prompt."

Darwin sat down on a log near the spring, and taking from his pocket a huge knife, began to whittle and to think. He was restless, and he made large whittlings. He was startled by a whistle, which, springing to his feet, he answered. Soon a stout, thick-set, rough-looking man emerged from a thicket and approached the spring. Darwin met him with the salutation, "Didn't you promise to be here as soon as it was light?"

"Yes, and I'd been here if it hadn't been for your bad calculation. The nag you wanted was'nt where you said I'd find him, and I had to hunt the critter."

"You got him?" said Darwin.

"I did that. He's in fine order, right out here on the edge of the woods."

"We'll go over, then," said Darwin. "When did you take him?"

"Night before last. It's safe to ride him away from here to-day, but maybe it wouldn't be to-morrow."

"I'll look out for that. You take care of yourself when I'm gone and don't git distressed about my luck. To-night I'll let the critter run, I don't care a curse where."

Conversing upon their villainous schemes for the future, the outlaws walked briskly through the woods until they reached the place where Darwin's companion had left the horse he had stolen.

Darwin untied the animal and sprang into the saddle. He then gave his hand to his fellow-outlaw and said:

"Now, Billy, good-by; one week from to-night we meet, you know where. You go back to the village and lounge about to-day, and to-night make tracks. Tell Sandys and Anstey I'll be at the grocery about eleven to-night. They'll wait."

"Good-by, Tom," answered Billy Mervin. "You can bet on me for Monday next. I'll tell the fellows at the grocery, and they *will* wait, that's a fact, and so'll somebody else. I don't care for the grocer nor the deacon. The devil take them. But otherwise, I'm a little compunctious, Tom. Sometimes I've a notion to crack a pistol."

"Bah!" said Darwin sneeringly, "let the thing work. After we've gone, I don't care if the whole of it comes out against that chicken-hearted, hypocritical old deacon. If that Brome aint got rid of, he'll fetch it out. I must be off. You go back to town like an honest man."

This conversation had been held as Billy Mervin walked beside Darwin's horse, while he rode through the woods toward the public road. The distance was short, only a few yards. They reached the highway as Darwin spoke. He struck his horse a sharp blow, and the animal, having high mettle, sprang into a swift gallop.

Taking a farewell look of Darwin as a cloud of dust began to envelop him and his stolen horse, Mervin proceeded to execute the command that he should visit the village.

It was rather an untraveled road along which Darwin galloped. He was obliged to travel for a few miles on another one, where he might expect to meet many persons, and when he approached it, he checked his steed. Though he burned with impatience, prudence required him to ride slowly. He was in sight of the point at which he could turn from the great highway into a by-road that led in the direction he wished to pursue. He congratulated himself upon his good luck, and again gave his horse the rein.

Just at the point where the by-road branched off, there was a turn in the main one, and Darwin's eyes were fixed suspiciously on this turn as he neared it. To his decided chagrin it was not more than a hundred yards distant when a buggy containing two men was driven around it. At first, Darwin saw nothing in their appearance to alarm him, but quickly he recognized Harry Brome and Constable Sedley, who, as Darwin was aware, held the office of deputy sheriff.

Brome's blood quickened in his veins as he recognized the outlaw. At once he reined up his horse and arose from his seat.

Darwin's liveliest suspicions were awakened. He thought it folly to turn back—he determined at all hazards to ride on. If it was the intention of Brome to arrest him, he should make the attempt at desperate risk. Darwin had confidence in his horse, and he would test his speed and bottom. He was a good horseman, and could impart to his steed something of the resolution which, at any time, might nerve himself. Rising in his stirrups, he applied his whip vigorously. Brome and the constable saw that Darwin would pass them, and in all probability escape, unless violent measures were employed to check his career. The constable sprang from the buggy. On came Darwin at breakneck speed. Brome raised his rifle to his face, and the outlaw saw that he designed to fire, but he did not heed the warning. Both Brome and the constable cried "stop!" but the outlaw passed them.

There was a sharp report—the horse and its rider were prostrated upon the road.

"You've killed him," cried the constable. "Rash, very rash, better let him gone."

"I shot at the horse, not at him," answered Brome calmly, "but I'll take the consequence. He's not dangerously hurt. See, he is getting up."

"Let us go to him," said the constable.

"Go on, but be a little cautious. He's armed, I'll warrant; I'll have a bullet in my rifle before I approach him."

Brome and the constable drew near the outlaw, who had

endeavored to rise, but finding himself unable, leaned upon his elbow. They were within pistol shot when, with a quick movement, he fired at them, and for Brome the shot had been fatal, but that the hand that held the pistol was more unsteady than it had ever before been.

"It's no use, Darwin," said the constable; "you may as well give up."

"Never, to you, dogs—take that;" with these defiant words Darwin fired a second pistol, but Sedley was watching him, and the bullet missed its aim.

Evidently Darwin was dangerously injured. The bullet had struck his horse in the shoulder, causing him to stumble, and Darwin was thrown forward violently; his skull was fractured, and blood-vessels in his body had been ruptured. Blood flowed from his mouth as he spoke. He felt that his final hour had come, and he said:

"Yes, you, Harry Brome, *Esquire*. You had been glad to have killed me outright. You wanted an excuse to shoot me. Dead men tell no tales; but I can talk yet, and I can tell it all, and I will. You've been after me to make folks believe I killed that young Etherege. You are a respectable man, I am a counterfeiter, but if I had strength enough I'd show you that I am not as much of a scoundrel as you are. Take that man, take him, Constable Sedley. I'm a dying man, and I tell you that he's a murderer. He killed his friend Etherege. He shot him for his money."

"Villain, you die with a monstrous lie on your soul. Your life has been one continued crime, and what can you expect to gain by this false charge? Nobody will believe it," cried Brome with vehemence.

"Ask Billy Mervin—ask Deacon Anstey or grocer Sandys, or—"

"Villains like yourself," cried Brome.

"They can show you up, though, and they will. They know who's got that chap's money. I aint the first man you've shot at, but maybe I'm the last." (Darwin raised himself up as he spoke.) "I'd be sure of *that* if I had a pistol. You'd go to hell with me."

Darwin gasped as he uttered this threat, and Sedley stooped down to support him, but the outlaw made a motion as if to grasp his knife, and the constable allowed him to fall back on the ground. It was evident he could not survive long, and Sedley wished to put him in Brome's buggy and convey him to the village, but he would not be moved. Brome and Sedley consulted upon the course they should pursue, and Brome said:

"You stay here; I'll go to the village and get help."

"No, no," gasped Darwin; "don't let him—he'll never come back."

Whether influenced by these words or not, the constable would not consent that Brome should depart, and as Darwin had grown so weak he could no longer resist, Sedley insisted that he should be put in the buggy. Brome assisted, and the outlaw was placed where he could be drawn to the village. Sedley supported him, and Brome led the horse. They had not gone far when Sedley said:

"It's over; he's dead."

CHAPTER VIII.

THE VILLAGE GOSSIP.

Slowly Brome's buggy, bearing the dead body of the outlaw, was driven into the village. Constable Sedley directed that it should stop at Barton's tavern, and immediately it was surrounded by an anxious, gossip-loving circle. Each one asked many questions, and then repeated what had not been answered. But few received definite information concerning the manner of Darwin's destruction, and the village buzzed with false rumors. The story most frequently told was that Brome had met Darwin; that the lawyer had charged Darwin with the murder of Etherege; that the outlaw returned the charge, and swore he saw Brome kill his friend; and that Brome then shot him. In all the rumors, facts were distorted to Brome's disadvantage, and it was the general impression that he had committed murder; some thought, in the shooting of Darwin; others, by destroying his friend. A few men and women who knew Brome, from a proper estimate of his character, indignantly branded these rumors as villanious, but many were not at all surprised. It was "just as they expected."

Among the latter class was a prominent member of Parson

Humiston's church—Mrs. Prime. She had often wondered that the Parson went so often to Brome Cottage, and came so seldom to her house. She never missed a sermon—the Bromes often did; she never disputed about doctrines—the Bromes often did; nobody ever saw her walking for pleasure on Sunday; she didn't even stroll in the churchyard, nor would she allow her children to pick flowers there. All of the ordinances of the church were observed by her, and more too. But few of them, according to her judgment, did the Bromes observe, and yet Parson Humiston was scarcely cordial to her, while he went every week, at least once, to Brome Cottage. He didn't preach as sternly as he had years before, and he must be falling from grace. Oh, it was enough to make any body fall from grace to be often in that Brome Cottage. There was a "*wicked pianer*"—and there were novels, a great many novels, and sometimes there was dancing; and some folks said there had been card-playing; and Harry Brome and Alice Brome went to meeting when they chose. No wonder he was a bad fellow! O, he had the worst temper. He must have, because his mother always had done just as wise Solomon said worldly women would *do*, "Spare the rod and spoil the child." No wonder he had committed murder. It was what Mrs Prime expected!

A soliloquy of this character Mrs. Prime indulged in the hearing of Mr. P. He was a quiet man. His wife had a will, and her will was enough for the whole family, but sometimes he dared indulge unexpressed opinions; and while Mrs. P. ran on about the Bromes, he gratified himself with the reflection, that if his wife was a little like Mrs. Brome he wouldn't complain; and as for Harry Brome's having committed murder, it was simply fudge.

In the gratification of this opinion, the quiet, humble man rather forgot himself, and he concluded his reverie by deliberately spitting on the floor, close by Mrs. P., who was industriously knitting, but not so industriously that she failed to observe the sin her careless husband had committed.

"Oh, la me," sighed she, "these men *are* all alike. Now, these fifteen years I've been talking, and talking, and it's no use."

Perhaps these latter words were addressed to Mr. P.'s actions, or perhaps bore reference to the lack of success in her talking. At all events, the humble man was exerting himself to eradicate all appearance of the stain he had made upon the home-made carpet.

Mrs. Prime (it ought to have been Prim) was a professing Christian, and she was precise in her profession, yet she was an idolater. She had a household idol, and incessantly she worshiped it. Every action, every movement, was a devotion to it, and it was an imp. Her thin form bore testimony in each article of dress, in every motion, to the ruling power of this household idol. Poor Mr. P., how often he wished that his wife could be converted from her idolatry. He would cheerfully have dispensed with his dinner every day for a year, could he by his own starvation have exorcised the imp which monopolized her affections.

"Every thing is very neat about you," said an intimate friend one day when Mrs. P. was not in hearing.

"Oh, Lord, yes," answered Mr. Prime; "but there's reason in all things, except some women, and my wife's one of them. I like order and neatness, but there are other comforts in the world besides order and neatness, only my wife don't know them. The 'imp of neatness is her idol.'"

"Hands off"—"don't put me out of place," could be read from every portion of Mrs. P.'s household as distinctly as if each article bore a printed label. The prevailing rule was that every thing was to be kept clean and in order. There were few things for use—ease; comfort was rarely, very rarely, calculated upon.

At Brome Cottage order and system were observed, but there was no severity, no stiffness. You felt at home in its parlors. When Mrs. P.'s parlors were entered, the visitor shrank like one intruding in a circle which was sacred to silence and severity. Mrs. P. never went to Brome Cottage but she said, "Oh, my, how things *are* knocked about here. There's no rule about this house. It's all vanity."

Therefore it was to be expected that when she heard the rumors about Brome and Darwin, she would half close her cold gray eyes, and looking down over her narrow chin, say:

"Well, well, any body might have known he'd come to *some* bad end."

Thus this precise woman concluded, from her own standard, without evidence, without reflection. The world is full of opinions just as shrewd; with just as good a basis.

While Madame Prime was giving Mr. P. a piece of her mind about a man's duty in his own house, and about the wickedness of such doings as she knew had been at Brome Cottage, Harry was conversing with his mother about the troubles which thickened around him. He said:

"I am the victim of a conspiracy, mother, and it comes from a quarter of which I had no suspicion when I first resolved to ferret out the counterfeiters. The outlaws, Darwin,

Anstey, Sandys, and the others, are but the servants, the hired instruments, of men who have bigger schemes than were ever yet projected in this country. I have only a hint of what they are at, but it comes from a reliable source, and soon I shall know it all; that is, I shall know it, if they do not triumph. I am in great danger, mother. There are men against me who have influence and money. They will not hesitate to take all possible advantage of Darwin's declaration against me, and circumstances will be brought forward that may enable them to make out a plausible case. They will have me arrested if they can, in the hope of keeping me from pursuing them, but, should they even succeed in getting a verdict against me, of branding me as a murderer, they shall not escape."

Harry had never so fully explained to his mother what he knew of, and what he had to fear from, the counterfeiters. She was now much moved at the picture he drew, but she had faith in the right, and she said:

"I must regret Darwin's death, but I cannot blame you. Let your enemies do what they may, they cannot sustain his charge against you, and unless they kill you, as they have poor Etherege, you will in the end triumph. I fear for your life, Harry."

"You need not, mother. The counterfeiters dare not assassinate me now. Such an act would ruin their schemes. But, mother, I do not believe they killed Etherege."

"And who did, then?"

"I am persuaded that he was not killed. I believe he was made a prisoner in some of their dens. They may let him starve to death, but I do not think they have assassinated him. Against all appearances, this conviction hangs to me."

"May your conviction prove correct and may he be restored to us," said Mrs. Brome, devoutly, "but I can see no foundation for such a hope. He is murdered, and you may be arrested as his murderer. Oh, my God, how little do we know what grief a day may bring forth. It had been better, Harry, if you had let the counterfeiters alone."

"But, mother, I could not."

"No, Harry, you could not. That is true. Now, you must triumph."

"I feel, mother, that severe trials are in store for us, but I am confident of triumph in the last hour, and perhaps it will be shown us that the kind offices of love and charity we have dispensed in this neighborhood have more power, when affliction overtakes us, than the enmity of narrow bigots who envy us, or the villainy of scoundrels who fear us. I know we have a few friends, mother, who can be relied upon. How does Alice take the bad news?"

"She is much distressed. She has never been herself since Etherege disappeared; and now she is inconsolable."

"I will find her and cheer her up."

Mrs. Brome went about her household duties with a troubled spirit, yet with a faith which enabled her to appear as if no fears oppressed her.

Harry sought Alice. They had a long and earnest conversation, and when they parted, Brome had renewed interest in the solution of the mystery which hung about the fate of Etherege.

CHAPTER IX.

COUNTERPLOTS.

Harry had determined while talking with Alice to go to the village, and, if possible, ascertain the character of the gossip concerning him. He walked immediately to Barton's tavern. When he opened the door, and allowed a breath of fresh air to disturb the fumes of whisky and tobacco which hung about the stove, there was quite a buzz among the loungers who had met to smoke, drink, and talk over the news. In this group there was a stranger, who took no part in the conversation, and who neither drank nor smoked. He had, however, been an attentive listener to the talk about Brome, and the speculations in regard to Darwin's death. Brome at once observed this man. There was commanding character in his face and form and bearing. Brome gazed at him intently. He did not meet the gaze frankly and boldly, and Harry puzzled his wits to answer to himself, why. The conversation stopped. Brome saw that he was an intruder, and, after exchanging a few words with Barton, went out. The door had not entirely closed behind him when the stranger arose, and inquired of the landlord:

"Can you tell me that young man's name?"

"I reckon I can—that's the chap they're talkin' about. He's the fellow that put a bullet in Darwin, a man who could drink twice as much whisky as any other man in this county."

The stranger immediately followed Brome, but he was not quick enough to observe that the young lawyer had been met by a man who on an important occasion had vowed to befriend him, and who was about to tell him that the tall, handsome man he had seen before Barton's bar-room stove was an individual from whom he had more to fear than from Sandys or Anstey, or any other of their village accomplices. Having communicated this information, Harry's friend said:

"You go home, and I'll watch. There's to be plotting done to-night, and I know where, and I mean to know what it is, but, Harry Brome, you will stand by me if I get in trouble by it. I am sober now. I have been all day, and I shall not drink to-night."

"You know you can depend on me, Tickell. Keep the promise you now make, and I can depend on you. Remember every thing depends on you to-night."

"You needn't fear," answered Tickell, as he wrung Brome's hand. Harry went directly home, while his companion stealthily returned to the village.

Tickell visited Barton's tavern, and made a hasty survey of the bar-room, then he turned his face toward Sandys' grocery. As he approached it he saw the door open, and the light which gleamed into the street showed him that the tall, handsome man who had attracted Brome's attention in the tavern, was about to give Grocer Sandys a call. Tickell was tempted to follow the stranger at once, but he had plans to further which could be best prosecuted, for the present, outside of the grocery. He had heard that Mervin, Tom Darwin's closest confidant, was in the village, and he wished to see him. Mervin and he had been old chums, and he was certain that if he could induce the villain to warm himself with a few social glasses, he could gain some profitable information from him. Tickell suspected that Mervin would visit the grocery, and it was his intention to watch for and fall in with him. While he was watching, Deacon Anstey entered the grocery. Tickell grew tired of his dull task, and determined to see why the handsome stranger and the sly deacon had called upon the grocer. When he presented himself before the counter he found no one in attendance but a flaxen-haired boy, who was known to be remarkable for his dullness. This boy was more dull than usual, being apparently half asleep, and Tickell could not ascertain from him whether Sandys had been at home that evening or not. The boy knew nothing. Tickell's suspicions were highly excited, and his curiosity to know why Anstey and the stranger had called on Sandys and gone into secret council was intense, but as he had received no intimation of the meeting, he dared not venture to intrude upon the circle. He was reluctantly obliged to retrace his footsteps back to Barton's. However, he did not give up hope of meeting Mervin. Barton knew the outlaw's friend, and Tickell applied to him for information concerning his hiding place.

"He's been wanting to see you," said Barton, "and I'll tell him you are here."

"You can give us a place for a little private confab, and something to keep us awake?"

"On terms, Tickell. You know, on terms."

"Of course; I'm in luck just now, and can stand one treat."

This was said in a tone Barton understood, and with a sly wink he conducted Tickell to a small back room, in which many dark and drunken scenes had been enacted, then went in quest of Mervin. He was not long absent, and when Mervin entered the den of secret carousal where Tickell awaited him, he cried:

"Good for a big time, old chum. I expected to've been out of this town to-night, but circumstances was agin me, and I'm not in the best of spirits. I'd just as lief take a jollify with you as any other fellow."

"All right, then," answered Tickell, shaking the rough hand extended to him. "You see I've got the documents."

"You're a clever chap, and you'll join me in a big glass to Tom Darwin. Curse my stars if I don't want to put a ball in that fellow who stopped him with his rifle, but then I won't. There's a worse trap set for him than I could manage."

"You mean Brome."

"I jist do."

"I understand, Mervin, but I'm afraid it won't work. That fellow's got some friends in this town, and they'll make a big fuss."

"Who cares? It must work. It's fixed right, and any how that fellow goes out of the way."

"Which fellow?" asked Tickell, with a knowing wink.

"Why, Brome, of course; t'other one's already fixed. Tom Darwin's not a man to half do things. But I'll tell you, Tickell, sometimes I'm a little squeamish. If it could have been done, I'd 've squared things up one way or t'other."

"Squared things up one way or t'other. I don't exactly understand."

"Then you don't know quite as much as I reckoned you did. You'll have to wait a spell before you do. You're all right, Tickell, but I can't let you in just yet. You know I am one of the chaps that can't be pumped."

"And I'm one of the chaps that wouldn't try to pump you, but I'll own up that I don't know all about this scheme you're in with Etherege and Brome, and I'd like to be a little better posted, because I've got to work, and I can't work in the dark, and what's more, I won't try. Neither Anstey nor Sandys, nor that handsome new fellow, Leyton, can make a blind tool out of me."

"You're right, Tickell, and that makes me think of it. I promised to sneak up to the grocery to-night, and if you come along, maybe your peepers will be opened."

To this proposition Tickell demurred. He said he had calculated on a good social time, and he didn't like to give it up, but Mervin said:

"Pshaw, come along; we'll have a good time up there. The old grocer will have to tap some of his choice kegs."

After feigning to take a starting drink with the outlaw, Tickell grasped his arm, and the two worthies marched cautiously toward the grocery.

CHAPTER X.

PLOTS THICKEN.

Deacon Anstey, Grocer Sandys, and the handsome stranger had been for several hours engaged in earnest conversation. The stranger whom Anstey called Colonel Leyton, with a submissive emphasis on the *Colonel*, had visited Cuyahoga village for the purpose of completing arrangements to prosecute a banking system, exceeding in magnitude any scheme of the character which had ever been prosecuted in America. He was quite surprised and very much chagrined to learn that the friends on whom he relied were suspected, and were involved in an enterprise, to relieve themselves, which threatened to explode his plans to their fullest extent.

"The whole of it is bad," he said. "I told you long ago Darwin wasn't to be trusted. He was always reckless. He never valued any body's life, and didn't care how much peril he brought on his associates."

"That's a fact, Colonel," said Anstey. "I was always afraid of him."

"And that's another fact," retorted Sandys, "I believe he hated you, and that's the reason we're in this scrape. Unless Harry Brome is got out of the way, we'll all wear striped trowsers."

"Come, come, friends, this is no time for wrangling. We're in a bad scrape, and must make the best of it. If I had known yesterday, however, what I know to-day, I had not been here to-night; but I am satisfied every thing depends on shutting up the fellow you call Brome. Can't he be bought?"

"Bought!" said Anstey. "Bought. You might as well talk about buying a flash of lightning if you were in a dark corner—"

"Them's my sentiments," said Sandys slowly.

"Then he must be convicted of the murder of the missing man you call Etherege. There's no other way," answered the Colonel.

"And as soon as he is arrested, he'll blow on us."

"That risk you must take, Mr. Sandys," said the Colonel. "But I don't believe he will. He's not had a chance to get enough to blow on, unless you have some traitor among you here. Do you suspect any body?"

"Let me see," said Anstey. "I guess Mervin's safe. He was a confidant of Darwin's, but I'm a little suspicious of Tickell. His folks live near Brome Cottage, and Mrs. Brome has often sent them things. He's a good-natured, easy fellow, and we'll have to watch him."

"You'd better watch him, and don't let him know any more than he now does. The plans I have revealed to-night, you must keep to yourselves. But where is that Mervin you spoke of? You tell me he's the only man who really knows whether the devil has that Etherege or not."

"He promised to come up here to-night," answered Sandys, "and it's about time he was coming."

"Well, I'm dry, Sandys," returned Leyton, "suppose you go and fill up the bottle, and see if he's not in the grocery."

Sandys went out of the council-chamber, and Leyton rose and walked backward and forward, while Anstey watched him with a sadly puzzled expression on his countenance.

When Sandys appeared behind his counter in his grocery, he was confronted by two persons who had for some time been waiting his appearance. The grocer was not pleased to see at least one of them, but he must appear as if he was right glad, so, after shaking Mervin's hand, he greeted Tickell with a great show of cordiality. This same show Tickell returned. While he was returning it, he did not fail to observe that Sandys gave Mervin a significant wink.

When Sandys went among his liquor casks in the back part of his grocery, Mervin followed him, and when Sandys again appeared where he could address Tickell, Mervin was not with him.

Tickell was accustomed to peculiar maneuvers on the part of Sandys and Anstey: he was quite disappointed in Mervin's disappearance, but he knew it would be vain to attempt to get in the council, and he resolved to ward off suspicion. He chatted with Sandys a few moments, because he saw that the grocer was itching to get away from him, and did not know how to accomplish it. When he relieved his host's perplexity by declaring that he must go down to Barton's, Sandys used an expression in which cowardly lies are often concealed, in more respectable and worthy company—"You needn't be in a hurry;" but Tickell's "call" to the tavern was peremptory, and he left Sandys rejoicing.

When Tickell went out of the grocery, he was wiser than when he entered it. Over Sandys' best brandy he had had a somewhat satisfactory chat with Mervin, and now, instead of going to Barton's tavern, he went to Brome Cottage.

The grocery door was no sooner closed behind Tickell than Sandys hastened whither he had sent Mervin. He found Leyton, Anstey, and the outlaw talking earnestly. Anstey had been remonstrating, but his influence was overpowered by the others, and Mervin said:

"I am satisfied, Colonel. Here's a witness to the bargain. I know a fellow who was followed by Harry Brome that day; he'll swear that Tom Darwin told the truth. I'll get an affidavit from him to-morrow, and the rest I'll finish before sunrise; but mind you, if the bargain aint kept, I'll blow the whole of you, if my neck is stretched for it."

"You needn't be afraid of us, and we won't of you. You can depend on us, because you know what is our interest, and we can depend on you because we know what is yours, and then you want to revenge Darwin's death."

"That I do, Colonel; and I will, you can bet your life."

Sandys, who had been till now a quiet listener, demanded explanations, which the Colonel gave him. He considered the plans a few moments, and then agreed to do whatever was required of him to further them. His own safety, as he thought, was involved in their success.

Anstey feared that his safety was involved in the same success, and he feared to have the plans put into execution. If never before in his life, he now regretted the hypocritically wicked career into which his inordinate avarice had led him. He was rich, but he was not respected—not even among his companions in fraud. All his life he had coveted cash, now he coveted character. He drank deeply to overcome his dread emotions, but when he went home, in spite of his maudlin condition, he was racked with accusing fears, wicked hopes and bitter regrets. His curses on himself for his first step in counterfeiting were more expressive than deacons generally are presumed to command.

When Anstey bid his confrères good night, he supposed that Sandys and Leyton had separated for that night. They deceived him. As soon as the Colonel, who went out with Anstey, parted from him on the street, he returned to the grocer's council-room—and when these two schemers had sat down to a third bottle of brandy, Leyton said:

"I believe you're right; Anstey's afraid. He'd back out now, square, if he could. We must hook him in deeper, and it must be done in connection with that devil you've waked up here."

"You mean Brome?"

"Of course I do. It's infernal bad that you should have let him get a clue."

"Let, thunder and lightning. There's no let about it. He saw us in the woods; but then, if it hadn't been for Tom Darwin's dare-devil propensity, and Anstey's cowardice, he'd never troubled us. Now, we're in for it, and he must swing—or at least be jugged till we are safe."

"And Anstey must make him swing."

"That'll be too hard, Colonel. He hates him like poison, but he's too much afraid to take a public stand. I wouldn't be in favor of trusting him—the first man who attacked him would find weak places. He used to have pluck, but he's lost it lately."

"If he don't go it who will?"

"We'll have to depend on Mervin. He's a trump. Excitement is high, and when Mervin's friend gets out a warrant, we'll throw our respectable influence in the scale."

"Our respectable influence—that's a fact, and it will be respectable influence. Let us get out of this fuss, and the scheme is clear."

"That reminds me, Colonel, you were going to give me some more particulars about what's been done."

"It's very late and I must be off, but I can tell you that a large amount of the currency is now ready. Nick Biddle himself couldn't detect the notes. Look at these."

The Colonel handed Sandys half a dozen counterfeit notes on the United States Bank. Sandys' eyes twinkled as he examined them, and when he pronounced them good, the Colonel continued:

"It's a good scheme. We've already made arrangements for a vessel at New Orleans; Johnston, who, you know, is a big merchant in Cleveland, is fully with us, and there are other big men in it. Just let us get our bark into the Gulf of Mexico once, and she shall go straight to China, where, with *our* currency, we can put in a splendid cargo, and before the notes can come back here, we can pocket the profits and take care of ourselves. Think if it is not worth some risk, Mr. Sandys."

Grocer Sandys did think. When Colonel Leyton went staggering to Barton's tavern, long after midnight, Sandys went to bed, but not to sleep. He could not sleep for thinking.

Had the intention of his thoughts been honest, they would not have disturbed his rest.

CHAPTER XI.

THE ARREST.

It was Tuesday morning. Joseph Etherege had been missing since Saturday afternoon. Diligent and thorough search for him had been fruitless. Public opinion declared that he had been murdered for his money. By whom and how? were the absorbing topics of speculation in Cuyahoga village and vicinity. At Brome Cottage speculations on the mysterious fate of its guest had occupied every mind. A thousand conjectures had been indulged, and a thousand plans discussed; but when Harry Brome came home the acknowledged cause of Darwin's death, and immediately was talked of as the only person who could tell what had become of his *friend*, all other plans and conjectures were merged in one comprehensive purpose—to crush his conspiring enemies by exposing their frauds, at the same time revealing the mystery of Etherege's fate, and the true cause of his death or abduction.

Mrs. Brome and Harry had met Tickell at a late hour in the night, and they were seated at a late breakfast when a servant entered the room and said a gentleman wished to see Mr. Brome.

Harry went out and met Constable Sedley. He invited

the officer into the cottage, but the invitation was declined. "My business is with you—it's a little particular and I don't like it, but I must do my duty, and I wouldn't like to alarm your mother and sister. I've only a little document to show you."

He handed Brome a small slip of paper, and Harry read it carefully, without any outward emotion. It was a warrant for his arrest as the murderer of Joseph Etherege. It had been issued upon the oath of Ben Danmer, an easy-going, indolent young man, who hung about Barton's tavern, and who drove a team, or chopped wood, when his necessities required him to work—when Barton would not trust him for board or for whisky, unless "the old score was wiped out." He had been chopping for Barton on Saturday, near the place at which Etherege disappeared.

"Walk into the house, Mr. Sedley. I must show this to my mother."

The constable was confused, and he made no reply, but mechanically followed Brome.

When he entered the breakfast-room, Mrs. Brome bid him good morning, and invited him to be seated, but he stood near the door changing his hat from one hand to the other, and said:

"It's mighty unpleasant, Mrs. Brome, but I'm a public officer, a servant, madam, and must do my duty."

Harry had handed the warrant to his mother, and she only bowed in response to the constable's apology.

"Who was with Mr. Danmer when this warrant was issued?" asked Mrs. Brome.

"Well, there was several at the 'Squire's. I recollect Deacon Austey," said the constable.

"There can be no bail given?"

"Not in such a case, madam."

"Harry must go with you to prison, then?"

"Yes, ma'am, but not just now to real jail. He's goin' to be examined in the village, maybe this afternoon, maybe to-morrow, and till then he'll have to be shut up in a room at Barton's."

"Your instructions are that he shall go there?"

"That's the distressing fact, ma'am."

As the constable spoke these words in a tone of sympathy, he looked sharply at Mrs. Brome. He could not understand her. She was so calm.

"Do you know any of the evidence on which it is expected to sustain this charge?" said Harry.

"Well, I can't say I do, but I heard Danmer say that he could swear what Tom Darwin told me was true, because he was with Darwin when it was done. I don't know as I ought to say any thing about it, but that's all I know."

"That's what I or any body else could have guessed, and you run no risk in telling it," returned Brome.

The constable did not like this response, and he said:

"Well, Mr. Brome, we needn't dispute, but we'll go to the village as soon as you are ready."

Harry looked at his mother inquiringly, and she said:

"Go, Harry, at once. Alice went over to Mr. Humiston's to see Edith, who came home last night. We'll all come down to see you when she returns."

"I am your prisoner, Mr. Sedley," said Harry.

The constable led the road and Harry followed, after whispering to his mother that Tickell must be seen before night.

Harry Brome had not been a prisoner at Barton's tavern

half an hour before all the people of the village were discussing the probabilities of his examination by the village 'Squire. The bar-room was crowded, and the landlord did a "thriving" business.

Mrs. Prime was not at all disappointed when the news of the arrest reached her ears. Of course she had expected it. But she was very sorry for Mrs. Brome. She would go at once and suggest the consolations of religion to her. When neighbors were in trouble it was Christian-like for their friends to give them religious counsel. Immediately Mrs. Prime was "fixed up" and on her way to Brome Cottage. It seemed to her that it was a long time before her knock was answered. But the folks were in trouble and she must excuse them, she supposed. At length Mrs. Brome answered the summons in person.

What a contrast there was in the appearance and bearing of those two women as they met. One was calm, and dignified and commanding. Her dress was of plain, soft material, and without ornament. Mrs. Prime was restless, suspicious, and forbidding. Two little tight curls, which peeped out from the lining of her bonnet, were kept in perpetual motion by her restlessness. She wore a plain black silk dress. The sharp lines of its folds, as they fell over her thin frame, were in keeping with the jealous severity of her character.

It always seemed to me that a generous-hearted, true woman should never wear harsh, black silk. There is a class of narrow-minded, ill-tempered, severe women, with whose characteristics it is in keeping. They admire it; it becomes them; and, as it is not in harmony with a liberal, hopeful character, to disappointed, soured spinsters, and wives and maidens who will be cross and jealous, and carry unhappiness wherever they go, it ought by other women to be wholly surrendered.

But though, in plain silk, Mrs. Prime, with jewels and ribbons, made quite a rich show. She never went visiting or to church without giving her neighbors good reason to believe that vanity, as well as gossip, was one of her characteristics, and, having an impression to make at Brome Cottage, as a matter of course, she appeared "to the best possible advantage."

Mrs. Brome did not invite her in. She stood in the hall with an inquiring expression on her countenance, which plainly enough said—"Mrs. Prime, what is the occasion of your call this morning?"

"You will excuse me, Mrs. Brome, but really I have heard that Mr. Brome had been taken by the constable this morning, and I didn't know but you might be in trouble, and I came to inquire if any of our church could render you any assistance."

"I thank you, Mrs. Prime, for any sympathy you may have, but you could afford us no aid. I know my son to be the victim of a wicked conspiracy, and he needs no defense which his character will not make for him."

"But it's terrible, Mrs. Brome, and you'll allow me to recommend to you the consolations of the Gospel."

"The same recommendation I have had before this morning from your worthy minister, with whom I was conversing when you knocked."

"Ah! then my poor words come late, but you'll have my prayers, Mrs. Brome."

"Thank you," said Mrs. Brome, bowing; and Mrs. Prime bowing in return, retreated, for she was not dull of apprehension, and she had become convinced that she was not needed at Brome Cottage.

As she went away she said to herself, "How she froze me off. I never did like her. I can't have any more charity. Parson Humiston! yes, I'll warrant he's there. He's most too thick there. I just believe Harry Brome will be convicted, and then what'll Parson Humiston say?"

Mrs. Brome had no uncharitable remarks to make when she parted from Mrs. Prime, but very likely she could not entertain very high respect for a person who, on the pretense of giving pious consolation, would endeavor to intrude upon her grief for the sake of getting materials for gossip. Poor Mrs. Prime, her selfishness and vanity and jealousy were transparent. She was one of a class which is quite numerous in even this day of "progress." When we are in deep trouble true friends are rare, but often those are numerous who pretend to give us sympathy for the sake of getting our confidence, that they may know how weak or how hardhearted we are, and make capital out of our infirmities.

CHAPTER XII.

THE PRISONER.

HARRY BROME had been a prisoner for one day. His mother and Alice, Parson Humiston and Edith Humiston, his daughter, had visited him. He was stronger in spirit than when his arrest was made, but he had yet been stronger if Alice had not appeared overcome with painful fears and conjectures. She would have been entirely prostrated, but that she leaned in spirit as well as body, upon Edith Humiston, who was as dear as a sister to her. She was older and sterner than Alice. They differed widely in appearance. Timidity and reserve were to be read in Alice's deep-blue eyes. Edith was tall and commanding. She was not unwomanly bold, but she was not timid. She had black hair, and very black eyes. They were small, bright, keen eyes. Alice had not feared to give Edith suspicions of her regards for the man whom her brother was accused of having murdered, but how eloquently had she plead that brother's innocence! Edith needed no eloquence to convince her of Brome's innocence. She would not have believed that he could decoy a friend into the woods and murder him for his money, even if his sister had feared that he was guilty.

During the visit of these friends, Brome had no opportunity to ascertain satisfactorily what Tickell was doing for him. Whenever company was permitted to enter his prison-room, he was closely watched. But Mrs. Brome had scarcely returned to Brome Cottage when Tickell slily visited her, and she was assured that he was yet true to their interests. Upon leaving Mrs. Brome with this assurance, he went to Barton's tavern, keenly on the alert for any hints which might aid him in his determination to serve Brome at the expense of the counterfeiters. He believed that Joseph Etherege had not been killed, but that, in some safe retreat about the village or in the woods, he was a prisoner like Brome, at the mercy of the counterfeiters. To satisfy himself whether his conjecture was true was now his purpose. He mingled in the throng at Barton's, and was not modest in his denunciations of Brome, but he met none of those from whom he expected to derive advantage in the furtherance of his design. He wished to meet either Mervin or Danmer, or both. While he searched for them, they were in secret council with Leyton, Sandys, and Anstey. In that council plans were fully arranged for the conviction of Brome before the magistrate. The examination would take place the following day. The "testimony" was all prepared. In company with a village lawyer who had long been one of Brome's jealous enemies, the task of this preparation had been committed to Deacon Anstey. Danmer's story was shrewdly concocted, and he had learned his "lesson." This accomplished, Mervin and Danmer were permitted to take leave of the leading conspirators, and when they were gone, Sandys said:

"I think it's a sure thing now. We need not appear in

it at all; Constable Sedley is completely our dupe, and he can make out case enough to jug Mr. Brome till court time, which is two months yet."

"It's all right, I think," answered Leyton. "Two months are enough. We can all take care of ourselves in that time."

"Maybe, and maybe not," said Anstey. "We've got to go on, I suppose, now, but we're only getting ourselves deeper into the trouble, and I wish I was out of the whole of it."

"As much of a coward as ever," retorted Sandys. "We know you, Deacon Anstey, and there's no escape for you. You must go on; if you don't, you're a dead man, if I have to shoot you myself. We're in a devil of a pickle now, that's a fact, but we've got to go through it, and then you can go to the devil if you want to; I'm going somewhere else."

"I'm not so much of a coward, Mr. Sandys, as to be afraid of your shooting," answered Anstey, "but I'm afraid your somewhere else will be to the penitentiary, and that we will all go together. If you'd taken my advice long ago, we would not have been in this pickle."

"Hold on!" cried Leyton. "It's no use to quarrel among ourselves now. Let's wait and see what's done to-morrow. I promised to see Lawyer Swift to-night, and it's time I was hunting him up."

The parting between Sandys and Anstey was sullen. Each was really afraid of the other. Sandys would have been glad to have seen Anstey in limbo could he have escaped himself; and if any friend of Brome's had gained Anstey's confidence that night, he might have learned the true cause of the young lawyer's imprisonment.

With fears and passions which threw him in a state of mind justifying such conclusions, Anstey sought for Danmer. He did not find him. Mervin, Danmer and Tickell had accidentally met, and Mervin bantered Tickell to finish the spree they began the night previous. Tickell was not slow to accept this banter. It was a short spree, for Mervin had important business to transact that night; but before it was over, Tickell learned that Anstey and Sandys somewhat suspected him, and when Mervin left him to transact the business on which he excused himself from longer remaining in his company, Tickell had a curiosity to know the nature of that business. He did not express that curiosity to his companions, but he gratified it by following their footsteps. They went to the office of Lawyer Swift, where they met Leyton, with whom Mervin had a few moments' secret conversation. Then he took leave of Danmer, telling him he would meet him early in the morning. Tickell cautiously followed the outlaw. He was impressed that something important to Brome depended on his actions that night, and he was determined to know whither he wandered and what he did.

Mervin went down through the village, and crossed the bridge over the falls of the river. There was no moon, but it was a clear autumn night, and Tickell found no difficulty in pursuing the conspirator. He followed the same path Darwin took on the morning they met at the spring in the woods. He walked rapidly, and sometimes talked to himself. Tickell saw that he was bearing toward that part of the forest where Etherege had disappeared, and his impression that with the fate of the missing man, Mervin's business for the night had some association, grew stronger.

For half an hour the pursuit was easy—then the wind rose, and occasional clouds crossed the sky—Mervin was, by this time, in the deep woods. He drew a small lantern from his coat pocket, and having lighted it, pushed forward with quickened steps. Tickell's difficulties multiplied, but he succeeded in keeping within sight of the lantern's glow. Mervin climbed a hill and descended into a ravine. He walked through this ravine till he reached a point where the rocks were large and numerous. Then he halted and opened his lantern so that it threw light on all sides. Tickell could now more easily follow the conspirator, notwithstanding the ruggedness of the path. He found himself at the opening of a cave. His heart beat heavily—his breath was almost suspended. In his anxiety he forgot necessary caution. He stumbled over a fragment of a rock, and fell with a groan. In an instant, Mervin threw the light of his lantern in the direction of the groan, and saw Tickell gather himself up. He did not recognize him, but he drew a pistol and fired. The aim was not sure, and Tickell gained his feet unharmed. With all his energy, he grasped a fragment of rock and hurled it at the conspirator. The aim was better than had been that of Mervin's pistol. The conspirator was knocked down; his lantern was broken, and its light extinguished.

CHAPTER XIII.

THE EXAMINATION.

It was cold, drizzly and dreary—that day on which Harry Brome was to be examined on suspicion that he, a young man who had borne a character previously above reproach, had deceived a guest at his mother's house, under base pretense of friendship, and had murdered him for his money. What dishonest speculation could he have engaged in, that he so pressingly needed the money as to go to so terrible an extremity to get it? was a conjecture often indulged among a portion of the villagers; others said it was possible that he did murder Etherege, but not for his money. Some sudden quarrel must have arisen. Perhaps there was jealousy between them—perhaps he might have revenged himself for some family insult, real or fancied.

These and many other suppositions were gossiped upon as the number increased whom curiosity had brought together to hear the examination. Notwithstanding the storm, which grew colder as the day advanced, not only the citizens of the village gathered in and around the tavern, but people came from the country, anxious to learn all that had transpired, and all the stories about what was expected to transpire. There was no office in the town large enough to hold half the people who wished to hear the trial. At length Constable Sedley succeeded in obtaining the school-house. The pupils were given a holiday in order that the curiosity of their parents and friends might be gratified in hearing the testimony which was expected to consign to infamy a fellow-being, who was just then at the threshold of active life.

About ten o'clock 'Squire Park carried his " authorities " to the school-house. He was followed by Constable Sedley, with Brome in custody. The prisoner was accompanied by his mother and sister. Parson Humiston and his daughter were not far from the Brome family. Behind and around the group which the constable conducted, swarmed men, women and children, who were determined to see all that was to be seen, and hear all that was to be heard.

Harry and his mother looked in vain among the faces staring at them, for Tickell's well-known features. They had been expecting tidings from him since the evening previous. Now they feared that his designs were suspected, and that the counterfeiters had dealt foully with him. On the other hand, the leading conspirators were disturbed by the non-appearance of Mervin. When last seen, he had promised to meet Danmer early in the morning. He had not again been heard from. Could he have fled? was he a traitor? or had he been waylaid? He was a slippery fellow. When he did not keep his appointments, there was reason to fear that he had gone over to the enemy for a bigger bribe.

All this Deacon Anstey considered, and he was very nervous. Leyton did not show himself. Sandys was quite as much disturbed as Anstey, but he could more successfully conceal his inquietude.

Brome had so far depended on Tickell that he had not prepared even the form of a defense without him. His own knowledge, combined with what Tickell was to secure proof of, was, in his judgment, sufficient to confound the conspirators and expose their infamous designs.

Tickell had failed to furnish the aid promised, at the hour when it could alone be made available in the examination. Brome must meet it alone. His lawyer was a tried friend, and a shrewd cross-questioner. He could be depended upon to sift the "testimony" thoroughly.

The 'Squire opened his court; the witnesses were called, and the examination proceeded in regular order.

It was proven that Brome and Etherege had gone away from the village in a buggy. The farmer, of whom Etherege bought land, testified to the particulars of their visit to him, and he was required to dwell particularly on the fact that Etherege had said he intrusted the use of his money to Brome. Other testimony of a technical character was adduced; then it was proven that Brome returned to the village in a great excitement—that he showed to several persons a handkerchief stained with blood, which had belonged to Etherege—that thorough search had been made for Etherege.

When Constable Sedley was called upon the stand, he gave clearly the incidents of the meeting with Darwin. Danmer was the next witness. Brome's lawyer had not as yet cross-examined one of the witnesses. He moved forward when Danmer took the stand and gazed intently at him. Danmer did not quail under the gaze. It had been anticipated that Danmer would be the first witness, but in Lawyer Swift's judgment, it was better that something of a case should be made out before Mr. Danmer subjected himself to scrutiny.

Just as Danmer had taken his oath, a note was handed to Brome. His face glowed as he read it. He showed it to his mother, and her face glowed more brightly than her son's had. His counsel read it without change of countenance and put it in his vest pocket, as if it were of little account, but Danmer had noticed the interest with which Brome and his mother perused it, and he was somewhat disconcerted. He managed, however, to answer calmly, when Lawyer Swift asked if he knew the prisoner.

"Did you see him on Saturday last?"

"Yes sir."

"Where?"

"I saw him at his mother's cottage in the morning, and in the afternoon I saw him in the woods below the village."

"What was he doing?"

"I had been chopping wood and was coming to the village with Tom Darwin, who said he'd been out shootin' squirrels, when I heard loud words. We listened a minute, and then we hurried up and saw Mr. Brome and Mr. Etherege."

"You had seen Etherege before?" said the lawyer.

"Yes sir—several times."

"What were Mr. Etherege and Mr. Brome doing?"

"Mr. Etherege was doing nothing. I thought Mr. Brome had been striking him with his rifle. I was going to rush on Brome, when Tom Darwin stopped me. He said he wanted to see a fight between them fellows, and nobody should interfere. He'd blow my brains out if I made a sign. I didn't care about having my brains blown out, and I kept still. It was good, Tom Darwin said; Brome knew a little too much about him, and now he'd got him. Let him kill t'other fellow. I knew Darwin didn't care what he did, and I was afraid of him."

"What kind of a place was it where this affray occurred?"

"It was in a ravine which many folks know out there. There's a big cave in the hill, and it was right close to this cave. I was on top of the hill when I heard the noise."

"What did Brome do with Etherege after you came up?"

"He didn't do any thing. Etherege was dead then, as near as I could see."

"Did you stay there and watch Brome?"

"No."

"And why didn't you?"

"Tom Darwin wouldn't let me. He said he'd shoot me if I didn't come away, and if I'd keep still a few days he'd pay me."

"What was Darwin's motive for requiring you not to tell what you had seen?"

"I don't know. He didn't give me any reason, only that he had a spite agin Brome, and he wasn't ready yet to blow on him."

"Did you see Brome strike Etherege?"

"No, but I'm sure he did."

"Why?"

"I know from his actions. He cut up like a guilty man."

There had been a death-like stillness in the court-room. When Lawyer Swift said he had asked all the questions he thought necessary, there was a buzz of conversation, but it stopped as he turned to Brome's lawyer and said, with a triumphant air:

"Take the witness."

Lawyer Farley looked sharply at Danmer and said:

"You were a friend of Tom Darwin's?"

"Not much."

"You know Deacon Anstey, and Grocer Sandys, and Billy Mervin?"

"Have seen them."

"Well, when did they concoct for you this story which you have just told?"

"I hope the witness will not be insulted," said Lawyer Swift.

"Not at all," replied Farley. "It's a civil question. He can answer it easily. Come, Mr. Danmer, give us the time."

The witness made no response. There had been a murmur of astonishment in the audience. Now all was hushed. Deacon Anstey and Grocer Sandys were very much interested. The witness was out of his "lesson." He was thrown on his own resources. The deacon and the grocer were anxious to know how he would "dodge" the lawyer.

"You don't answer my question, Mr. Danmer," said the lawyer. "Yonder is Mr. Anstey, and right behind you is Mr. Sandys. They can correct you if you should not give the right date."

"May it please the court," said Lawyer Swift, "I should like to understand the motive of these insinuations against the witness and other respectable citizens of this village."

"May it please the court," answered Lawyer Farley, "we make no insinuations. We mean to show a conspiracy between persons who are now in this house, and some others, to convict Mr. Brome of a crime which their confederates committed. It is a conspiracy to prevent Mr. Brome from bringing them to justice for their villainy. The scheme was well laid, but not so well that it cannot be exposed. We ask that

Mr. Sandys and Mr. Anstey be brought forward and detained as witnesses for the defense."

The order desired in this request was given, and Deacon Anstey and Grocer Sandys were brought within view of all the spectators. They exchanged significantly perplexing glances, and thought with serious emotion of what Brome had seen them at in the forest. Neither of them had ever in the slightest degree imagined that he could be put on the witness stand for Brome. They were very impatient to know what Lawyer Farley would ask next.

" May it please the court," said Lawyer Swift, " it is now afternoon. It is past the usual time for adjournment. I would suggest that the court take a recess."

" We beg the gentleman not to be quite so anxious. We have no objection to a recess, but we shall demand that the witness on the stand be taken into custody," said Farley.

" On what ground ? " demanded Swift.

" That he is perjured," replied Farley.

" This is a remarkable proceeding," said Swift.

" You will think it more remarkable still, when our evidence is all in," answered Farley.

There was a strange feeling of mingled hope and distrust in the audience. The 'Squire felt it. Lawyer Swift perceived it, and rose to take advantage of it.

" May it please the court, I hope this irregular proceeding on the part of the defense may be stopped. It is all founded on presumption—impudent presumption. There is not a particle of proof—"

" There is," rang shrilly from a voice in the back part of the school-house.

At this moment the crowd swayed with excitement, and

cries of "Clear the way," "Clear the way," were uttered by many voices.

From the central aisle the mass of men parted as if a magical wand had fallen between them; at the same time two persons were hurried toward the bar.

"Etherege!" cried Harry Brome.

"Tickell!" cried Anstey and Sandys simultaneously, and with the cry both rose to their feet. In the confusion they would have dashed from the school-house, but Lawyer Farley watched them, and he cried:

"Stop the conspirators!"

Anstey, Sandys and Danmer were immediately in safe custody.

> "The best laid schemes o' mice an' men
> Gang aft a-gley."

Of the meeting between Etherege and Brome and Mrs. Brome, and Alice and Etherege, it is enough to say that there were cries of joy, and tears and congratulations, and rapid questions and quick answers.

CHAPTER XIV.

THE LAST.

The evening after Brome's examination, there was a remarkable revolution in the public opinion of Cuyahoga village. He, who had been a wretch for whom "hanging was too good," was regarded as a deeply-injured young man —a shrewd, useful young man. It was strange, many people said, that so much confidence had been put in the charges of the conspiring counterfeiters.

What of these counterfeiters? Tickell had managed to inform himself of the treacherous designs of Tom Darwin, and of the distrust Leyton and Sandys entertained for Anstey. When he told the whole story of plotting and counterplotting, the penitent deacon was quite vexed, and in his vexation he talked wildly, so wildly that Tickell learned fully the object of Colonel Leyton's visit to Cuyahoga village. It was not hard, then, to persuade the deacon to agree to divulge all his knowledge of the counterfeiters, upon the assurance that he should escape the law's reward. Harry Brome did not learn from the deacon the motives of Etherege's imprisonment, but he did learn fully those for the subsequent conspiracy against his own liberty. Etherege was able, however, to tell a satisfactory story about his capture and detention. His friends were impatient for this story as soon as congratulations on his escape had been given him. Before the Brome family and friends left the school-house, many questions were put to him. He answered them as fully as was possible at the time, but while he and Harry, and Alice and Edith, rode in a carriage from the village to Brome Cottage, he detailed at length the story of his wrongs. He said that Brome had not been absent from him more than a quarter of an hour, when a blow from an unexpected and unseen foe, felled him to the ground. He was rendered insensible. When his consciousness returned, he was a prisoner, in a lone, dark, damp cell, and Tom Darwin was his companion.

"Where am I? What am I a prisoner for?" were his first words.

"You're in *my* jail," answered Darwin with an oath, "and you'll stay here till you learn the fun of spying after other folks's business."

"Where is Harry Brome? What has been done to him?"

"Nothing *yet*," said Darwin with a sinister smile. "He has gone home to tell his folks that you're lost or murdered. They'll hunt you, but they'll not find you. You're safe."

"Safe!" answered Etherege, "in the power of an outlaw—an unscrupulous counterfeiter? Why not murder me at once?"

"That wouldn't suit my purpose," returned Darwin with provoking calmness.

Securely bound, Etherege was too much of a philosopher to indulge impotent rage, and he endeavored to speak calmly to his jailor and learn the cause of his imprisonment, but

Darwin only taunted him. He was compelled to lose his temper or be silent. The outlaw went out from the cell, and was absent several hours. When he returned he was accompanied by Billy Mervin, and, from their conversation, the prisoner learned that his friends at the village were alarmed, and that thorough search was to be made for him. When his captors left him alone again, he hallooed until his strength failed him, in hope some one searching for him would hear the cry. He had no idea, however, of the locality of his prison. For aught he knew, it might be some subterranean vault in the village. His calls for help were therefore given with forlorn hope. There was no light in his cell. He could not distinguish between night and day. Before the second morning of his imprisonment arrived, it seemed to him that many days and many nights must have passed. He could take no note of time. When Mervin and Darwin left him, they had loosened the cords with which his arms were tied, and he had slipped his hands from them. He would have groped about his dungeon, but he feared some trap was left, some pitfall, by which his life would be destroyed, and he dared not venture many steps. He could have welcomed death, but that he hoped for rescue. It was not a flattering tale hope told, but there was encouragement enough in it to render the prisoner tenacious of life. During the first hours, or, as they seemed to him days, of his imprisonment, this tenacity was a sustaining power. It grew weaker and weaker, until he deliberately made up his mind that he must die, in darkness, a lingering death, and no friend ever know his sad fate. No one came to bring him food or drink. When first imprisoned he would have spurned it, but he grew weak and faint, then hungry—intensely, desperately thirsty and hungry. He felt his strength departing. His gnawing hunger and burning thirst seemed to have consumed themselves, and he was left reckless of life; he prayed for death. He thought of the world and all its gladness for a young, healthful, hopeful man, and he wished for death. Whether he thought of Brome Cottage and its inmates especially, he did not say, but his eyes told tales which were, to those who listened, a satisfactory revelation that bitter regrets were blended with his forced resignation.

He wondered how long a man could live without nourishment. He wished to calculate how many days had passed since he was taken prisoner. He could not decide satisfactorily, not because he had not been informed of the power of human endurance, but he could not estimate how much strength had gone from him. At times he was resolute—again he was faint and weak. He passed into a state of forgetfulness—it was not sleep—it was only forgetfulness of his present situation. He lived over again scenes which were dear in his memory. Sweet pleasure surrounded him, when he was startled by a sharp cry—a flash of light pained his eyes. Some one shook him and spoke kind words to him. He aroused himself enough to ask:

"Where am I?"

"With a friend, who comes from Harry Brome. Get out of this dungeon quick, for God's sake," was the answer.

Leaning upon the friend who thus encouraged him, Etherege was assisted from the dungeon into a large underground chamber, where daylight dimly shone. He was too weak to ask explanations. He submitted himself to his guide, and was conducted into the open air. Then he was assisted over and around rocks which jutted from a hill-side. When he reached the bottom of a deep ravine, his guide showed him a horse and wagon. Disguised in a farmer's slouched hat and great coat, he was driven to Cuyahoga village, and ushered into the place where his friend Brome was undergoing examination on suspicion of being his murderer. He recovered his astonishment just in time to complete the "argument" Brome's counsel had interposed to expose the counterfeiters' conspiracy. Tickell had told his story of Etherege's rescue to Brome at the school-house, and when Etherege concluded, Harry briefly sketched Tickell's exploits, beginning with incidents which the course of our Romance has revealed.

When Tickell was left in the cave with Mervin, he dared not call for fear his voice would tell the outlaw where to make a fresh attack, not knowing whether that individual was seriously or slightly wounded. He held his breath and listened. He heard deep groans, then oaths, then the exclamation:

"Come out there, whoever you are; if you wasn't bored when I shot, you needn't be afeard. You did the business for me."

Tickell did not know whether to believe this a sham or the fact, and he kept quiet.

Again and again, the outlaw cursed and called. His voice grew weaker. He swore he was dying. He said:

"I know it—my time's come, and I'll tell you that fellow you're after's here, but I'll be damned if you'll find him. If you'd let me alone a little while, I'd fixed him."

"Damned you'll be, then, Billy Mervin, for I *will* find him," cried Tickell, assured that Mervin could do him no harm.

"Holy Mother! you traitor dog," groaned Mervin.

"Take it easy," Billy, responded Tickell, "the game is up."

Mervin answered with curses, and Tickell groped his way toward the spot, whence the curses proceeded. Accidentally his foot struck some light object. He picked it up, and to his joy discovered that it was Mervin's lantern. Tickell was a smoker, and had with him the means of striking a light. In a moment he was enabled to examine the extent of Mervin's injury. He was not so badly hurt that Tickell dared trust him, and he tied his arms with his handkerchief, and then promised he would help him to escape if he would tell him where to find Etherege.

The stone Tickell hurled struck Mervin on the breast. He was not hurt as badly as he feared. Tickell had no doubt he would recover, and told him so.

Mervin cursed and threatened for some time, but when he became satisfied that he was securely in Tickell's power, and that there was hope of his recovery if he could be taken care of, he consented to give Tickell directions which led him to the dungeon where Etherege pined.

Tickell at once assured himself that Mervin did not deceive, and when daylight came, he went to the nearest farm-house, procured a horse and wagon, and conveyed the outlaw to his own house in the village. He left there the note which was handed to Brome in the school-house, after the examination had opened, then, in hot haste, returned to the cave, and rescued the prisoner.

While the people of Cuyahoga village were gossiping about the remarkable operations of the counterfeiters, and the circumstances of the acquittal of Brome, Tickell arranged for the pursuit of Colonel Leyton, who, early on the morning of the examination, had disappeared. The handsome, accomplished Colonel, he who, while scheming to defraud on a large scale, had been a favored guest of the proudest citizens of not only Cuyahoga village, but of larger towns in Ohio, was arrested and thrown into prison. Subsequently, upon the testimony of Tickell and Anstey, he and Grocer Sandys were sent in company to the penitentiary.

Meantime Constable Sedley was ordered to New Orleans to check the scheme for defrauding people of foreign lands, which Anstey had divulged. It was discovered that a ship had been purchased and was partly laden with stores. Several of the "stockholders" were arrested; others escaped and became restless wanderers, fleeing from justice—fearing recognition—shunning observation.

When the excitement attending his rescue and its results had passed away, Joseph Etherege fell violently sick. For several weeks his life was in imminent danger, but after a favorable crisis, he recovered rapidly. During his illness a "ministering angel" often brought sunshine to his bedside, sunshine that warmed his heart. When his health returned he begged the company, the consolation, the sympathy of that "angel" through health as well as sickness, so long as both should live.

It was Christmas eve. A gay company had assembled at Brome Cottage. There were two brides and two grooms in that company. The drifting snow and the whistling winds were unheeded. The houseless, the homeless, on that stormy night were forgotten by the merry revelers, who were rejoicing in the happiness present and in prospect.

Suddenly there was a wild alarm. A startling cry rang on the night air. It was "FIRE! FIRE!!"

A portion of Brome Cottage was in flames. The wedding guests were driven into the night-storm. Brides and grooms, male and female guests, were soon engaged with hot and nervous energy in efforts to subdue the flames. Water enough could not be procured. The wind was high. Before citizens of the village could reach the scene of painful disaster, the handsome cottage was wrapped in flames. Only a small portion of its valuable furniture was snatched from the fire.

"An incendiary did this," every body said. The morning after the fire, a man was found near the cottage—frozen to death. He was recognized as Billy Mervin. In his death grasp, he had an expired torch.

He had avenged, in his wicked way, the death of Darwin.

Tickell had kept him at his house several weeks, and would have kept him longer, but one night, though weak and penniless, he secretly crept away.

The people of the village never saw him, but Barton the landlord knew he was not far distant, and Barton also knew that, on Christmas eve, he was very drunk, and had made mysterious threats.

"The way of the transgressor is hard."

Anstey was obliged to move west. Tickell chose to emigrate westward also, and so did Barton, whose tavern had become a place of bad repute.

Brome Cottage was not rebuilt, but Harry Brome and Edith his wife, and Mrs. Brome his mother, had a happy home in the village, and there was another happy home there, and Mr. Joseph Etherege and Mrs. Alice Etherege were its master and its mistress.

THE
Bright Eye of the Settlement.

THE BRIGHT EYE OF THE SETTLEMENT.

"When?"

"At seven o'clock, on Thursday morning. We start at eight."

"All right. You can depend on me."

These words were exchanged by two young men in the shaded streets of a quiet New England village.

They had been schoolmates, and were intimate friends. One was about to take leave of the associations of his youth, and of his early manhood—the other had been invited to witness a ceremony which would unite to his friend, through sickness and health, through prosperity and adversity, one who had been to both of them a playmate in youth, but who had been more than a playmate to the elder in manhood. For a few days there had been wide-spread excitement in the little town. A colony for emigration had been organized. The bride and groom of Thursday morning were to join the band of emigrants. They would be the youngest married people in it.

The morn was propitious. There was a joyful wedding—then there were prayerful good wishes, and sad partings.

The honeymoon had passed, and autumn succeeded summer; when, in the midst of a prairie, whose regular undulations reminded the settlers of the ocean, from whose shores they had come, nearly a score of pleasant cottages surrounded a small, white church, and a white school-house.

Remote from other settlements, rarely having society other than that which they found among themselves, being congenial in tastes and opinions, the New England settlers were more cordial—much more closely interested in each other's prosperity or adversity than they had been in the village from which they emigrated.

From gardens around their dwellings they had gathered one rich crop; and a second time flowers had bloomed for them in the apparently boundless field, which stretched away in beautiful lines toward the distant horizon—when the census of their colony numbered one more than it did on the morning their white church was dedicated. There had not been a death—and the youngest bride was a mother.

The little immigrant was what all the maids and all the matrons called a sweet babe. He was a large, fair child, with light, curling hair, and expressive countenance, and clear, blue eyes.

When he grew large enough to run out of doors, and the men met him, as they went to or came from their labors, they called him Bright Eyes. The women often talked of him as a promising child, and all were proud of him as the first-born of the settlement.

Remarkable for beauty, intelligence, and goodness, when he was two years old the settlers were, toward him, as one family. The women were hard workers; the men had rough hands and bronzed faces, but they had tender hearts. Frequently, pains were taken to save nice presents of cake or pie for Bright Eyes, and sometimes a settler took many steps out of his way to carry him a flower, or a handful of berries.

Recognizing a bond of union in love for a little child, the colonists were happier than men often are where honors and riches command the choicest and rarest of the peculiar privileges of refined society.

Whether over all the prairie the fresh beauty of spring, the maturing glory of summer, or the pensive loveliness of autumn attracted attention—whether deep snow reflected the winter sun, or cutting wind swept dark clouds over the settlement, the colonists had time for, and took pleasure in, cheerful, social gatherings, singing-schools, and prayer-meetings.

Often, old and young meeting together, social visiting, singing lessons, and concert of prayer blended their attractions, their enjoyments, and their consolations.

On a dark night, in the last winter month, at one of those reunions, a few words, whispered from ear to ear, saddened every heart, and put a new fervor into the closing prayer.

Bright Eyes, the child around which the pride and affection of the settlement clustered, had been suddenly taken ill.

In childish enterprise and glee he clambered after some pictures on a book-shelf, and had fallen. He did not, at first, appear to be much hurt, and his father joined the winter-evening party. But before the hour at which the settlers were expected to seek their homes, a violent fever disturbed his brain, and filled his mother's heart with grievous apprehensions.

Though the succeeding morning was severely cold, and a fierce wind filled the air with drifting snow, scarcely had the day broken, ere the sad news was known at every fireside, that the hope of the settlement was dangerously ill with fever —in a brain unusually developed. There, around a neat cottage, near the church, centered the entire interest of all the settlers. Little Bright Eyes knew no rest. Soon he did not know his father or his mother. Violent spasms seized him, and irregular moans expressed a most painful struggle between firm disease and a strong frame.

At length, while his father held him in his arms, and his mother kneeled by his side, watching for a last look of recognition, he sank into a deep stupor, from which death took him peacefully.

It was Sabbath morning. Little children in their classes at Sunday-school were told that Bright Eyes had gone to heaven.

In the white church, that day, a sermon from this text, "Suffer little children to come unto me, and forbid them not," moved the sternest men, as well as the tenderest women. The head of the household from which Bright Eyes had been taken was the preacher.

Every settler felt then that affliction hath bonds of union closer than the ripest pleasure can furnish. To each other they renewed those vows, the keeping of which would enable their beloved pastor to lead them the way Bright Eyes had gone.

On the following evening, when the first-born of the prairie was laid in his little grave, every man, woman and child able to brave piercing cold, heard the clods fall on his coffin. Their hearts bled in sympathy. The pastor knew that the shadow which had fallen over his threshold, crossed also every threshold in the settlement.

At his saddened home he took leave of his people in only these words: "The Lord gave, and the Lord hath taken away. The Lord chasteneth whom he loveth. Blessed be the name of the Lord."

———

Whoever visits now the village of ———, in ——— county, Iowa, may witness mutual respect and forbearance among all the people, from children in the street to men at their business, and women in their homes, which will puzzle his understanding as much as it will challenge his admiration unless, spending a Sabbath there, he hears the village pastor preach the Gospel, and, affected by his pensive countenance, learns the story, I have poorly told, of The Bright Eye of the Settlement.

The features of this story, as true to real occurrence as my pen can make them, furnish a striking contrast to the features of a story, which faithfully depicts pioneer life, as it was in the west fifty years ago.

www.ingramcontent.com/pod-product-compliance
Lightning Source LLC
Chambersburg PA
CBHW021157230426
43667CB00006B/445